BAPTISM AND CHRISTIAN IDENTITY

BAPTISM AND CHRISTIAN IDENTITY

Teaching in the Triune Name

Gordon S. Mikoski

.

WILLIAM B. EERDMANS PUBLISHING COMPANY
GRAND RAPIDS, MICHIGAN / CAMBRIDGE, U.K.

Published 2009 by
Wm. B. Eerdmans Publishing Co.
2140 Oak Industrial Drive N.E., Grand Rapids, Michigan 49505 /
P.O. Box 163, Cambridge CB3 9PU U.K.

Printed in the United States of America

15 14 13 12 11 10 09   7 6 5 4 3 2 1

Library of Congress Cataloging-in-Publication Data

Mikoski, Gordon S.
Baptism and Christian identity: teaching in the Triune name /
Gordon S. Mikoski.
p.   cm.
Includes bibliographical references.
ISBN 978-0-8028-2460-8 (alk. paper)
1. Baptism. 2. Trinity. 3. Reformed Church — Doctrines.
4. Identification (Religion)   I. Title.

BV811.3.M55   2009
234′.161 — dc22
2009006931

www.eerdmans.com

For Nancy

and

To all of my teachers

Contents

Introduction: Search for a Standpoint   ix

The Point of View of the Author   ix

*Why This Book Matters to Contemporary
Mainline Churches in America*   xiii

Methodological Considerations   xv

Plan of the Book   xxv

1. Baptismal Practice in Congregation and Text   1

On the Centrality and Importance of Baptism   1

The Baptismal Rite at St. Peter's Presbyterian Church   8

Stepping Back from Baptismal Rite   28

2. Depth Soundings in Theology and Christian Education   39

Depth Soundings in Trinitarian Theology   41

Depth Soundings in Christian Education   57

*Toward a Trinitarian Practical Theology of Education
and Formation for Discipleship*   66

3. Baptism, Trinity, and Ecclesial Pedagogy
in the Work of Gregory of Nyssa   69

Background and Context   72

Contents

The Baptismal Rite   83

Stepping Back from the Baptismal Gestalt   89

Summary and Assessment   124

4. Baptism, Trinity, and Ecclesial Pedagogy
   in the Work of John Calvin   131

   Background and Context   133

   The Baptismal Rite   142

   Stepping Back from the Baptismal Gestalt   153

   Summary and Assessment   183

5. Baptizing and Teaching in the Triune Name   191

   What We Can Learn from Gregory of Nyssa and
        John Calvin about the Baptism-Trinity-Pedagogy Nexus   192

   Reflections on the Contemporary Context   197

   Strategic Principles for Baptizing and Teaching
        in the Triune Name   203

6. Baptizing and Teaching in the Triune Name
   at St. Peter's Presbyterian Church   217

   Worship   217

   Education and Formation for Discipleship   221

   Epilogue: An Overture to a Trinitarian Practical
   Theology of Christian Formation   235

   Bibliography   237

   Index of Subjects and Names   247

   Index of Scripture References   253

Search for a Standpoint

Thinking begins in what may fairly be called a forked-road situation, a situation that is ambiguous, that presents a dilemma, that proposes alternatives. As long as our activity glides smoothly along from one thing to another, or as long as we permit our imagination to entertain fancies at pleasure, there is no call for reflection. Difficulty or obstruction in the way of reaching a belief brings us, however, to a pause. In the suspense of uncertainty, we metaphorically climb a tree; we try to find some standpoint from which we may survey additional facts and, getting a more commanding view of the situation, may decide how the facts stand in relation to one another.

John Dewey, *How We Think*

The Point of View of the Author

I came late to Christianity. Christian beliefs and practices were largely unknown to me during the first seventeen years of my life. My conversion to Christianity came as the culmination of a search for ultimate truth. Christianity was the very last place I looked for anything having to do with truth. As I read the Gospel of Matthew one spring morning during my senior year of high school, I had the strong sense that Jesus Christ was alive and somehow speaking to me through the text of the Sermon on the Mount. At that moment I knew that he was truth embodied. Everything

Introduction

changed for me after that encounter with the risen Lord mediated by the text of Scripture.

In a way that I have only recently begun to comprehend, the faith in search of understanding to which this study bears witness began when I emerged from the baptismal font several months after my conversion. During those first few years of my pilgrimage into deeper understanding of the mystery of God and the Christian life, I focused mainly on Jesus Christ and matters related to the character of the Christian life. My experience of post-baptismal formation, or mystagogical catechesis, continued as I entered seminary in order to prepare for full-time ministry in the Presbyterian Church (USA) (hereafter PC[USA]). At my ordination trial in February 1990, I worried that someone would ask me a question about my understanding of God as Trinity. After four years as a religion major and an additional four years of seminary, I realized in those moments of fear and trembling that I did not know very much about the doctrine of the Trinity. Greatly relieved that no one posed any questions along these lines, I resolved to make the study of trinitarian theology a priority during my pastoral ministry.

I began service as associate pastor for education at the Grosse Pointe Memorial Church in suburban Detroit in 1990. During the eight and a half years that my wife, Nancy, and I enjoyed teaching the Christian faith to children, youth, and adults as associate pastors in that congregation, I worked to develop my understanding of the doctrine of the Trinity and to deepen my grasp of Christian education. I found great help in my early investigations into the doctrine of the Trinity from the senior pastor with whom we worked, the Rev. Dr. V. Bruce Rigdon. Having taught church history for over twenty years at McCormick Seminary in Chicago prior to accepting a call to serve as senior pastor and being something of an expert on Russian Orthodox theology, Dr. Rigdon greatly aided my growing understanding of trinitarian theology. Through conversations with Dr. Rigdon and by reading works by German Reformed theologian Jürgen Moltmann, I eventually found my way to the Cappadocian fathers: Gregory Nazianzen, Basil of Caesarea, and Gregory of Nyssa. These pastor-theologians from the fourth century helped me to see that the doctrine of the Trinity provides the grammar for Christian belief and practice.

One day during my ministry in Grosse Pointe, I came across the opening lines of Catherine LaCugna's book, *God for Us: The Trinity and Christian Life:*

> The doctrine of the Trinity is ultimately a practical doctrine with radical consequences for Christian life. That is the thesis of this book. The doctrine of the Trinity, which is the specifically Christian way of speaking about God, summarized what it means to participate in the life of God through Jesus Christ in the Spirit. . . . The life of God — precisely because God is triune — does not belong to God alone. God who dwells in inaccessible light and eternal glory comes to us in the face of Christ and the activities of the Holy Spirit. Because of God's outreach to the creature, God is said to be essentially relational, ecstatic, fecund, alive as passionate love. Divine life is therefore also *our* life. The heart of the Christian life is to be united with the God of Jesus Christ by means of communion with one another. The doctrine of the Trinity is ultimately therefore a teaching not about the abstract nature of God, nor about God in isolation from everything other than God, but a teaching about God's life with us and our life with each other.[1]

LaCugna's assertion stimulated my emerging quest to relate the doctrine of the Trinity to Christian education. If practical, then surely the doctrine of the Trinity could relate in some significant way to the curriculum and methods whereby children, youth, and adults come to, grow in, and live out the Christian faith. The doctrine of the Trinity must lend itself to deep connections with the theory and practice of Christian education.

With growing questions about how to relate the doctrine of the Trinity and Christian education and with an ever intensifying sense of call to serve the church primarily as teacher, my family and I left Michigan in the summer of 1998 so that I could pursue doctoral study of these questions at Emory University in Atlanta, Georgia. I came to doctoral study in the practical theological discipline of Christian education with a clear sense of the "forked-road situation" described by John Dewey in the epigraph to this introduction.[2] I have reflected for a long time on how to bring together the doctrine of the Trinity and Christian education in a way that would avoid the pitfalls of beguiling abstraction, fawning nostalgia, and reductionistic pedagogy on the one hand while affirming embodied discipleship, creative particularity, and democratic engagement on the other. In what follows I

---

1. Catherine Mowry LaCugna, *God for Us: The Trinity and Christian Life* (San Francisco: HarperSanFrancisco, 1991), p. 1.

2. John Dewey, *How We Think,* Great Books in Philosophy series (Amherst, N.Y.: Prometheus, 1991), p. 11.

have attempted to develop a trinitarian approach to Christian education that aims to equip disciples for faithful Christian participation in the context of contemporary American democratic society.[3]

Two of my academic mentors, James W. Fowler and Craig R. Dykstra, contributed much to the shaping of the perspectives I articulate in this book. Jim Fowler helped me to see Christian education as a form of practical theology. He greatly encouraged my thinking about the practical dimensions of the doctrine of the Trinity in relation to ecclesial pedagogy. He and I have often discussed the possibility of developing a trinitarian practical theology. This book aims to take some faltering first steps in the direction of that larger project.

In addition to being a key mentor in seminary, Craig Dykstra has helped me to see the importance of religious practices in Christian education. His sponsorship of the growing body of literature about the importance of religious practices for shaping vital Christian faith in congregations has influenced the attempt made here to bring the doctrine of the Trinity and Christian education together into a generative framework.[4]

---

3. In this study I will often use the term *ecclesial pedagogy* to refer to the range of activities involved in fostering the development of Christian faith in individuals and congregations. While I could and sometimes do use such terms as *religious education, Christian education, catechesis,* or *formation,* I increasingly prefer the term *ecclesial pedagogy.* The reason for my preference for this particular term stems from my conviction that it combines an emphasis on intentional teaching and learning in congregational settings with a flexibility that allows for both the traditional patterns of education and the broader ways in which the whole life of a congregation fosters the development of vital Christian faith. My colleagues and I in the Christian education subarea of the practical theology department at Princeton Seminary recently decided to change the name of our area to "Education and Formation for Discipleship." I will occasionally use that term as another synonym for the area of ministry traditionally known as Christian education.

4. For example, see Dorothy C. Bass, ed., *Practicing Our Faith: A Way of Life for a Searching People* (San Francisco: Jossey-Bass, 1997); Craig R. Dykstra, *Growing in the Life of Faith: Education and Christian Practices* (Louisville: Geneva, 1999); Stephanie Paulsell, *Honoring the Body: Meditations on a Christian Practice* (San Francisco: Jossey-Bass, 2002); Dorothy C. Bass, *Receiving the Day: Christian Practices for Opening the Gift of Time* (San Francisco: Jossey-Bass, 2000); and Miroslav Volf and Dorothy C. Bass, eds., *Practicing Theology: Beliefs and Practices in Christian Life* (Grand Rapids and Cambridge: Eerdmans, 2002). More recent books in the Practices of Faith series include Thomas G. Long, *Testimony: Talking Ourselves into Being Christian* (San Francisco: Jossey-Bass, 2004) and Don Saliers and Emily Saliers, *A Song to Sing, A Life to Live: Reflections on Music as Spiritual Practice* (San Francisco: Jossey-Bass, 2005).

The Neo-Aristotelian substructure of much of the religious practices discussion that he and Dorothy Bass have sponsored has helped me to rein in my sometimes impetuous Platonic tendencies.

I do not remember exactly when in my studies at Emory I came to the realization that the practice of baptism holds the key for bringing together the doctrine of the Trinity and ecclesial pedagogy into a dynamic nexus. I do know, however, that when I read Dykstra and Bass's introductory essay, "A Theological Understanding of Christian Practices," in Miroslav Volf and Dorothy Bass's edited volume, *Practicing Theology: Beliefs and Practices in Christian Life,* I had the sense that I was onto something significant.[5] I have since become convinced that focusing on and privileging the sacrament of baptism offers a particularly helpful way to see the inherent connections between the doctrine of the Trinity and Christian education. Thus, through the influence of the Dykstra and Bass-inspired religious practices discussion, this book came to focus on the interplay of baptism, the doctrine of the Trinity, and ecclesial pedagogy.

If it is true that all research projects are at some level autobiographical, then I have discharged at least part of my duty to my readers by sharing a bit of the story and background that have given rise to this book. It represents my attempt to integrate the various trajectories of ecclesial and academic interests with which I have been concerned for nearly a decade. I offer it in the hope that others will gain something for their own thinking and practice from the discoveries I have made along the way.

Why This Book Matters to Contemporary Mainline Churches in America

This book, though, is more than simply an attempt to think through my own intellectual and ecclesial preoccupations. I believe that there is something of significance here for contemporary mainline churches in America. Among the many issues facing Protestant congregations in contemporary America, the challenge to find a basis for unity in the midst of much internal conflict and acrimony seems increasingly serious. Protestant churches also need to find ways to form disciples that are deeply rooted in the partic-

5. Craig R. Dykstra and Dorothy C. Bass, "A Theological Understanding of Christian Practices," in Volf and Bass, eds., *Practicing Theology,* pp. 13-32.

ular beliefs and practices of the Christian faith while equipping them to engage creatively in an increasingly pluralistic social and political context.

Christian faith is never lived in the abstract; it is always rooted in congregations. For this reason, I engage a particular congregation in this book as a way to locate and concretize the issues with which I deal. The congregation, which I will call St. Peter's Presbyterian Church, located in a large metropolitan area in the Southeast, will provide some concrete mooring for the argument I lay out in the book. After investigating the interrelationship of baptism, Trinity, and pedagogy in the central part of the book, I will circle back around to the St. Peter's congregation in order to discuss a number of constructive proposals for educating and forming disciples in light of the insights gained from my investigations.

At another level, this book attempts to address some of the challenges faced more broadly by American society. With a burgeoning number of identity and interest groups, the question of unity and diversity confronts American society as never before. In religious terms alone, America has become the most religiously diverse nation on the planet.[6] The increasing diversity not only of American religious life but also of race, ethnicity, economic status, and cultural identification raises many important and pressing questions. Some of those questions have to do with the role of the churches in the realm of the public. Should the churches pull back from public engagement into enclaves of homogeneous Christian identity? Or should they, instead, dilute their particular beliefs and practices so as to build bridges with non-Christian communities? I do not find either of those strategies particularly satisfying. I argue, instead, for a trinitarian approach to Christian formation that aims to develop a strong sense of specifically Christian identity and creative engagement with those individuals and groups in American society who are not Christian. Along these lines, I find Princeton moral philosopher Jeffrey Stout's three critical questions for Radical Orthodox theologian John Milbank helpful:

- Is it not possible to discern the workings of the Holy Spirit, and thus some reflection of God's redemptive activity, in modern democratic aspirations?
- Is there nothing in the political life of modern democracies, or in the

---

6. Diana L. Eck, *A New Religious America: How a "Christian Country" Has Become the World's Most Religiously Diverse Nation* (New York: HarperSanFrancisco, 2001).

lives of those who are struggling for just and decent arrangements within them, that a loving God would bless?

· If the plenitude of God's triune inner life shines forth in all of creation, cannot theology discern some such light in democratic community?[7]

I believe that positive answers to such questions as Stout poses can serve as pointers to ways in which the relationship between baptism, the doctrine of God as Trinity, and ecclesial pedagogy may profitably take shape in churches — particularly those in the Reformed tradition — which are situated in the contemporary American context. However we might construe the relationships between baptism, Trinity, and pedagogy, we must, I believe, do so in a way that makes sense for the particular historical context in which we live. We cannot and should not allow ourselves the dangerous luxury of thinking that we can return to any golden age of the past — whether, for example, of the fourth or of the sixteenth centuries. Now is the time and this is the place into which we, as the baptized, are called to bear witness to the saving work of the Triune God in and on behalf of the world in which we find ourselves.

Methodological Considerations

I approach the issues at play in this book as a practical theologian working in the mode of ecclesial pedagogy. While theological reflection upon the complexities of lived human experience takes place in several parts of the theological curriculum, I find that the tools, literature, and methods of the field of practical theology provide indispensable help in carrying out my task.

For most of the modern history of practical theology, ministerial or clerical practices provided the predominant organizing principle for the field. Even today, many departments of practical theology in theological schools divide up into subdisciplines related to ministerial practice: homiletics, liturgics, pastoral care and counseling, and Christian education. In the latter decades of the twentieth century, several attempts were made to move beyond the tendency to apply theological concepts to ministerial practice. Practical theologians like Don Browning, James Fowler, and

---

7. Jeffrey Stout, *Democracy and Tradition* (Princeton and Oxford: Princeton University Press, 2004), p. 104.

Johannes van der Ven have worked ~~to reconceive the field of practical the-~~ ~~ology in terms of theological reflection upon the complexities of individ-~~ ~~ual and social experience.~~[8] These efforts have resulted in the expansion of the field beyond its original preoccupations with theory applied to ministerial practice into communal and public paradigms.[9] The communal paradigm in practical theology focuses on the dynamics of whole communities. The public paradigm seeks to do practical theology in and for the wider public beyond the churches. While these paradigms often compete for supremacy, they often exist side by side or in complex interplay.

Most practical theologians today share a commitment to explore the many dimensions of the complex interface between theological norms and thick descriptions of human experience. Modern practical theologians interact at significant depth with the empirical data provided by the human sciences of psychology, sociology, ethnography, and anthropology. Inasmuch as the human sciences have emerged from the Enlightenment turn to the complexities of the human subject, the recent character of the field of practical theology bears a distinctly modern impress.

Much modern practical theological work has operated within the assumptions of modern moral monotheism as exemplified by H. Richard Niebuhr's radical monotheism. This is not to say that all modern practical theologians are necessarily unitarian in outlook. Many practical theologians do, in fact, hold implicit trinitarian beliefs; they very often, however, express the explicitly theological dimensions of their work in terms of an undifferentiated moral monotheism. Often this moral monotheism moves in the direction of a binitarianism as articulated by H. Richard Niebuhr in which the transcendent God creates and sponsors the moral universe and the Son works to redeem it by moral example or gracious transformation. The pattern can be seen in the work of two leading practical theologians, Don Browning and Johannes van der Ven.[10]

---

8. Don S. Browning, *A Fundamental Practical Theology: Descriptive and Strategic Proposals* (Minneapolis: Fortress, 1991); James W. Fowler, *Faith Development and Pastoral Care,* Theology and Pastoral Care series, ed. Don S. Browning (Philadelphia: Fortress, 1987); and Johannes van der Ven, *Practical Theology: An Empirical Approach,* trans. Barbara Schultz (Kampen: J. H. Kok, 1990; reprint, Leuven: Peeters, 1998).

9. See for example, Richard R. Osmer and Friedrich L. Schweitzer, eds., *Developing a Public Faith: New Directions in Practical Theology: Essays in Honor of James W. Fowler* (St. Louis: Chalice, 2003).

10. Van der Ven, *Practical Theology.* In personal conversation with van der Ven at the

In his work *A Fundamental Practical Theology: Descriptive and Strategic Proposals*, Don Browning advocates a practice-theory-practice approach to practical theology broken out into four theological moments: descriptive theology, historical theology, systematic theology, and strategic practical theology.[11] He employs a sophisticated version of theologian David Tracy's revised correlation method along with powerful insights taken from hermeneutics and moral philosophy. In principle, Browning allows for engagement with the doctrine of the Trinity as part of the second movement (historical theology) in which human experience interacts dynamically with classic Christian texts. At one level, then, Browning clears a path for practical theological engagement with the doctrine of the Trinity.

At another level, however, Browning implicitly forecloses this possibility. When he lays out his set of normative assumptions that guide his approach to practical theology we see that he advocates for a classically liberal Protestant position heavily influenced by Kantian moral monotheism. Browning claims that his views have been shaped by liberal Protestantism tempered by neo-orthodoxy.[12] He distances himself from Barthian forms of neo-orthodoxy in favor of the vision of the Niebuhr brothers.[13] Like them, he confesses to having a difficult time dealing in any meaningful way with the Holy Spirit, except through the symbolic language used by a Pentecostal church that he studied.[14] In fact, Browning's operative doctrine of God comes from the Niebuhr brothers.

From Reinhold Niebuhr, Browning espouses a view of God who acts in three different modes: Creator, Judge, and Redeemer.[15] Behind the three metaphors that describe differentiated aspects of God's activity stands an

---

International Society for Empirical Research in Theology (ISERT) in Bielefeld, Germany, in April 2004, he maintained that he holds an orthodox trinitarian theological position. Because of the social and political position of practical theology in European universities, van der Ven intentionally downplays the dogmatic perspectives that lie in the deep background of his work and tends to emphasize the unity of God. One might say that for van der Ven the doctrine of God is implicit in his work, while the oneness and the transcendence of God forms the explicit public framework of it.

11. Browning, *Practical Theology*, pp. 7-9. For a description of the various movements in his vision of practical theology, see pp. 47-58.

12. Browning, *Practical Theology*, pp. 63-64.

13. Browning, *Practical Theology*, pp. 63 and 143ff.

14. Browning, *Practical Theology*, pp. 65, 29-33, and 261-66.

15. Browning, *Practical Theology*, pp. 143ff.

implicit belief in a single, undifferentiated divine Person. The single divine Person acts in history to establish, judge, and redeem human beings.

Jesus plays an important role in Browning's theological perspective as moral exemplar. Jesus reveals more clearly than any other human being the character of the divine Person in his life of agapic love that culminated on the cross.[16] In this, Browning sees a high degree of resonance with Kantian and Neo-Kantian moral philosophy: "My point is this: Christian neighbor love and Kantian or Neo-Kantian moral principles are formally the same, but the symbol of the cross adds a dimension that the Kantian principle lacks [that is, self-sacrifice]."[17] Jesus' humanity and transparency to God have been brought to the fore. Browning makes no mention of the historical Christian claims of Jesus' divinity as the preexisting Second Person of the Triune God.

Browning's inability to incorporate a meaningful pneumatology into his normative theological perspective on practical theology combined with his moral exemplar Christology and his emphasis on the single divine Person of God demonstrates that he places no particular value on the historic Christian claim of God as Triune. This does not mean that Browning fails as a Christian or as a practical theologian. On the contrary, Browning provides a worthy ideal of both scholarship in practical theology and authentic Christian discipleship. It only means that the understanding of God as Trinity plays no effective role in his practical theological vision. It means, further, that Christian particularities have been played down in service to a laudably wide moral vision for the improvement of American society.

Along similar lines, Dutch practical theologian Johannes van der Ven advocates for a thoroughgoing empirical approach to practical theology in his work *Practical Theology: An Empirical Approach*. He writes: "Empirical theology is a product of the combination of empirical and hermeneutic-communicative methods: the hermeneutic-communicative approach functions as the frame of reference within which the meaning and significance of empirical research unfolds."[18] Much like Browning, van der Ven seeks to engage in theological reflection in close proximity to human experience using the complex methods of hermeneutics and empirical research

16. Browning, *Practical Theology,* pp. 147-48.
17. Browning, *Practical Theology,* p. 233.
18. Browning, *Practical Theology,* p. 32.

to shed light on traditional religious symbols. Van der Ven holds up the symbol of the divine reign, or *basilea,* as the norm that forms the goal of practical theological engagement.[19] This eschatological reality is marked by "the normative principles of freedom, equality, universality, and solidarity."[20] In van der Ven's vision, God functions as a solitary divine Person who rules all things as a benevolent monarch. Jesus teaches about and demonstrates the principles of God's rule with authority. Like Browning, for van der Ven Jesus functions as moral exemplar with exceptional religious insight and power; he is not referred to as divine or as a member of the Trinity.[21] The Holy Spirit finds no place or mention in van der Ven's discussion of the doctrine of God that guides his work.

Van der Ven came closest to a trinitarian point of view when he worked to identify in quantitative terms the religious beliefs and opinions held by a population sample about each of the Triune Persons.[22] Due to the political location of his research in the context of a secular university, van der Ven deemphasizes confessionally oriented aspects of his work. In part, this makes empirical research into the contours of contemporary patterns of religious belief about God easier to operationalize and the results more widely accessible to academic and general public audiences.

As was the case in my interpretation of Browning, I do not intend to highlight problems with the theologically normative character of van der Ven's work at the point of the doctrine of God in order to take away from the importance of his contributions to the field of practical theology. His work has, in fact, contributed greatly to the development of the field, particularly with regard to developing rigorous empirical research methods and results. Drawing attention to the lack of an explicit and meaningful trinitarian normative framework serves only to underscore the need to find an effective way to build interdisciplinary bridges between the extraordinarily helpful work of practical theologians like Browning and van der Ven and the practical turn that contemporary trinitarian theologians have taken. But why is it important to do so?

Linkages between contemporary trinitarian theology and practical theological discourse need to be made for at least three reasons. First, trini-

19. Browning, *Practical Theology,* pp. 73-76.

20. Browning, *Practical Theology,* p. 74.

21. Browning, *Practical Theology,* pp. 69-73.

22. Johannes van der Ven, personal conversation with the author, ISERT conference, Bielefeld, Germany, April 2004.

tarian theology with its increasing orientation toward all things practical needs to interface with the perspectives, tools, and insights provided by the field of practical theology. Doing so will give depth, texture, and nuance to the claim that the Trinity is ultimately the most practical of all Christian doctrines. Second, practical theologians need to find ways to connect not only with wider moral and academic audiences but also with the Christian churches. This can be done quite effectively by connecting with the trinitarian theological grammar at work in most congregations. While the work of practical theology can have a tremendously helpful influence on congregational life, most of the literature of practical theology seems limited to academic discourse among other practical theologians. Only by speaking the language and grammar of the historic Christianity that guides life in the pews can practical theology begin to shape the life of the churches in any significant way. Third, the dynamics of the doctrine of the Trinity can function to complement and expand the goods provided by undifferentiated moral monotheism. For example, it may make some real difference if normative visions for the transformation of society in the direction of love find sponsorship in a community of Persons marked by diversity in unity and unity in diversity, rather than in a solitary divine monarch.

A few practical theologians have actually begun to move in the direction of an explicitly trinitarian approach to their work. Jim Fowler at Emory and James Loder and Richard Osmer at Princeton Seminary have worked in recent years to engage in practical theological investigation and reflection within the framework of a thoroughly and explicitly trinitarian framework.[23]

Jim Fowler, one of H. Richard Niebuhr's ardent followers in the field of practical theology, has worked for some time now to integrate a full-

---

23. For a comprehensive discussion of Fowler's efforts to integrate a full-orbed trinitarian perspective in his work, see my chapter "H. Richard Niebuhr and Fowler's Evolution as a Theologian," in Osmer and Schweitzer, eds., *Developing a Public Faith*, pp. 101-16. For trinitarian approaches in recent practical theology, see James E. Loder and W. Jim Neidhardt, *The Knight's Move: The Relational Logic of the Spirit in Theology and Science* (Colorado Springs: Helmers and Howard, 1992), pp. 22-24 and 287-306; James E. Loder, *The Logic of the Spirit: Human Development in Theological Perspective* (San Francisco: Jossey-Bass, 1998), pp. 74-77 and 339-42; Richard R. Osmer, *The Teaching Ministry of Congregations* (Louisville: Westminster John Knox, 2005), pp. 157-58 and 203-9. See also Ray Anderson, *The Shape of Practical Theology: Empowering Ministry with Theological Praxis* (Downers Grove, Ill.: InterVarsity, 2001), pp. 35-46.

orbed Niebuhrian vision of the intersection of God's activity in the complexities and vicissitudes of human life and a robust and explicit practical trinitarianism. In order to do this, Fowler has pushed against the confines of Niebuhr's Spirit-wary Neo-Kantianism and has gravitated toward more Hegelian-inspired pneumatologies. Fowler's efforts to meet this challenge have assumed the form of a recovery of the notion of a statement of the providence of God, or as Fowler prefers, the "praxis of God" in human history. His efforts to stake out a thoroughly trinitarian standpoint continue into the present.[24]

From a somewhat different practical theological starting point, James Loder also attempted to integrate a thoroughly trinitarian framework into his work before his recent and untimely death. Standing on orthodox conciliar trinitarianism, Loder based his practical theological framework for understanding the dynamics of human transformation in terms of the "relational logic of Chalcedonian Christology" as refracted through the lens of Kierkegaard.[25] Loder looked to the relational dynamism described by the trinitarian notion of *perichoresis* for the interpretive key that unlocked the bipolar mysteries of the incarnation, theological anthropology, and "the inner life of the trinitarian God."[26]

Fowler and Loder, whose practical theological perspectives differed considerably on the question of the nature and development of Christian faith, increasingly converged on the necessity of a deep trinitarian framework when engaging in theological reflection upon the complexities of human formation and transformation. As a student of both of these practical theologians, I pick up and seek to develop here a convergent theme in their work.

Finally, my Princeton Seminary colleague, Richard Osmer, has increasingly engaged the trinitarian perspectives of Jürgen Moltmann in his practical theological endeavors. Osmer writes:

> Just as the theology of the Hebrew Scriptures takes its bearing from the salvific experiences of exodus and covenant, Christian theology takes its bearings from the patterns of divine action discerned in the Son and Spirit that leads it to form a trinitarian understanding of God. Long before church councils and theologians forged an explicit doctrine of the

---

24. Mikoski, "H. Richard Niebuhr and Fowler's Evolution as a Theologian," in Osmer and Schweitzer, eds., *Developing a Public Faith*, pp. 110-14.

25. Loder and Neidhardt, *Knight's Move*, pp. 58-59.

26. Loder and Neidhardt, *Knight's Move*, p. 308.

Trinity, the early church was developing trinitarian practices that gave expression to the mystery at the heart of the Christian understanding of God. As early as the Gospel of Matthew, Christ is portrayed as telling his disciples that they are to baptize new converts "in the name of the Father, and of the Son and of the Holy Spirit" (Matt. 28:19). Prayers are offered to the Son and the Spirit, and they are worshipped along with the Father. The Spirit is portrayed as uniting disciples to Christ and through him to the Father.

A trinitarian understanding of God is basic to Christian belief and practice. . . . Throughout the centuries, Christian theologians have struggled to find ways of honoring both the unity and differentiation of the Trinity. I follow the lead of Jürgen Moltmann, emphasizing the distinct personhood of each member of the Trinity. This is commonly known as a *social doctrine of the Trinity*. Unity is pictured as being like a fellowship of persons who are so closely related to one another that the actions and "subjectivity" of one always impact and influence the others. The divine persons are bound together in a community of mutual love.[27]

Osmer sees great potential for advancing practical theological research by embracing the kind of normative practical trinitarianism that Moltmann has articulated. Such a vision offers new possibilities for thinking in a practical theological mode about how to foster harmonious communal life in the midst of real and profound differences, whether in churches or in the wider society. Along with our colleague, Kenda Dean, I have a high degree of resonance with Osmer's efforts to develop a thoroughly trinitarian approach to practical theological work in the area of education and formation for discipleship.

While the doctrine of God as Trinity has recently emerged as an important theme in some quarters of practical theology, baptism as the rite of initiation into communities of trinitarian faith and life has received little attention from any practical theologians. The turn to religious practices, spearheaded by Craig Dykstra and Dorothy Bass, has opened up some new possibilities for practical theological research in relation to such important ecclesial practices as baptism. In the introductory essay to an anthology on the implications of the recent religious practices discussion

---

27. Osmer, *The Teaching Ministry of Congregations*, pp. 204-5.

for theological education, Dykstra and Bass identify baptism as the core of the matter. They write:

> At its heart baptism is not so much a distinct practice as it is the liturgical summation of all the Christian practices. In this rite, the grace to which the Christian life is a response is fully and finally presented, visibly, tangible, and in words. Here all the practices are present in crystalline form — forgiveness and healing, singing and testimony, sabbath-keeping and community shaping, and all the others. Unlike each particular practice, baptism does not address a specific need, instead, it ritually sketches the contours of a whole new life, within which all human needs can be perceived in a different way. . . . *Part of the work of Christian theologians in every age is to reflect on the shape and character of the new way of life Christians enter when we rise from the watery death of baptism. . . . Exploring this question involves us both in contemplating the deepest foundations of Christian faith and in figuring out the shape our living should take amidst the immediate concerns of each day.*[28]

With their assertion that baptism functions as the core constituting practice of the church in relation to several Christian religious practices, Dykstra and Bass point the way to a potentially fruitful line of research focused on the importance of communal practices. In this endeavor, they anchor practical theological reflection in the practices of the Christian community. This move allows them to avoid the narrowing of the field that characterized the earlier clerical paradigm in practical theology while simultaneously providing a formational basis for ecclesial engagement in the public realm. Dykstra and Bass have rightly identified the locus (that is, baptism) for the dynamic intersection of fields and concerns that may well, when successfully negotiated, lead to advancements in theological reflection on the Trinity, Christian education, and practical theological research more broadly.

In this study, I use the rite of baptism as a kind of lens through which to explore the practical and formative character of the doctrine of the Trinity, especially in relation to practices of ecclesial pedagogy. I will anchor my trinitarian reflections on the theory and practice of Christian education precisely in the sacrament of baptism.

28. Dykstra and Bass, "A Theological Understanding of Christian Practices," pp. 30-31; emphasis mine.

In this endeavor I will follow, in basic outline, the practical theological method described by my colleague Richard R. Osmer. He points to four "core intellectual operations," or moments, of practical theological method.[29] The four interrelated components and the defining question associated with each moment are as follows: the descriptive-empirical moment (What is going on?); the interpretive moment (Why is this going on?); the normative moment (What ought to be going on?); and the strategic moment (What can be done to reshape what is going on?).[30] Inasmuch as these four moments reciprocally influence and interpret one another, practical theological studies do not necessarily need to follow a strictly linear sequence from the descriptive moment through to the pragmatic moment.[31] Ordinarily, however, the practical theological process will follow a linear progression from the descriptive moment through to the strategic moment.

Another feature of Osmer's model for engaging in practical theology that has some relevance here concerns the modality in which the practical theological inquiry takes place. Practical theologians and pastoral practitioners can use these four moments of practical theology in the mode of pastoral or leadership formation. In this mode, the emphasis lies with the behavior of and implications for clerical leadership in congregations. Alternatively, practical theologians and pastoral practitioners might use the four moments of practical theology in service to the communal or congregational mode. In this approach, practical theological inquiry using the method described by Osmer would pay special attention to the practices and ethos of congregations taken as a whole. Those engaging in practical theological research might also use these four core activities of practical theological investigation in the mode of public engagement. Practical theology in this paradigm would pay particular attention to the dynamics of interface between the church and the wider social context.[32] Lastly, the four moments of practical theology could be put to use in the mode of multi-faith conversation. Here, researchers and practitioners could use Osmer's method as a tool of comparative work across religious lines.

To be sure, there are advantages in seeing this practical theological

---

29. Osmer, *The Teaching Ministry of Congregations*, pp. xiv-xvii and 303-6.
30. Osmer, *The Teaching Ministry of Congregations*, pp. xiv-xvii and 303-6.
31. Personal conversation with the author.
32. Personal conversation with the author.

method not as a linear but as a circular and dynamically reciprocal process. I will leave that discussion for another day. For the sake of clarity and simplicity, I will proceed from a descriptive and interpretive account of a currently situated baptismal rite, through a normatively oriented conversation with two relevant historical thinkers, and conclude with some strategic perspectives and implications for education and formation for discipleship in a congregational setting. This whole effort also aims to gesture toward the larger undertaking of developing a full-blown trinitarian approach to practical theology.

Plan of the Book

The thesis of the book can be stated rather briefly: *the development of a trinitarian practical theology of Christian formation proceeds best by way of the dynamic interplay of the sacrament of baptism, the doctrine of the Trinity, and the practice of ecclesial pedagogy in which the sacrament of baptism serves as the orienting center.* This study aims to articulate a way to address these interlocking concerns by advancing the argument that the sacrament of baptism, the doctrine of the Trinity, and the practice of ecclesial pedagogy should be seen as elements of a larger differentiated whole. Further, I argue that showing their deep interconnectedness involves making the sacrament of baptism the starting point and the orienting center of the inquiry.[33]

In chapter 1, I describe the sacrament of baptism in its situatedness in an actual Presbyterian congregation. I begin to illustrate how baptism in all its fullness can provide the orienting center that brings together trinitarian theology and Christian education in a particularly compelling manner.

In chapter 2, I begin to explore some of the reasons why I think my thesis is necessary and helpful for developing an approach to ecclesial pedagogy in a trinitarian mode or framework. I work to substantiate and to reflect further through a series of "soundings" in the academic fields of systematic theology and Christian education in relation to the concerns I have identified in the situated account of baptismal practice. In this chap-

---

33. Others may well devise approaches for accomplishing a similar objective. By setting up and pursuing the problem in the way that I propose, I do not intend to foreclose other ways of addressing these issues. I intend only to offer a compelling way of engaging the issues I have identified.

ter I argue that discussions about the practical nature of the doctrine of the Trinity among contemporary systematic theologians would be strengthened by paying further attention to the situatedness of local congregations, as well as to the bodily and pedagogical dimensions of human life implied by the term *practical*. While there has been a turn to practice in recent discussions of the recently revitalized doctrine of the Trinity, further work in relating this discussion to local congregations and to the practice of baptism and Christian initiation would provide the nuance and depth required to put into operation the transformative promise of the recent claims about the practical character of the doctrine of the Trinity.

On the other side of the coin, I argue that Christian education must do more to reclaim its voice as a serious and generative conversation partner in theological discourse. The field stands to gain much by generating frontline theological insights based on extrapolations of the complexities of the teaching-learning enterprise. In further developing the theological dimensions of the field, Christian educators stand to gain a great deal by entering into dynamic interdisciplinary conversation with those contemporary trinitarian theologians who emphasize the practical character of the doctrine.

In chapters 3 and 4, I demonstrate that privileging the baptismal rite lays bare the inherent interconnections between baptism, the doctrine of the Trinity, and practices of ecclesial pedagogy in the thought of two eminent trinitarian pastor-teachers: Gregory of Nyssa and John Calvin. These giants of trinitarian thought — one from the fourth century and one from the sixteenth — will help me make my argument that baptism, the Trinity, and ecclesial pedagogy belong inseparably together.

In chapter 5, I argue that Gregory of Nyssa and John Calvin can only take us so far. Inasmuch as the world we live in is a markedly different situation than either the fourth or the sixteenth century, I argue that we need to do an old thing in some very new ways. By baptizing and teaching in the Triune Name, pastors and teachers in contemporary American mainline churches should aim to form Christians who hold together both a well-developed sense of Christian identity and a strong sense of openness to creative engagement with non-Christian individuals and communities in and for the furtherance of the common good in contemporary American democratic society. We do not live in fourth-century Cappadocia or sixteenth-century Geneva. We live in the increasingly pluralistic and, hopefully, still democratic America of the twenty-first century. Now more than ever, those charged with responsibility for ecclesial pedagogy need to think carefully about the outcomes of ecclesial pedagogy in reference both to the life of the churches and to the larger social and political contexts in which the churches live. I return to the St. Peter's congregation in chapter 6 because I believe that the implications of the perspective I articulate will be most fully played out at the congregational level.

It is not likely that by the end of this study I will have found a way to address definitively every challenge I have identified in this introduction. Integrating my own trajectories of thought, finding resources to address the festering conflicts of mainline Protestant churches by forming people in faith who have vision and skill requisite for negotiating unity in the midst of diversity, the need for constructive strategies of creative Christian engagement in the public square, and the search for more effective approaches to theological education could each result in a major research project. I seek here only to articulate a frame of reference from which such complex issues may be addressed more fully in subsequent work. It is my hope that the way I approach my own particular "forked-road situation" will prove helpful to some and will provide others with a few useful insights that will stimulate further conversation.

CHAPTER 1

Baptismal Practice in Congregation and Text

Pour out your Holy Spirit upon them, that they may have the power to do your will, and continue forever in the risen life of Christ. To you, Father, Son, and Holy Spirit, one God, be all praise, honor, and glory, now and forever. Amen.

PC(USA) Book of Common Worship

On the Centrality and Importance of Baptism

Many contemporary treatments of the doctrine of the Trinity begin with theological ideas and move toward practical application. Such treatments usually exemplify something of an intellectualist fallacy. To know the good does not necessarily translate into doing the good, even if the good of which we speak is the Triune God. For all of the talk about the practical import of the doctrine of the Trinity, much contemporary trinitarian theological discussion continues to remain a highly technical academic phenomenon not yet fully or explicitly connected to the lives of ordinary embodied human beings.

I propose that at least some aspects of the discussion about the practical dimension of the doctrine of the Trinity can advance significantly by beginning with the congregationally situated practice of baptism. Proceeding in this way will help to keep theological reflection "in close proximity to human experience."[1] If the conversation about practical trinitarianism begins at the point of the local, the concrete, the bodily, and the communal, then we may be able to overcome some of the difficulties involved in relating ideas and practices. Because it only exists in local, concrete, bodily, and communal terms, the trinitarian practice of baptism seems uniquely suited to such an approach.

Religious Practices and the Practice of Baptism

Today, we find much talk in mainline Protestantism about the nature and importance of religious practices in relation to the revitalization of churches and their ministries.[2] Most of these discussions have taken their cues from a renewed interest in Aristotelian moral philosophy as interpreted by Alasdair MacIntyre in his work *After Virtue: A Study in Moral Theology*.[3] MacIntyre argues that the current cacophonous mélange of moral discourse in which adherents of different frameworks talk past one another results from the wrong-headed and ill-conceived project of modernity with its supposed sacred/secular split, possessive individualism, hegemony of disembodied reason, and so forth.[4] As remedy for the bankruptcy of modern liberal culture, MacIntyre calls for a recovery of the Aristotelian tradition of virtue ethics by which individual character is formed

1. James W. Fowler, personal conversation with the author.

2. See these works: Craig R. Dykstra, *Growing in the Life of Faith: Education and Christian Practices* (Louisville: Geneva, 1999); Dorothy C. Bass, ed., *Practicing Our Faith: A Way of Life for a Searching People* (San Francisco: Jossey-Bass, 1997) and *Receiving the Day: Christian Practices for Opening the Gift of Time* (San Francisco: Jossey-Bass, 2000); Christine D. Pohl, *Making Room: Recovering Hospitality as a Christian Tradition* (Grand Rapids: Eerdmans, 1999); and Miroslav Volf and Dorothy C. Bass, eds., *Practicing Theology: Beliefs and Practices in Christian Life* (Grand Rapids: Eerdmans, 2002).

3. See especially Alasdair MacIntyre's *After Virtue: A Study in Moral Theory*, 2nd ed. (Notre Dame, Ind.: University of Notre Dame Press, 1984). For a sustained and incisive yet appreciative critique of MacIntyre — particularly with respect to problems in his "fall" narrative of Western moral philosophy — see Jeffrey Stout's works *Ethics After Babel: The Languages of Morals and Their Discontents* (Princeton: Princeton University Press, 1988), pp. 191-242, and *Democracy and Tradition* (Princeton: Princeton University Press, 2004), pp. 118-39.

4. MacIntyre, *After Virtue*, pp. 35-75. For a series of essays on the hidden religious character of modernity, see David S. Pacini, *The Cunning of Modern Religious Thought* (Philadelphia: Fortress, 1987).

through extended engagement in a constellation of communal practices oriented toward seeking the moral good. MacIntyre writes:

> My own conclusion is very clear. It is that on the one hand we still, in spite of the efforts of three centuries of moral philosophy and one of sociology, lack any coherent rationally defensible statement of a liberal individualist point of view; and that, on the other hand, the Aristotelian tradition can be restated in a way that restores intelligibility and rationality to our moral and social attitudes and commitments.[5]

MacIntyre's disdain for modern pluralism leads him, ultimately, into a nostalgic appeal for a contemporary version of medieval communal life.[6] Ironically, MacIntyre uses the tools of the Enlightenment — especially critical reason and historical analysis — to make his case against modernity.[7]

Even though I have serious qualms with MacIntyre's overarching social agenda and antimodernity stance, I do think we can be helped in our thinking about practices by affirming — along with Jeffrey Stout and others — MacIntyre's less boisterous and more modest claims about the definition of a practice.[8] MacIntyre defines a practice in this way:

> By a "practice" I am going to mean any coherent and complex form of socially established cooperative human activity through which goods internal to that form of activity are realised in the course of trying to achieve those standards of excellence which are appropriate to, and partially definitive of, that form of activity, with the result that human pow-

---

5. MacIntyre, *After Virtue*, p. 241.

6. MacIntyre, *After Virtue*, pp. 244-45.

7. Stout observes, "The book [*After Virtue*] belongs to a prominent strand of Romantic ethical discourse that has never been hard to find in the modern period and has always relied, in just the way MacIntyre does, on the rhetoric of ruin and fragmentation. It is a very modern form of ethical discourse, but also a form that has a stake in not being able to recognize itself as belonging to the setting against which its criticism is directed" (*Democracy and Tradition*, pp. 134-35). Stout goes further to observe, "For at the time he wrote *After Virtue*, his long-standing hatred for all things liberal combined with his loss of faith in Marxism in a way that seems to have occluded his historical memory. The *modern* intellectual traditions to which he owes the most receive no acknowledgement whatsoever. This peculiar form of amnesia has everything to do with his grim conclusion that the exhaustion of Marxism, 'is shared by every other political tradition within our culture' (AV, 262)" (*Democracy and Tradition*, p. 138).

8. Stout, *Ethics After Babel*, pp. 266-72.

ers to achieve excellence, and human conceptions of the ends and goods involved, are systematically extended. . . . In the ancient and medieval worlds the creation and sustaining of human communities — of households, cities, nations — is generally taken to be a practice in the sense in which I have defined it.[9]

MacIntyre has articulated a rich understanding of what constitutes a practice, and we can profitably bear this definition in mind as we proceed. MacIntyre helps us to see that baptism goes beyond the realm of mere activity. Baptism is a core constituting practice of the Christian life that possesses a trinitarian grammar and calls forth disciplined patterns of ecclesial pedagogy. How and to what extent this is the case will come into view as the exploration progresses through this and subsequent chapters.

An extended focus on baptism as a practice will help to provide some of the nuance and depth that the current religious practices conversation in Protestantism needs in order to sustain its current momentum over the long haul. In addition to focusing on deep-level epistemological issues and rigorous empirical investigation of actual practices, the next phase of the religious practices conversation must concern itself with how to adjudicate among competing configurations of religious practices.

The religious practices field is not at all level. Some practices function more centrally in religious communities than others. Some practices derive their existence and character from core practices. Some practices constitute individual and corporate identity (for example, baptism), whereas other practices function in a more auxiliary or derivative mode. Some practices are rather quotidian; others are more liminal in character. Yet still another set of religious practices serves a mediational function in that it forms linkages between the religious communities and their larger social context (for instance, the practice of hospitality). This multivariable situation points to the importance of sustained and contested conversation about the many plausible ways in which we might construe the constellation of religious practices.

In my view, liturgical practices function as primary constituting practices for Christian communities. All Christian practices derive their meaning and function from their relation to the core practices associated with the corporate worship of the gathered community; particularly, practices

9. Stout, *Ethics After Babel*, p. 175.

4

related to the Word, sacraments, and prayer. For example, the practice of hospitality finds its depth, direction, and meaning primarily in relation to the more basic practice of the celebration of the Eucharist.[10] The larger point here is simply that the whole subset of religious practices concerned with how people come to Christian faith, grow in that faith, and live it out find their proper grounding and orientation in the core constituting practices of the Word and sacraments.

Reformed Liturgical Practices and Baptism

The Reformed tradition has usually privileged those liturgical practices associated with the ministry of the Word. Reading, preaching, and hearing of the Word have usually overshadowed or even, at times, eclipsed other primary liturgical practices. The sacraments, too, have been largely subordinated to the ministry of the Word. While we might adduce many reasons for asserting the primacy of practices associated with the Word, this tendency has often had the effect of treating the sacraments as if they were merely audiovisual aids for the preached Word.

This underlying pattern manifests itself in several aspects of the Reformed and Presbyterian churches. For the most part, sanctuaries in this tradition function as austere lecture halls. These spaces usually feature a large, centralized pulpit from which the Scriptures are read and expounded upon. The Eucharistic table often stands below the pulpit in a subordinate position. Likewise, the baptismal font, often rather small and unadorned, usually sits off to the side of the table, if not on the margins of the sanctuary itself. Rarely does one find a worship space in which pulpit, font, and table stand in juxtapositional parity.[11]

In general, the Reformed tradition more broadly and American Presbyterianism in particular have come down squarely on the prophetic side of the biblical inheritance. Calvinist churches of all stripes tend to emphasize the centrality of the proclaimed Word. Religious rituals and rites tend to be viewed as secondary matters. While there is much to commend

10. Ana María Pineda hints at this in her article "Hospitality," in Bass, ed., *Practicing Our Faith*, p. 36.

11. The notion of "juxtaposition" as an interpretive category is taken from Gordon Lathrop, *Holy Things: A Liturgical Theology* (Minneapolis: Fortress, 1993; paperback ed., 1998), pp. 10-11.

this Word-centered, or logocentric, orientation, the downside of it has been the denigration of the sacraments. The long-standing pattern of interpreting the sacraments as visual aids for the proclamation of the Word has resulted in a tendency to subordinate all practices to the hegemony of theological theory. Over time, the effect of this has been to privilege the mind, the theoretical, and the decontextualized while downplaying the bodily, the situated, and the contextual in both liturgy and life.

The effects of this logocentric pattern are strongly evident in patterns of ecclesial pedagogy in the PC(USA). For a very long time baptized infants and children were not allowed to participate in the sacrament of communion until they had successfully negotiated their way through communicants' class. This class was, essentially, a condensed course in the rudiments of Presbyterian theology. The upshot of this theological "fencing" of the Lord's Table was simply that a baptized person could only be admitted to the Eucharist upon the transmission and mastery of a prescribed minimum level of biblically based theological knowledge.[12] Here again, as with the arrangement of liturgical space and the order of the liturgy, we can see quite clearly that the Word and the attendant emphasis upon theological theory has tended to trump participation in sacramental rites and, further, has led to the diminishment of the importance of religious practices of all sorts and varieties.

What was true of the practice of adolescent transition into active church membership by means of the mini-seminary character of the communicants' class was also true of the entire range of practices comprising the church's educational ministry. Christian education in PC(USA) churches tends to be seen as an auxiliary function of the ministry of the Word. In this view, a good and effective educational ministry provides excellent Bible study in service to the promotion of Bible knowledge for all ages and stages. To be sure, there is much to commend in this approach — especially in view of rampant biblical illiteracy and the perpetual specter of religious superstition, not to mention the crucial role of Scripture in divine revelation — but this emphasis by itself is insufficient to form a thoroughly Christian pattern of life. The argument I am making here about the centrality of baptism in Christian education should not be misconstrued, however, as a call to replace or demote the importance of the Word in ecclesial pedagogy. On the contrary, I take for granted the continuing

---

12. The reasons for this will be discussed in greater depth in the chapter on Calvin.

strength of the emphasis on the Word and seek only to bring the sacraments into some kind of dynamic parity with the Word in Reformed worship, education, theology, and life.

Today there are signs of significant change to this pattern of the primacy of the Word — and the implicit bent toward the hegemony of theological theory — in the life of many congregations. In many places, churches have begun to move in the direction of an appreciation of the importance of symbolic, nonverbal ritualization. One sign of significant change came with the rethinking of the patterns of pedagogical practices in relation to baptism and the Eucharist. For example, in the 1970s both antecedent churches of the PC(USA) did away with the minimum theology requirement as the threshold for admittance to the Lord's Supper. As a result, it is now possible — at least technically — for baptized infants to receive the Eucharist on the very day of their baptism. Very few infants and small children baptized in the PC(USA), however, actually partake of the bread and the cup today. The decisive shift away from a minimum theological requirement for admission to the Lord's Supper has yet to be fully grasped by pastors and laity alike. Much work remains to be done in the direction of fully integrating this shift into congregational practice. Much confusion and misconception reigns in Presbyterian churches today about the question of when sessions should allow baptized children to participate in the Lord's Supper.

Such changes point forward to a recovery of a fuller meaning of the sacrament of baptism as paradigm for the entirety of the Christian life. Changes in the practice of the sacrament of baptism and in the wider ecology of faith formation at the congregational level require a fundamental rethinking of the meaning and place of baptism in the life of the church as a whole. Concomitantly, the complex enterprise of ecclesial pedagogy — inasmuch as it connects to and depends on the sacrament of baptism — will have to be reexamined and, quite possibly, reconceptualized. Changes in the baptismal liturgy open anew questions about the kind of teaching and learning called for both leading up to and following from the celebration of the baptismal rite. Early Christian traditions conceived of this as a comprehensive process of initiation into the church and the Christian life.

I want to contribute to a shift in the theory-practice relationship in the formational ecology of PC(USA) congregations by means of a baptismally based trinitarian pattern of faith formation. In some way, my efforts here resonate with the vision of Orthodox liturgical theologian Alexander

Schmemann (1921-83), who intended that his liturgical theology of baptism would "overcome the fateful divorce between theology, liturgy, and piety."[13] In such a view, doxological praise of the Trinity, theological reflection, and patterning of the Christian life function together in differentiated unity.

As the practice of Christian initiation, baptism functions as the central rite that constitutes and reconstitutes the church as the Body of Christ. Baptism serves as the rite of initiation into participation in the church, liturgy, and the Christian life.[14] In words that John Calvin himself could well have affirmed, Schmemann wrote: "Baptism is truly the beginning, the foundation, and the key. The whole life of the Church is rooted in the New Life which shone forth from the grave on the first day of the new creation. It is this new life that is given in Baptism and is fulfilled in the Church."[15]

Baptism, then, is the core liturgical practice that connects persons and whole communities to the orienting narrative of the life, death, and resurrection of Jesus Christ. It initiates and continues to orient persons with regard to the Christian life. For this reason, it is highly desirable and essential to begin a consideration of the deep interrelatedness of a practical doctrine of the Trinity and practices of ecclesial pedagogy by means of a close examination of an actually enacted baptismal rite.

The Baptismal Rite at St. Peter's Presbyterian Church

I have come to know the St. Peter's Presbyterian congregation and its dynamics over the course of some four years of regular involvement in the congregation's life, particularly in its educational ministry. In many ways, it typifies the kinds of issues facing many American Presbyterian congregations of its size and social location.

---

13. Alexander Schmemann, *Of Water and the Spirit: A Liturgical Study of Baptism* (Crestwood, N.Y.: St. Vladimir's Seminary Press, 1974), p. 12.

14. A correspondent study of the interweaving of baptism and the Eucharist in relation to the doctrine of God as Trinity, theological anthropology, and practices of ecclesial pedagogy or faith formation would certainly be in order on another occasion.

15. Schmemann, *Of Water and the Spirit*, p. 12.

Congregational History, People, and Programs

St. Peter's Presbyterian Church is located in a growing suburb of a large and fast-growing metropolitan area of the southern part of the United States.[16] Over the course of its forty years, the congregation grew from a small, committed group of charter members into a burgeoning 1,500-member congregation. Longtime members recount with pride the building of the congregation's campus by stages. Most of the current facilities had been built by the late 1970s, when the congregation was at its peak in terms of numbers and vitality. As the result of a series of difficulties with several senior pastors and a couple episodes of internal conflict, however, the congregation precipitously declined in membership until it leveled off in the mid-1990s at approximately 550 members. Currently, new members slightly outnumber losses through deaths and transfers.

White, middle-class families and individuals along with a handful of refugee families from West Africa make up the bulk of the membership of the congregation. While many European American families form the core of the population in the community in which St. Peter's is located, the area is currently in the midst of demographic transition. Hispanic immigrants make up the fastest-growing group in the area immediately surrounding the church. One nearby suburban neighborhood holds the distinction of being the most culturally and linguistically diverse municipality in the greater metropolitan area due to the recent influx of political refugees from several deeply conflicted regions of the world. The surrounding area in which the church is located became home to many white, middle-class families who left the city limits in the late 1960s due to integration and racial unrest. Many white, middle-class people who left the city to settle in the suburban neighborhoods in the immediate vicinity of St. Peter's have begun to move even farther out from the metropolitan center in recent years.

St. Peter's Church has sponsored several refugee families from a politically tumultuous nation in West Africa over the course of the past decade. While several African refugee families have joined St. Peter's, to date there are no members from the Hispanic community. There are only a couple of African American members. In an effort to promote racial reconciliation in the area, the congregation maintains a partnership relationship with

16. I have changed the name and disguised the precise location of this congregation.

9

two African American congregations in the vicinity. Recent initiatives by the senior pastor to begin a Hispanic ministry aimed at serving the needs of the burgeoning Latino/Latina community in the area around the church have been met with promising, but somewhat mixed results.

One finds considerable theological diversity at St. Peter's Presbyterian. People in the congregation sometimes joke, "We have liberals, conservatives, and everything else in between." Only about one-third of current members are lifelong Presbyterians. Many members have come from one strain or another of the Baptist tradition. Several members also have come to the congregation as former Catholics, Lutherans, and Methodists. The recent debates over ordination, the placement of the American flag, and the Hispanic ministry initiatives have put the congregation's ideological diversity to the test.

The recent arrival of a moderate and affable head of staff has had the effect of reducing antagonism between various ideological factions within the congregation. He emphasizes the development of congregational fellowship in the hope that a healthy fabric of relationality across ideological differences will mitigate the emotional intensity around controversial issues. He also puts a premium on inclusive, open, and fair processes when dealing with the various challenges facing the congregation.

New energy and vision fuel the many programs of St. Peter's. A vital and growing children's ministry, including a solid church school and vital midweek programs for children, have contributed to a sense that the congregation could eventually recover its peak size and dynamism. The congregation increasingly now attracts one of the crucial demographic groups for congregational vitality: families with young children. Large numbers of adults — parents and non-parents alike — share in the leadership of children's ministries. This fact also points to renewed energy and the potential for numerical and spiritual growth.

The youth program serves a relatively small, but recently growing number of middle and senior high school students. Five years ago, the congregation began a high-commitment midweek program of Christian nurture for children and youth in grades one through twelve called Logos. Upwards of fifty children and youth along with an equal number of parents and adult volunteers from St. Peter's participate weekly in this dynamic program.

Worship Space

The original master plan for facilities called for the current sanctuary to serve as a chapel. Due to lack of funds and a dramatic fall-off in membership due to controversies associated with pastoral leadership, the congregation did not build the envisioned larger sanctuary and bell tower. The existing single-story buildings that form a generous quadrangle are set back a considerable distance from the busiest thoroughfare running through town. Non-church members who pass by the church on a regular basis are often not aware of the presence of St. Peter's Church. This spatial fact contrasts rather dramatically with the three other very visible and imposing church edifices in town.

The congregation built the relatively unadorned sanctuary of St. Peter's in the 1960s. The amber wood of the ceilings, pews, and chancel furniture conveys a sense of comfort and warmth. The carpeting and pew cushions add to a sense of informality and welcome. The pews in the sanctuary on either side of a center aisle can hold up to four hundred people for any one service. Only on Christmas and Easter will one find the pews filled to capacity.

The chancel area rises several steps above the main floor. The clean lines of the imposing organ case in the front of the church communicate beauty without ostentation. As one faces the chancel, one sees an ample wooden pulpit on the left-hand side of the chancel. On center stage, one sees the moveable communion table with the words, "Do this in remembrance of me" carved into a header running around the table. To the right of the table stands a relatively small baptismal font. The wooden font rises to a height of three and a half feet. A small wooden cross graces the cover. The silver bowl inside the font comfortably holds a quart of water. Farther to the right, one will find a wooden lectern. The birth of a new baby in the life of the congregation results in the placement of a red rose bud in a simple vase on or near the baptismal font. A life-sized wooden cross, mounted on the organ case, provides symbolic orientation and unity for the whole sanctuary.

Worship Times

On Sunday mornings there are usually two services of worship during the period from Labor Day to Memorial Day. During the summers, the congregation gathers for a single service. During the academic year, the 8:45 service usually contains thirty-five to fifty people, most of whom are above the age of fifty. While the pastors make efforts to ensure that most everything remains the same between the two services, the sacrament of baptism is rarely celebrated at the early service. At the 11:00 service during the school year, one can easily count two hundred people. A wide range of ages characterizes this service. Most of the time the sanctuary feels comfortably populated for this service. The full choir always sings. The congregation energetically participates in the responsive prayers and in the singing of hymns. Because most families with young children attend this service, one of the pastors usually offers a children's sermon. Following the children's sermon, most of the children leave the sanctuary in order to participate in an educational enrichment program designed to equip them for active participation in regular worship.

Between the two services, St. Peter's offers education classes for all ages. The number of children, youth, and adults participating in the Sunday morning education programs averages around 150 persons. Teams of adult volunteers teach denominational materials in the children's classes. The six to eight middle school students alternate between computer-based Christian education curricula and discussion of biblical themes related to their lives. The senior high class varies its content from minicourses on a variety of youth-related "hot topics" to discussion of films that have religious themes. Three of the four adult education classes function as support or fellowship groups and use curricular material to strengthen relationships and to further Christian understanding. The fourth Sunday morning adult education class focuses mainly on current theological and ethical issues.

The schedule changes during the summer months. The congregation gathers for only one service of worship at 10:00. Education classes for all ages precede the service of worship by one hour. The summer worship services maintain all the elements of the services during the rest of the year, except for children's messages and a pick-up choir instead of the chancel choir.

The head of staff preaches three out of four Sundays throughout the year. The associate pastor preaches about once a month. Occasionally, a seminary intern will preach. The sermons usually consist of thoughtful reflections on the intersection of biblical texts and contemporary issues in the congregation and the cultural issues facing white, suburban, middle-class families.

The Administration of the Sacrament of Baptism

The pastors administer the sacrament of baptism at St. Peter's three or four times a year during the regularly scheduled Sunday morning services. In keeping with the norms of the PC(USA) and the larger Reformed tradition, the pastors do not administer emergency baptisms. Nor do baptisms occur as a private, family-only ritual. Baptisms always take place in the sanctuary on Sunday mornings during the regularly scheduled services of worship.

Infants and small children make up the largest percentage of candidates for baptism. Occasionally, one can see the baptism of a teenager as a part of the confirmation process. Rarely, it seems, does an adult seek baptism as part of the new members' class.

One cannot simply show up on any given Sunday, infant in arms, and demand baptism for the child. Presbyterian polity requires that the pastors and the session follow a "decent and orderly" process of pedagogical and administrative preparation prior to the celebration of baptism. This process entails submitting a formal request for baptism to the church's governing body (the session) and meeting with one of the pastors for preparatory education about the meaning of the practice of baptism.

In the polity of the PC(USA), only the session of the local church may approve requests to receive the sacrament of baptism. The session, a group of ordained laypeople serving on three-year rotation together with the two pastors, thoughtfully considers each request for baptism. The session determines the suitability for baptism on the basis of evidence of Christian faith by the candidate or by at least one parent who has a record of church membership, usually in that congregation. Under special circumstances, a request for baptism may be approved by the session even if the candidate or the candidate's parents belong to another Christian tradition or to no tradition at all, as in the case of those who are just now coming to the Christian faith.

The second part of the preparatory process involves meeting with a pastor. This meeting usually takes place a few days to several weeks in advance of the baptismal event. The purpose of this meeting is primarily educational. The pastor explains the meaning of the rite according to biblical teaching and denominational convictions as refracted through the essential tenets of the Reformed tradition. In these meetings the pastor will often initiate a conversation with the candidate or with the candidate's parents about the linkage between baptism and living a pattern of Christian life in church and society. These meetings typically focus on liturgical choreography and administrative procedures related to the upcoming event.

On a baptismal Sunday, the elder in charge of worship reserves the first one or two pews at the front of the sanctuary on the baptismal font side for the baptismal candidate, family members, sponsors, and assorted close friends. Usually, an observer of the congregation can easily recognize baptismal Sundays due to the presence of five to ten very dressed up visitors armed with camcorders and seated with the candidate's family in the first two rows of pews on the right side of the sanctuary.

PC(USA) congregations have great flexibility with respect to the ordering of worship.[17] At St. Peter's, baptism comes before the ministry of the Word. There is no particular theological commitment behind this pattern. The placement of the sacrament of baptism immediately before the reading of Scripture and the preaching of the sermon encourages the children in the congregation to participate in the rite. It also allows the parents of restless or cranky infants to take them to the nursery immediately following the event.

One never finds baptism and the Eucharist celebrated on the same Sunday. Neither the pastors nor the session make any discernible effort to coordinate baptisms with high holy days in the liturgical calendar. Baptisms are primarily administered according to demand.

At the appointed moment in the service, the pastor presiding over the sacrament gets up and calls all the children of the congregation forward to sit on the chancel steps. As the children bound up the aisles and arrange themselves on the chancel steps, the pastor then calls up the candidate for baptism and the appropriate members of the candidate's entourage, usually the parent or parents and a sponsor or two. At the same time that the children and the appropriate members of the baptismal party move to their appointed locations, the elder from the session appointed for the day moves into the pulpit. The pastor and the baptismal party gather around the baptismal font.

When everyone is in place, the rite begins.[18] The pastor begins the pre-

17. PC(USA) polity allows for considerable flexibility with regard to the ordering of worship in particular congregations. See *Book of Order,* W-1.4001 and W-3.1001-2 for more detailed discussion.

18. "The Sacrament of Baptism," in *The Book of Common Worship* (hereafter *BCW*), prepared by the Theology and Worship Ministry Unit for the Presbyterian Church (U.S.A.) and the Cumberland Presbyterian Church (Louisville: Westminster John Knox, 1993), pp. 403-15.

sentation of the candidate with a reading of the Great Commission from
the end of Matthew's Gospel:

Hear the words of our Lord Jesus Christ:

All authority in heaven and on earth
has been given to me.
Go therefore and make disciples of all nations,
baptizing them in the name of the Father,
and of the Son,
and of the Holy Spirit,
and teaching them to obey everything that I have commanded you.
And remember, I am with you always,
to the end of the age. (Matt. 28:18-20)[19]

The recitation of this Gospel text not only opens the rite but also orients
the interpretation of the event about to unfold. This text functions effectively to renew and to make specific God's covenantal promise with regard
to the rite of baptism. It also links together the explicitly trinitarian event
of baptism and the practices of faith formation before and after the event.
In the initial moments of the rite, teaching, baptism, and the Trinity are indissolubly, if embryonically, linked together.

The presiding minister continues by reading one or more of five brief
selections from the Acts of the Apostles or one of the epistles.[20] On this
particular occasion, the pastor chose to read the passage from the sixth
chapter of the Epistle to the Romans:

Do you not know
that all of us who have been baptized into Christ Jesus
were baptized into his death?
Therefore we have been buried with him by baptism into his death,
so that, just as Christ was raised from the dead
by the glory of the Father,
so we too might walk in newness of life.

(Rom. 6:3-4)[21]

19. *BCW*, p. 403.
20. Eph. 4:4-6; Gal. 3:27-28; 1 Pet. 2:9; Rom. 6:3-4; Acts 2:39.
21. *BCW*, p. 404.

This biblical text serves further to introduce and interpret the rite. It signals to all present the inner meaning of the rite. It reminds the listeners that they also have a personal stake in what takes place in this rite because they have been baptized. They, too, have entered into the reality and way of life to which the sacrament bears witness. This particular celebration provides an occasion for the whole congregation to recall and to renew their own baptisms even as they witness and participate in someone else's baptism.

The Romans text further signals to all that the water rite has a much deeper significance than simply applying a bit of water to the baptizand's head. The rite intends a mystical or spiritual meaning for the baptizand as well as for the already baptized. It signifies nothing less than some sort of participation in or entering into the death and resurrection of Jesus Christ. The seemingly innocuous act of sprinkling with a few drops of water is merely the surface manifestation of a deep and profound transformation from death to life.

After the recitation of two scriptural texts, the minister continues to introduce and to interpret the rite by reading a few lines of carefully crafted prose from the text of the baptismal liturgy. These lines intend to provide further framing for the water act:

> Obeying the word of your Lord Jesus,
> and confident of his promises,
> we baptize those whom God has called.
>
> In baptism God claims us,
> and seals us to show that we belong to God.
> God frees us from sin and death,
> uniting us with Jesus Christ in his death and resurrection.
> By water and the Holy Spirit, we are made members of the church,
> the body of Christ,
> and joined to Christ's ministry of love, peace, and justice.
>
> Let us remember with joy our own baptism,
> as we celebrate this sacrament.[22]

In this statement, the denomination's doctrine of baptism is succinctly communicated to the congregation and to the baptismal party. The rite

---

22. *BCW*, pp. 404-5.

unmistakably lifts up themes of divine promise, election, liberation, church membership, and faithful activism in society. Through this well-crafted prose the minister locates the meaning of the rite not only in the broad flow of Christian religion but also in the particular historical stream of the Reformed tradition in which the PC(USA) stands. Additionally, we find here an interesting interplay between tenses. The present event recalls past celebrations of baptism for the gathered congregants. It also calls the gathered assembly to look forward to the ongoing effect and vocational import of the baptismal rite. The rite brings together past, present, and future at the point of identity and vocation.

The initial phase of the rite continues in a distinctively Reformed and Presbyterian modality. The latter half of the presentation section of the rite follows a covenantal pattern of action and interpretation. The elder appointed to participate in the rite on this day now addresses the congregation. The elder represents the session in presenting the candidate for baptism. The elder declares that the session has approved the candidate for baptism. Thus, the rite calls forth in synecdochic form the fundamental polity of the church characterized by partnership between ordained pastors and ordained laity or elders.

Proceeding on, the focus now shifts back to the minister, who poses questions of intent to the baptizand's parents (or to the baptizand) and to the sponsors, if any happen to be present.[23] Instead of the minister, the elder from the session assigned to the celebration of this rite poses a covenantal question to the congregation. These covenantal questions run as follows:

[To parents:] Do you desire that N. be baptized?
Relying on God's grace do you promise to live the Christian faith, and to teach that faith to your child?

[To teens and adults:] N., do you desire to be baptized?

---

23. In the case of young children, there are no prescribed age demarcations that determine when a pastor may pose the question directly to the child instead of to the parents. The pastor usually makes this determination in consultation with the parents of the baptizand. In some cases, a pastor will pose a basic form of this set of questions to a child as young as four or five years of age. The rite also allows for sponsors, but does not require them. Most baptizands at St. Peter's have no sponsors.

[To sponsors:] Do you promise, through prayer and example,
to support and encourage N.
to be a faithful Christian?

[To the congregation:] Do you, as members of the church
    of Jesus Christ,
promise to guide and nurture N.
by word and deed
with love and prayer,
encouraging him/her to know and follow Christ
and to be a faithful member of this church?[24]

These questions effectively involve everyone present as active participants in the rite. There are to be no passive observers in the baptismal rite. All present participate actively in some fashion, except for nonbaptized adults who may happen to be present in the pews on that particular occasion. Each baptized person present who is a member of that (or some other) Christian congregation is given the opportunity to make a solemn promise with regard to the person undergoing baptism.

At St. Peter's, the presiding pastor poses an additional set of questions. The pastor directs them to the children of the congregation seated on the chancel steps watching the event unfold. One of the pastors or the seminary intern poses the following question not found in the PC(USA) baptismal liturgy. The minister asks the children:

Do you promise to be a friend to N.? If s/he needs directions will you show him/her the way? If s/he falls down will you pick him/her up? Will you play with him/her and share with him/her the stories of Jesus?

This set of questions for the children of the congregation will not be found in the official liturgical texts of the denomination. They represent an embellishment of the rite common to many PC(USA) churches in the southeastern region. The origin of these supplemental questions for the children of the congregation is not known with certainty. The various pastors of St. Peter's have used them regularly over the course of the past couple of decades.

When all of the parties present for the establishing of the baptismal covenant have indicated their intent to carry out their respective responsi-

24. *BCW*, pp. 405-6.

bilities and duties, the initial phase of the rite concludes. The rite has thus far been introduced and interpreted in reference to the trinitarian narrative of salvation with a Christological focus and within a covenantal frame. Pertinent groups — the baptismal party, the session, the pastoral leaders, the sponsors, and the congregation — have been actively engaged in making solemn covenantal vows. Past, present, and future come together in the rite in order to establish the identity and vocation of the baptizand.

The second phase of the rite calls for public profession of faith. The minister seamlessly continues in the liturgy without signaling a shift to this second phase of the rite. Another section of prose interpretation opens this phase of the rite:

> Through baptism we enter the covenant God has established.
> Within this covenant God gives us new life,
> guards us from evil,
> and nurtures us in love.
>
> In embracing this covenant we choose whom we will serve,
> by turning from evil and turning to Jesus Christ.
>
> [Turning to the candidate or to the candidate's parents:]
> As God embraces you within the covenant I ask you
> to reject sin, to profess your faith in Christ Jesus,
> and to confess the faith of the church,
> the faith in which we baptize.[25]

This material provides a conceptual bridge between the end of the previous section, which posed covenantal questions to all parties present, and the expressions of Christian faith that follow in the section immediately preceding the water act. The distinctively Reformed character of the rite now incorporates demythologized elements from the ancient West Syrian twin practices of renunciation *(apotaxis)* and adherence *(syntaxis)*.[26]

> Trusting in the gracious mercy of God,
> Do you turn from the ways of sin
> and renounce evil and its powers in the world?

---

25. *BCW*, pp. 406-7.
26. E. C. Whitaker, *The Baptismal Liturgy*, 2nd ed. (London: SPCK, 1981), pp. 22ff.

Do you turn to Jesus Christ
and accept him as your Lord and Savior,
trusting in his grace and love?

Will you be Christ's faithful disciple,
Obeying his Word and showing his love?[27]

Having received affirmative answers to these questions the minister now turns to the whole congregation and invites everyone to stand, as they are able, in order to join in a common profession of faith by reciting the Apostles' Creed. The liturgical text at this point provides an option. The pastor may decide to lead the congregation in a seriatim recitation of the three articles of this trinitarian creed. Alternatively, the creed may be offered in its original tripartite interrogational form in which the recitation of each article is preceded by a question formally posed by the minister. Even though this particular creedal affirmation developed out of the substrate of the baptismal liturgy, the pastors at St. Peter's usually opt to omit the historical interrogatives at the head of each of the sections of the creed.[28] The use of the Apostles' Creed definitively locates this liturgical act and the attendant community within the Western or Latin Christian tradition because this particular creed arose out of the baptismal practices of the Western Christian tradition. No churches of Eastern Christianity use this creed in their baptismal rite.[29]

In the case of infants, this second section concludes with the recitation of the Apostles' Creed. If, however, an adult or teenage member is being baptized on the basis of an active profession of faith in Jesus Christ, then the profession of faith phase of the rite concludes with a further question posed to the baptizand:

Will you be a faithful member of this congregation,
share in its worship and ministry
through your prayers and gifts,
your study and service,
and so fulfill your calling to be a disciple of Jesus Christ?[30]

27. *BCW*, p. 407.

28. J. N. D. Kelly, *Early Christian Creeds*, 3rd ed. (New York: Longman, 1972), pp. 30-61.

29. For a fuller treatment of the historical development leading up to the current form of the Apostles' Creed, see Kelly, *Early Christian Creeds*, pp. 368-434.

30. *BCW*, p. 408.

The juxtaposition of this question with the trinitarian profession of faith intends to join Christian belief and Christian practice. The rite does not make any explicit verbal linkages between them; the explicit and intentional linkage between the rite of baptism, trinitarian belief, and constitutive practices of the Christian life as understood in the Reformed tradition is left undeveloped in the rite.

With these preliminary steps completed, the gathered company now moves into the heart of the rite. The liturgical text calls for water to be poured into the baptismal font "visibly and audibly."[31] This rarely occurs at St. Peter's. The rite provides no prose interpretation for this act. Seeing and hearing this most basic of elements — associated with the sustenance of living things on the earth and with its full range of symbolic resonances — signals the transition into the central act of the rite. The pastors of St. Peter's generally do not follow the stage instructions supplied by rubrics. Instead, while praying the prayer over the water, they usually lift out some of the water already in the font and allow it to gently cascade back into the font. More often than not, the congregation does not see or hear the water. Usually, only the presiding pastor, the family, and the gathered assembly of children strewn across the chancel steps experience the aesthetic dimensions of the rite. For the most part, the words of the rite overshadow the sensory aspects of the rite until the epicenter of the baptismal liturgy.

Immediately upon pouring the water into the font, the presiding minister leads the congregation in a prayer of "Thanksgiving Over the Water." This water prayer has three main sections.[32] It begins with the traditional Western church dialogue between minister and congregation. In this way, the opening section of the central section of the rite links it with the celebration of the Eucharist. Unlike the form used for the Eucharistic celebration, however, the second dialogical exchange does not find a place in the baptismal prayer.[33] In the main body of the prayer, the presiding pastor gives thanks to the Triune God on behalf of the congregation by means of a highly selective recounting of water-related moments in salvation history:

---

31. *BCW*, p. 410.

32. Actually, *BCW* makes two prayers available for use. I have selected the first of the two. Both prayers have the same basic structure and pattern.

33. "Lift up your hearts. We lift them to the Lord." *BCW*, p. 69.

The Lord be with you.
And also with you.
Let us give thanks to the Lord our God.
It is right to give our thanks and praise.

We give you thanks Eternal God,
for you nourish and sustain all living things
by the gift of water.
In the beginning of time,
your Spirit moved over the watery chaos,
calling forth order and life.

In the time of Noah,
you destroyed evil by the waters of the flood,
giving righteousness a new beginning.

You led Israel out of slavery,
through the waters of the sea,
into the freedom of the promised land.

In the waters of Jordan
Jesus was baptized by John
and anointed with your Spirit.
By the baptism of his own death and resurrection,
Christ set us free from the power of sin and death,
and opened the way to eternal life.

We thank you, O God, for the water of baptism.
In it we are buried with Christ in his death.
From it we are raised to share in his resurrection.
Through it we are reborn by the power of the Holy Spirit.

Send your Spirit to move over this water
that it may be a fountain of deliverance and rebirth.
Wash away the sin of *all* who *are* cleansed by it.
Raise *them* to new life,
and graft *them* to the body of Christ.
Pour out your Holy Spirit upon *them,*
that they may have power to do your will,
and continue forever in the risen life of Christ.

To you, Father, Son, and Holy Spirit, one God,
be all praise, honor, and glory,
now and forever.
Amen.[34]

The tenses and trinitarian grammar of this prayer convey the sense that the event being celebrated has a wide and deep significance. By this rite, the baptizand and the gathered company participate in and are grafted into the entire sweep of the Triune economy of salvation taking place within history. Funded by the past and swept up into the future, the present act discloses Triune meaning. The third part of the prayer has the character of an epiclesis, a liturgical prayer invoking the presence of the Holy Spirit. The community through the prayer of the pastor requests that the First Person of the Trinity send the Third Person in order to join the baptizand with the Second Person in and through participation in the church on behalf of the world.[35]

We should note in passing that the presiding pastor at St. Peter's often shortens this prayer in order to save time and to keep the worship service within the tacitly agreed-upon time limit of one hour. When this tactical shortening takes place, much of the theological richness and precision of relating this event to the grand sweep of the Triune economy gets left on the liturgical cutting room floor.

At the conclusion of the prayer over the water, the presiding pastor gestures for the parents to give the child to the pastor. In the case of school-aged children or adults, the pastor motions for the baptizand to kneel on the chancel steps. The pastor receives the infant or young child and then positions it comfortably in her or his arms. Then the pastor reaches into the baptismal font, scoops up a small amount of water, and applies it to the baptizand's head. The pastor repeats this gesture three times corresponding to each member of the Trinity:

N., I baptize you
In the name of the Father,
And of the Son,
And of the Holy Spirit.
Amen.[36]

34. *BCW*, pp. 410-11.
35. *BCW*, pp. 410-11.
36. *BCW*, p. 413.

These words reflect the standard pattern of the Western churches.[37] The words used in this rite assume that the Holy Spirit works through the agency of the church and through the leadership and ministry of the presiding pastor to make the baptizand a member of the Body of Christ.

The presiding pastor follows the application of the sanctified water with the laying on of hands and a blessing. The current senior pastor of St. Peter's has anointed baptizands with oil only in response to specific requests for it, even though the liturgical rubrics for the rite suggest it.[38] In the liturgical rubrics for the rite supplied by the PC(USA), the anointing with oil is suggested, but remains entirely optional. The senior pastor and the majority of members tend to view anointing with oil as an undesirable Roman Catholic practice.

The baptismal rite concludes with a series of actions related to welcoming the newly baptized into the life of the church. In the case of infants and small children, the presiding pastor walks down the chancel steps with child in arms, careful to avoid tripping on the assembled body of children from the congregation who have witnessed the event. Once on the main level of the sanctuary, the pastor walks down the central aisle and usually says something along the lines of the following:

> See what love the Father has given us that we should be called the children of God and so we are. I want to you to welcome N. to the family of God. This child is our newest member. Please remember the promises you made today when someone calls you and asks you to teach Sunday School or to volunteer to help out with Vacation Bible School or with the midweek Logos program for the children and youth program of our church.

After processing up and down the center aisle, the presiding pastor climbs the chancel steps and returns the child to its parents. Sometimes the pastor asks the congregation to join in a very short impromptu prayer of blessing for the newly baptized. The closing acts of the rite called for in *The Book of Common Worship* — a unison liturgical response of welcome by the con-

---

37. The Eastern churches, by contrast, use an intentionally passive construction provided by John Chrysostom, "you are baptized in the name of . . . ," which is meant to emphasize the work of the Holy Spirit in the act of baptism. See E. C. Whitaker, *Documents of the Baptismal Liturgy*, 2nd ed. (London: SPCK, 1970; paperback ed., 1977), p. 36.

38. *BCW*, p. 413.

gregation and the exchange of peace — rarely find their way into the pattern of practice at St. Peter's Church. Sometimes, the choir will sing a transitional anthem with a baptismal theme to close the rite and to provide transitional music to the next section of the service of worship. The music also functions as "travel music," allowing for the baptismal party to remove the newly baptized infant from the sanctuary and for the designated adults to usher the rest of the young children from the sanctuary steps, out of the sanctuary, and into their supplemental liturgical education program in one of St. Peter's education buildings.

The rubrics at the end of baptismal rite note that if the Eucharist is celebrated during the same service in which baptism is celebrated, it is appropriate for the newly baptized to receive the communion elements first. The rubrics do not stipulate minimum age requirements for admission to the Lord's Table. Current PC(USA) policy leaves this matter to the discretion of parents in consultation with the pastor and with the approval of the session. In actual practice, Presbyterian congregations differ rather widely in their policies concerning the admission of baptized children to the Eucharist.[39] For the most part, at St. Peter's any linkage between the two rites is so muted as to be almost nonexistent.

Patterns of Post-Baptismal Ecclesial Pedagogy

Following the administration of baptism, the church expects the newly baptized to participate in a pattern of ecclesial pedagogy for a number of years. For those baptized as infants, this means moving from the nursery through the graded Sunday morning church school as well as participation in a concentrated week of study in the summer. It may also imply partici-

---

39. See the following sections of the *Book of Order* on the subject: G-5.0301.b, W-2.4011.b, and W-4.2002. There seems to be some incoherence on this subject in the church's polity. The first text cited seems to indicate that all baptized children are welcome to partake of the Eucharist even prior to any explicit profession of faith in Jesus Christ. The second statement seems to stipulate that as long as baptized children receive some instruction about the sacrament of the Lord's Supper they are welcome to participate in it. The third text puts the accent on the subjectivity of the child, emphasizing that the key variable is the child's conscious desire for communion. This seeming incoherence may well mask or cover over a deeper-level problem about the fundamental relationship between the sacraments of baptism and the Lord's Supper.

pation in the Logos midweek program. Parents are also encouraged to teach the basics of Christian life and belief at home. Many parents at St. Peter's avoid this because they feel ill-equipped to do so and fear that they would lack appropriate answers for potential questions that their growing children might pose to them.

The next major event connected with baptism for most baptized children at St. Peter's comes in early to mid-adolescence with the experience of the confirmation class. The church offers this program to help baptized children who are entering into the early stages of adulthood to appropriate the faith for themselves. After a period of teaching and preparation, confirmands are presented to the congregation, and they confirm the promises made on their behalf at the time of their baptism as infants by making their own covenantal promises as they publicly profess the Christian faith.

The practice of confirmation has a long history. It is a distinctively Western church phenomenon. In the ancient church, the baptismal rite was divided up. The profession of faith and the application of water portions of the rite were performed together. The third section of the rite, the confirmation or sealing, was often delayed until the bishop could be present. The completion of baptism might, therefore, be delayed for a period of months or years. By the Middle Ages, this split within the sacramental rite eventuated in the elevation of confirmation to sacramental status in its own right. The sacrament of confirmation functioned as a rite of passage from childhood into adulthood.

The Protestant churches demoted confirmation from its medieval sacramental status, but they maintained the basic pattern of practice, only now the emphasis was placed on the transmission of sets of doctrinal beliefs. In the Reformed tradition, confirmation became the gateway to participation in the Eucharist. In order to participate in the Lord's Supper in a worthy manner, it was thought that a young person needed to demonstrate a minimum level of doctrinal proficiency. In this framework, the course was usually called communicants' class, indicating that it provided the doctrinal requirement for admission to the sacrament of Holy Communion.

This system was criticized and reevaluated in relatively recent decades. The chief criticisms were that preadolescent children routinely demonstrated a vital and active Christian faith and that putting a doctrinal fence around the sacrament functionally excommunicated the developmentally disabled and the mentally infirm, not to mention the recognized fact that no one — not even Calvin himself — actually understood fully what was taking place in the sacramental event. In the 1970s, the preparation for communion paradigm gave way to the commissioning paradigm. In this framework, the required adolescent class became the occasion to prepare and equip emerging young adults to take up their ministries of service as active church members working for reconciliation in society.

In recent decades, the church has moved toward a confirmation model that includes a commissioning emphasis but ties the whole process directly to the sacrament of baptism, completing and bringing to fulfillment what was set in motion when their parents brought them to the font as babies.

Some attempts have been made in the PC(USA) liturgical resources to connect baptism with other significant life events in addition to confirmation. For example, an optional text in the covenant-making part of the wedding service explicitly links baptism and the marriage covenant.[40] The "Service of Witness to the Resurrection" at the time of death also makes provisions for seeing death as a completion and fulfillment of baptismal transformation.[41] Additionally, baptismally based liturgies are available for the renewal of a congregation, for the reception of new members, for various occasions of growth in the faith, and for certain situations of pastoral care and counseling.[42] The pastoral staff at St. Peter's Church has adapted the baptismal service for use in commissioning participants in youth mission trips and as a unit in the two-year cycle of the children's liturgical education program. Renewal of baptism has been incorporated into the Sunday morning liturgy of the congregation twice in recent years.

To summarize, the ritual aspect of the practice of baptism takes place in a congregation with particular bodies and with a complex interplay of words and gestures. The concrete, particular, bodily practice of baptism provides the substrate out of which theological reflection, understandings of the Christian life, and ecclesial pedagogy arise.

In order to explore this situated account of the baptismal rite in greater depth, we need to step back from describing the details of the ritual dimensions of the practice as celebrated in the St. Peter's Presbyterian Church in order to reflect more deeply upon the meaning of the rite as

40. *BCW*, p. 843.
41. *BCW*, pp. 912 and 921-23.
42. *BCW*, pp. 431-88.

practiced. This move will both afford deeper insights and raise a number of important questions that we will want to take with us as we move further into this study.

Stepping Back from Baptismal Rite

The Meaning of Baptism

In order more fully to interpret the rite in its complexity and richness, it will be necessary to step back from the rite itself in the attempt to parse out some of the main threads of meaning tightly interwoven into its texture. By detaching from the immediacy of the intricate interweaving of text and action in the rite, I will seek at this point to trace some central thematic developments and to raise a series of questions that will guide the unfolding investigation into the relationship between baptism, the doctrine of the Trinity, and ecclesial pedagogy. We will not seek to interpret the baptismal rite and its initiatory implications in an exhaustive fashion. To do so would require a project devoted solely to this purpose. For now, we will focus on the themes of Trinity and pedagogy as tools for interpreting the deeper meaning of the situated account of the rite.

The Doctrine of the Trinity

The structure of the rite is thoroughly trinitarian in character. The PC(USA) baptismal liturgy uses explicitly trinitarian language from beginning to end. Proceeding from the scriptural recitations and the theological interpretation provided — during the initial phases of the rite, the corporate profession of the Apostles' Creed, the grammatical structure of the prayer of "Thanksgiving Over the Water," and in the words said during the application of the water — trinitarian language predominates. What makes the rite a distinctively Christian washing has to do with the linkage of the act of washing and the narrative of the economy of the Triune God's dealings with humanity across the sweep of history. This becomes clear as we seek to interpret the meaning of what has taken place in the baptismal celebration. Revisiting relevant portions of the rite will aid us in the examination of what it teaches and what questions it raises with regard to the

Trinity. Later, we will follow a similar procedure with regard to ecclesial pedagogy in relation to the baptismal liturgy.

The use of Matthew 28:18-20 in the presentation phase of the rite signals that this event is a religious practice with a trinitarian valence. The church takes in new members through baptism into "the name of the Father, and of the Son, and of the Holy Spirit."

The Triune character and language of this text at the head of the rite raises a number of important questions. In what ways do the baptized relate to the mystery of the Triune God? Does it mean that they somehow appropriate the activities or the energies of the Trinity? Do they bear the Triune Name like a union card or as a symbol of allegiance? What does it mean to be baptized into the one name, which is multiple? How might this shape an understanding of the Christian life in the context of the church and the wider society? The rite implicitly poses these questions and others like them.

Another set of insights opens up for us when we consider the Triune baptismal formula in reference to the context in which it appears. Immediately before and immediately after the explicit linkage between baptism and the Trinity in the Great Commission, we find the address of the risen Jesus Christ to the proto-church. On the basis of the authority given to him, he commands his followers to go out over the face of the entire world, making disciples and instructing those newly formed disciples in his commands. The passage concludes with Jesus Christ's promise to be with the church continually until the end of the age. The interplay in this Scripture used at the beginning of the rite suggests a dynamic interaction between Christology and trinitarian convictions. These two doctrinal loci suggest perhaps that Christology and trinitarian doctrine must mutually interpret one another and do so in relation to living a baptismally oriented Christian life in the context of the church and for the good of the wider world.

The interpretive prose section immediately following the scriptural citations employs trinitarian grammar. It shapes and guides the interpretation of the event and the life issuing forth from it. The risen Lord Jesus, the Second Person of the Trinity, gives commands and makes promises to the church. The First Person of the Trinity calls, claims, and seals people by freeing baptizands "from sin and death." The First Person unites them with the crucified and risen Second Person of the Trinity. The Third Person of the Trinity works to make baptizands members of the church and to join them to "Christ's ministry of love, peace, and justice." The rite intends to convey that the divine Persons work together in differentiated unity in both the rite and in the life of the baptized. It also communicates that the Trinity interrogates all of our living and dying. The Triune character of the Christian life comes through in the juxtaposition of the work of the Triune God "for us" in baptism and the life of love, peace, and justice to which baptizands are called. The baptized will come to know this life of love, peace, and justice partly through occasions for baptismal renewal in common worship and partly through participation in ecclesial pedagogy, which explores the meaning of baptism for the Christian life.

In the profession of corporate Christian faith, defined by the recitation of the Apostles' Creed, we find ourselves in deeper trinitarian waters. The location of the explicitly trinitarian Apostles' Creed at this point in the PC(USA) baptismal liturgy indicates that as participants move closer to the epicenter of the rite, they also move ever more deeply into the mystery of God as Trinity as the theme of the Christian life. The profession of the creed signals not only an historical or conceptual connection with the three divine Persons at work in the economy of salvation, but also that this reality shines through the present liturgical proceedings. The creed epitomizes the beliefs and implicitly points to the practices of the Christian life.

Again, the language of the rite provides clues as to how to interpret the rite and poses many questions. For example, we may ask about the nature of the interrelationship between the three Persons and about how this trinitarian pattern of divine activity relates to the life into which the baptized is initiated in the rite. How does the Triune grammar of this rite relate to the variety of frames of meaning among the various participants in the rite? Is the doctrine of God as Trinity merely a set of ideas to which one must give assent, or does it also provide orientation for a pattern of living in the church and for the world? In what sense might doctrine and patterning of life be intertwined? What difference does being baptized into the One Name That Is Three make for living with people who differ in both church and society? Does being baptized into the Triune Name provide any resources for living with others in differentiation and unity? What would constitute the basis for a unity in the midst of diversity in the church and in society? These questions highlight the fact that attempts to interpret the rite lead both to some notion of the doctrine of God as Triune and to a number of questions about the character of a baptismally based trinitarian pattern for the Christian life, which require further exploration outside of the celebration of the rite.

The prayer of "Thanksgiving Over the Water" further manifests trinitarian commitments at the heart of the baptismal rite. Addressed to the First Person of the Trinity, it recounts key events in salvation history in which the Triune God has been at work in and through water: creation, the judgment of sinful humanity and the deliverance of righteous Noah and his family, the Exodus, the baptism of Jesus by John, Jesus' death and resurrection, and the sacrament of baptism. The prayer locates baptism in the context of these events in the Triune economy of salvation. The concluding element of the prayer reiterates and reinforces the practical trinitarianism embedded in the prayer as a whole:

> We thank you, O God, for the water of baptism.
> In it we are buried with Christ in his death.
> From it we are raised to share in his resurrection,
> Through it we are reborn by the power of the Holy Spirit.[43]

When set in the context of the proclamation and prayers of the church to the Triune God, the water becomes an instrument of Triune transformation in the baptizand's life. By the work of the Holy Spirit and through the will of the Father, baptized persons are united with Jesus Christ in his death and resurrection. The gathered community prays with the presiding pastor that through this liturgical event the Holy Spirit will bring the baptizand to rebirth into a life of faithful discipleship in relation to Jesus Christ and to the glory of the Father. In some fashion or another, the water ceremony seeks to fund and shape the many patterns of everyday ritualizations that make up Christian daily life.

Further, this prayer calls upon the First Person of the Trinity to send forth the Third Person in order to sanctify the water and to transform the person who will undergo the sanctified washing:

> Send your Spirit to move over this water
> that it may be a fountain of deliverance and rebirth.
> Wash away the sin of *all* who *are* cleansed by it.
> Raise *them* to new life,
> and graft *them* to the body of Christ.
> Pour out your Holy Spirit upon *them*,
> that *they* may have the power to do your will,

43. *BCW*, p. 410.

and continue forever in the risen life of Christ.
To you, Father, Son, and Holy Spirit, one God,
be all praise, honor, and glory,
now and forever.
Amen.[44]

The epiclesis here is reminiscent of the long-standing practice in the Eucharistic "Great Prayers of Thanksgiving" in which the gathered company calls upon the Holy Spirit to bless and transform the gathered company, connecting them to the risen Christ. In both baptismal and Eucharistic epicleses, prayers call upon the First Person of the Trinity in the hope that the Third Person will be made present to work in and through the elements in such a way as to effect unity with the Second Person of the Trinity. The epicletic prayer attends not only to the present context of liturgical celebration but also to the whole extent of the baptizand's life. The liturgy forges a link between the baptismal rite, the Trinity, and the unfolding course of the baptizand's life. Thus, the treatment of the Trinity comes in the context of the conjunction of liturgical rite and biography.

Beginning with baptism and working outward, so to speak, the doctrine of the Trinity aims to function as a crucial part of the formation of individuals and communities. Baptism links the Trinity to concrete, embodied, historical people and communities and the lives they lead. Viewed through the lens provided by the baptismal rite, the doctrine of the Trinity ceases to function as a complicated abstraction and becomes the deep grammar for a whole way of life.

The climax of the rite comes with the application of water to the baptizand in the Triune Name. While the minister applies water to the baptizand, she or he interprets the act in explicitly trinitarian terms. Some pastors make three gestures with the water; others use only a single gesture. In both cases, the presiding pastor says:

N., I baptize you
in the name of the Father,
and of the Son,
and of the Holy Spirit.[45]

44. *BCW,* p. 411.
45. *BCW,* p. 413.

At this critical juncture, all of the themes, trajectories, and Persons come together into a simple, yet profound crescendo. In the context of the gathered congregation, water is applied to the body of the baptizand, marking that person as part of not only the church, but also and most especially of the Triune God. The ironic interplay of the quotidian symbol of water and the sublime affirmation of One God in Three Persons points to the character of the life embarked upon in this rite as well as to the qualities of the pedagogy that will make such a life possible. The baptizand, as adopted child of the Triune God, will spend the rest of his or her life becoming what he or she already is by virtue of having water applied to him or her in the Triune Name.

Laying on of hands, anointing, welcome, and sharing the peace conclude the rite. These ritual moments tend not to employ fully and explicitly trinitarian language, even though an underlying trinitarian grammar appears to be assumed. Instead, the texts call upon only one or two members of the Trinity. The laying on of hands and the anointing sections focus on the Third Person of the Trinity, while the act of welcome centers on the Second Person of the Trinity. The dense trinitarianism at the epicenter of the rite makes possible a focus on one or two Persons of the Godhead without concern for eroding the fundamental grammar of the rite as a whole. Correspondingly, with the assumption of a practical trinitarianism at work in the whole of the Christian life it becomes possible to focus on the Father, the Son, or the Holy Spirit at various points and for a variety of purposes along the way. The rite seems to point to some flexibility in the way in which the Triune grammar gets used in relation to the Christian life. Once duly established, Christian communities need not slavishly employ explicitly trinitarian language to describe divine activity. Conversely, particular focus on one or two of the divine Persons can be translated into a wider trinitarian framework.

The application of water and oil and the laying on of hands are all very concrete, bodily gestures. They involve human beings touching one another in specific ways in specific communal contexts for specific purposes. In baptism, the affirmation of the Triune God is inscribed upon the body of the person being baptized. Trinitarian grammar shapes a way of life precisely at the point of the body. Baptism brings the concrete, the sensory, the contextual, and the local aspects of human life together with the Triune mystery. Baptism demands that the doctrine of God as Trinity avoid speculation divorced or alienated from the corporeal and the local. Baptism gives trinitarian reflection a street address.[46] By extension, baptism provides a uniquely practical way to understand the doctrine of the Trinity in relation to the formation of individuals and communities. To reiterate: pursued by way of the baptismal rite with its deep trinitarian grammatical structure, the doctrine of the Trinity becomes a pervasive grammar for an entire way of life.

Thus, as we step back from the baptismal gestalt, we can see quite readily that the rite communicates a number of very significant convictional conceptualizations about the mystery of the Triune God. The rite conveys some of these messages explicitly while others are implied just below the surface of the text. The messages conveyed in the rite about the mystery of God are not promulgated for their own sake; rather, these messages teach powerfully and synecdochically what it means to live as human beings before the Triune mystery. In particular, they proclaim that human beings need vital relationships with the Triune God and with other human beings. The rite affirms implicitly that humans exist as relational creatures from beginning to end. By implication, aggressively asserted autonomous individuality, in which the person stands cut off from all other persons, represents the fundamental problem of human life. The baptismal rite, inasmuch as it involves an intense focus on the baptizand in the context of concentric circles of ecclesial community and vital relationship with the Triune God, points to a vision of human life characterized by uniqueness and clear differentiation of personhood in the context of interlocking webs of personal relationality. The baptized receive both uniqueness and connection with others in the baptismal rite. Baptism confers Christian identity and provides a basis for deepening that identity in the communal context of the church.

The baptismal rite affirms, too, that human beings are able to be called by God. This means that the baptizand is determined as a "response-able" being. Self-determination, in the most exaggerated sense of the term, expresses something crucial about the fundamental crisis of human existence apart from the Triune God. The rite proclaims that we are not left to our own devices in the seemingly "natural" condition in which we find ourselves apart from baptismal grace. In our so-called normal state we are

---

46. This line of reflection has been inspired in part by the discussion of Alexander Schmemann on the significance of water in the baptismal rite. See Schmemann, *Of Water and the Spirit*, pp. 37-43.

actually "mal-onomous"; that is, we are subject to the law of evil and corruption. The rite calls baptizands from self-trust to trust "in the gracious mercy of God."[47] In so doing, adherence to and dependence upon evil and the ways of sin must be publicly and decisively denounced. Response to the Triune God through trust in and adherence to Jesus Christ must follow immediately the renunciation of evil and sin. The rite summons the baptizand to theonomy; that is, the Triune God calls her or him to a life lived in loving relationships with the Triune God and with her or his neighbors. Triune determination sets the first and last words about human existence. Baptized children will have to grow into an understanding of this gift. The fundamental importance of the Triune grace bestowed in baptism requires frequent remembrance on the part of the whole congregation for this awareness to come to the fore and serve as determinative for the Christian life.

Finally, the baptismal rite communicates something crucial about human vocation. The Triune God calls and claims people for lives of authenticity and public witness. This same God also commissions and empowers people for lives of service to others in church and in society. God calls the baptized to live "joined to Christ's ministry of love, peace, and justice."[48] They are to participate in and serve as agents of the *Missio Dei* in the world.[49] They are called to participate in and to further the Triune work of redemption in the world.

Many of the questions raised about the character of the Christian life implicit in the trinitarian thematics of baptism point to the possibilities for human growth and transformation. While participants at each stage of the lifecycle may experience something of the numinous in the baptismal rite, they will each have a very different sense of the implications of the rite for belief and life. This line of interpretative probing of the baptismal rite pushes directly into the realm of ecclesial pedagogy.

---

47. *BCW*, p. 407.

48. *BCW*, p. 405.

49. On this concept, see Jürgen Moltmann, *The Church in the Power of the Holy Spirit: A Contribution to Messianic Ecclesiology*, trans. Margaret Kohl (New York: Harper & Row, 1975), pp. 10-11.

Practices of Ecclesial Pedagogy

The baptismal rite assumes and calls for a set of para-liturgical practices of ecclesial pedagogy. Such practices lead to and follow from the baptismal event itself. The rite asserts that in the natural state, human beings exist in alienation and separation from the Triune God. Human beings are not born into right relationship with God or with their neighbors. Right relatedness to God and neighbor — to which baptism serves as both initiation and proleptic witness — requires a lifetime of growth and maturation resultant from the subtle pedagogical work of the Triune God in and through the church. Candidates for baptism cannot simply show up for baptism, receive it upon demand, and leave as if it were an event with merely punctiliar significance. The revolutionary transformation in inner life and outer behavior does not come as a magical event. Baptism marks the entrance into an entire way of life characterized by ongoing transformation into deeper apprehension of the Triune mystery and its implications for daily life. Such a life requires serious preparation as well as lifelong effort in order to appropriate fully the gift of grace given in baptism. Inasmuch as this is the case, baptism requires a well-developed system of preparatory and implicative pedagogy that aims to form people in Triune faith, belief, and life.

Baptism assumes some pattern of preparatory ecclesial pedagogy. The headlining statement from Matthew 28:18-20 points to the complex task of faith formation that must precede baptism. Making disciples may take a variety of forms and involve a number of widely divergent processes. In whatever way churches conceive of the disciple-making task, it doubtless involves some complex set of intentional practices of teaching and learning. People grow into vital Triune faith and practice through a series of planned pedagogical interactions within the community of faith. Churches intentionally and tacitly — sometimes well, sometimes badly — engage in disciple-forming practices. In so doing they are involved in a part of the larger work of the sacrament of baptism. What ought these preparatory practices of formation into the Triune pattern of the Christian life entail? How would the preparation of parents of infants differ from the preparation of older children, youth, and adults? How long should such preparatory catechesis take? What might the curriculum include and exclude? The current PC(USA) baptismal rite does not provide explicit specifications for ecclesial pedagogy; it only provides hints and suggestions.

Practices of formation into Christian beliefs and practices also proceed from the rite of baptism. The risen Christ commands his followers to teach the baptized "to obey everything that I have commanded you." The text implies that this work of forming people into the Christian life requires ongoing effort. By implication, the baptized never graduate from the school of faith in the church. The rite sets the stage for viewing the entire range of formal and informal practices of ecclesial pedagogy as preparation for and extension of baptism. More than that, it calls forth ecclesial pedagogy. Baptism in all its fullness can only come to realization through sustained and intentional processes of ecclesial pedagogy spread over the entire lifecycle.

The rite of baptism conveys that this event involves much more than a ten-minute episode on some Sunday morning. Ongoing and intentional practices of faith formation ought to pervade the life of a local congregation. Such ecclesial pedagogy ought to foster commitment to doxological praise of the Trinity and a pattern of living out the Triune grammar of the Christian life.

The baptismal liturgy communicates several further messages about practices of ecclesial pedagogy. The baptismal rite places the complex set of practices aimed at formation into Christian faith and life within the context of promise making and promise keeping. The baptismal rite calls for practices of faith formation. These practices address head-on such basic human dramas as death and life, bondage and liberation, and sin and forgiveness. In a very condensed way, the rite points to and even makes possible a doxological way of life.[50] Through baptism, one enters into a particular kind of relationship with the Triune God. To be sure, all humans have a relationship with the Triune mystery all of the time. The author of the Acts of the Apostles attributes a particularly germane Pauline appropriation of Hellenistic poetry, "In him we live, move, and have our being" (17:28). Baptism represents moving into an awakening to the reality of a right, or reconciled, relationship with the Triune God.

Patterns of ecclesial pedagogy arising from the baptismal rite will require some developmental sensitivity if they are to address the needs and

---

50. I understand the phrase *doxological way of life* to entail love for and worship of the Triune God as the primary determination in a person's life. A life devoted to singing praise to the Triune God also implies being so transformed by encounter with the mystery of Triune love that one experiences increased capacity for love of one's human neighbors.

connect with the frameworks of meaning of baptizands across the lifecycle. We would do well to ask about pedagogical practices arising from and in service to the baptismal rite in its most fulsome sense. How might the baptismal rite provide the crucial organizing principle for the complex of activities and practices associated with the entire range of ecclesial pedagogy? In what ways might this highly specialized initiatory ritual exert shaping influence over patterns of daily ritualization in family and society?

This situated account of the PC(USA) baptismal rite begins to point toward ways by which baptism, the doctrine of the Trinity, and ecclesial pedagogy may be held together in dynamic tension.

In the following chapter we will see what can be gained by engaging scholarly reflection on the doctrine of the Trinity and on Christian education. We will then turn to two historical figures — one from the early church and one from the Reformation — who will afford insight into ways by which baptism, the Trinity, and pedagogy can be held together in a differentiated whole. The exploration of this dynamic nexus and the reconstruction of this nexus in our two exemplars will greatly aid the effort to articulate a constructive approach to this dynamic nexus for contemporary American mainline Presbyterian congregations.

CHAPTER 2

Depth Soundings in Theology
and Christian Education

At its heart baptism is not so much a distinct practice as it is the li-
turgical summation of all the Christian practices. In this rite, the
grace to which the Christian life is a response is fully and finally pre-
sented, visibly, tangible, and in words. Here all the practices are pres-
ent in crystalline form — forgiveness and healing, singing and testi-
mony, sabbath-keeping and community shaping, and all the others.
Unlike each particular practice, baptism does not address a specific
need, instead, it ritually sketches the contours of a whole new life,
within which all human needs can be perceived in a different
way. . . . Part of the work of Christian theologians in every age is to
reflect on the shape and character of the new way of life Christians
enter when we rise from the watery death of baptism. . . . Exploring
this question involves us both in contemplating the deepest founda-
tions of Christian faith and in figuring out the shape our living
should take amidst the immediate concerns of each day.

Craig Dykstra and Dorothy Bass,
"A Theological Understanding of Christian
Practices," in *Practicing Theology*

The baptismal rite at St. Peter's Presbyterian provides a concrete case to
anchor our reflections on the relationship between baptism, the Trinity,
and pedagogy. In the latter part of the previous chapter, we began to step

39

back from a description of the details of the rite as it functions in the whole ecology of formation in the congregation. This chapter will continue the effort to explore the links between the three elements of the crucial nexus of baptism, the Trinity, and pedagogy. In order to gain further insight into the meaning of baptism in relation to the doctrine of the Trinity and to ecclesial pedagogy, we will turn to the disciplines of theology and Christian education. We will track key threads in those two disciplines to see what further light can be shed on the issues under investigation.

Over the course of the past twenty years or so, many theologians have turned their attention to the doctrine of the Trinity. With each passing month, more and more books appear that aim to contribute to a revitalized approach to the doctrine of the Trinity. Many of these works claim that the doctrine is thoroughly practical in character. Some of these works have begun to pay attention to the formative and educational dimensions of the doctrine. While these efforts move in the right direction, much more remains to be done in order to make good on the promising beginnings of a practical doctrine of the Trinity, particularly with respect to the ways in which this distinctive Christian teaching can interface with the congregational efforts in education and formation for discipleship.

The field of Christian education — nearly moribund in recent decades with respect to theological vitality and depth — stands to gain a great deal by engaging the ferment around the doctrine of the Trinity taking place in theological circles today. A few signs of such engagement have recently begun to appear. Anchoring the discussion of trinitarian approaches to Christian education in the sacrament of baptism, the field may find its way back to theological vitality.

In this chapter, I explore what assistance we can find for thinking about the relationship of baptism, the Trinity, and Christian education in the fields of theology and Christian education. I take some "depth soundings" in both fields around this theme. In what follows I do not pretend to provide an exhaustive treatment of the relevant themes and thinkers; instead, I lift up some key episodes and issues that will bring into focus the possibility and need for an effort that brings this crucial nexus into bold relief.

Depth Soundings in Trinitarian Theology

Many trinitarian theologians today claim that the doctrine of the Trinity is the most practical of all Christian doctrines. This may seem a rather odd claim given the somewhat obscure history of the doctrine of the Trinity in much of Western Christianity. Until only fairly recently, the doctrine of the Trinity was thought to be a matter best left to academic theologians.

Contemporary theologians offer a variety of opinions concerning the point at which the doctrine of the Trinity lost its deep connection with the practices of the Christian life. Let us consider three such "fall" narratives concerning the severance of theory and practice in relation to the doctrine of the Trinity. Catherine Mowry LuCugna (1952-1997), Wolfhart Pannenberg, and Ellen Charry have each pointed to a particular period in church history when theological reflection lost its mooring in the quotidian practices of the Christian life.

We begin with the period of the early church. An examination of the early history of Christian doctrine provides evidence for a close association with Christian life and practice in the oldest strata of theological reflection. Perhaps no one stated so clearly as Prosper of Aquitaine (c. 390–c. 463) the primary understanding of the relationship between theory and practice during those early centuries of the church's life. His apt phrase, "the pattern of prayer determined the pattern of belief," applied equally well to the development of the doctrine of the Trinity as it did to other central doctrines of the faith.[1]

In his study of the development of early church creeds, J. N. D. Kelly articulated this sense of the close connection between the liturgical practice of baptism and the development of catechetical-liturgical or declaratory creeds in the following manner:

> Declaratory creeds may . . . be regarded as a by-product of the Church's fully developed catechetical system. At the same time, as Eusebius's remark helps to remind us, the traditional bridge joining them to baptism should not be ruthlessly demolished. It would be false as well as misleading to minimize the connection between them: it was in fact extremely intimate. The catechetical instruction of which declaratory

---

1. "Legem credendi lex statuat supplicandi." Quoted by Aidan Kavanagh, *The Shape of Baptism: The Rite of Christian Initiation,* Studies in the Reformed Rites of the Catholic Church, vol. 1 (New York: Pueblo, 1978), p. xii.

creeds were convenient summaries was instruction with a view to baptism. The catechumen was all the time looking forward to the great experience which would set the crown on all his intensive preparatory effort. So closely did the catechetical instruction dovetail into the ceremony of initiation which was to be its climax that the single word baptism, in an extended sense, could be used to cover them both taken together. Thus St. Irenaeus could speak of "the rule of truth . . . which he received through baptism (διὰ τοῦ βαπτισμός)." Furthermore, the catechetical preparation was dominated by those features of the impending sacrament which constituted its essence, the threefold interrogation with the threefold assent, and the threefold immersion. Consequently the instruction deliberately aimed . . . at elucidating and expounding the three aspects of the Divine Being in Whose triune name the baptism was to be accomplished, and the catechetical summaries whose formation it prompted were inevitably cast in the Trinitarian mould.[2]

During some of the earliest layers of Christian history, theological reflection always had to be squared with the traditional practices of prayer and praise operative in the churches of the day. Theological reflection unfolded in close proximity to liturgical and pedagogical practice.

Catherine Mowry LaCugna pointed out in her work *God for Us: The Trinity and Christian Life* that the patterns of prayer and liturgical practice were also reformulated in light of theological controversies in the early church.[3] Thus, it would seem that Prosper's axiom worked — unhappily so, according to LaCugna — in reverse fashion. She argued that the first Council of Nicea (325) effectively reversed the earliest and more desirable pattern: "In the entire process of doctrinal development, Prosper's axiom that 'the law of worship funds or constitutes the law of belief' was reversed: the law of belief, namely the doctrine of the Trinity, came to constitute the law of worship. Orthodoxy (*ortho doxa* = right opinion or right belief) ac-

---

2. J. N. D. Kelley, *Early Christian Creeds,* 3rd ed. (New York: Longman, 1972), pp. 51-52, citing *Adv. Haer.* 1.9.4 (*P.G.* 7:545).

3. "Prosper of Aquitaine coined the axiom that 'the law of prayer funds the law of belief' *(legem credendi lex statuat supplicandi).* On the other hand, the patterns of liturgical prayer were forced to change in light of the resolution of those same Christological and Trinitarian controversies." Catherine Mowry LaCugna, *God for Us: The Trinity and Christian Life* (New York: HarperCollins, 1991; New York: HarperCollins Paperbacks, 1993), p. 112.

quired the sense, particularly in the creeds, of right teaching."[4] LaCugna argued that theologians in the fourth century in both East and West "followed a course that significantly relaxed, or depending on one's point of view, even compromised the pre-Nicene connection between *oikonomia* and *theologia*."[5] LaCugna argued that this change resulted in a loss of the thoroughly practical character of the doctrine of the Trinity from the early third century until the mid-twentieth century. She further argued that the disjunction of Christian practice and theological reflection has been effectively addressed only by her theological mentor, Karl Rahner (1904-1984), in his assertion that the economic Trinity (God's relations with us) is identical to the immanent Trinity (God's internal relations apart from creation).[6] Rahner's claim, or axiom, makes it possible once again to talk in a meaningful way about the mystery of God as Trinity in relation to the complexities of lived human experience. In her view, the Triune God is at work in the history of creation and redemption in order to bring about healing, restoration, and transformation of human life. So, LaCugna blames the "fall" of theological reflection on the first ecumenical council and the advent of Constantinianism.

Wolfhart Pannenberg offers a different account of the "fall" of theological reflection from its integration into the life and work of the church. In his work *Theology and the Philosophy of Science,* he explores the character of theology in relation to scientific inquiry.[7] Part of Pannenberg's study involves an investigation of the character of theology in the early church as sapiential wisdom *(sapientia)*. This wisdom was contrasted with a more disconnected and abstract knowledge *(scientia)*.[8] In his view, the predominance of the "practice funds theory" approach generally prevailed in Western Christianity precisely until the rise of a *scientia* that was increasingly disconnected from the life and practices of the church. This shift took place primarily in the medieval universities in the twelfth and thirteenth centuries.[9] With the relocation of the context for theological reflection away from the cathedral and the monastery and into the universities, the

---

4. LaCugna, *God for Us*, p. 135.

5. LaCugna, *God for Us*, p. 12.

6. LaCugna, *God for Us*, pp. 2 and 211-24.

7. Wolfhart Pannenberg, *Theology and the Philosophy of Science*, trans. Francis McDonagh (Philadelphia: Westminster, 1976).

8. Pannenberg, *Theology and the Philosophy of Science*, p. 8.

9. Pannenberg, *Theology and the Philosophy of Science*, p. 228.

configuration of the theory-practice relationship gradually shifted toward the primacy of theological theory, or an Aristotelian-inspired *scientia.*

Pannenberg points out that there were voices at the time of this shift who argued strongly for the practical character of theology; yet the arguments supported by William of Auxerre (c. 1180-1249) and Bonaventure (c. 1217-1274) did not carry the day. Scholastic theologians like Thomas Aquinas (c. 1225-1274) prevailed in promulgating the primacy of a more purely theoretical and speculative conception of theology.[10] Unlike LaCugna's pointing of the finger of blame at Nicea, Pannenberg points to the rise of the medieval universities and scholastic theology as the crucial moment in the severance of theological theory and ecclesial practice.

Ellen Charry's version of the "fall" emphasizes the seismic changes that occurred in theological reflection as a result of the Enlightenment. In her book *By the Renewing of Your Minds: The Pastoral Function of Christian Doctrine,* Charry points out that theology up to a certain point had what she calls an "aretegenic" character (from the Greek term relating to the formation of excellence or virtue).[11] Theological reflection and teaching was intrinsically oriented to the Christian life and the acquisition of practical wisdom. It aimed to "assist people to come to God."[12] According to Charry, most theological reflection was aretegenic, or sapiential, in character up to the Enlightenment of the seventeenth and eighteenth centuries. Reflecting on the wrong turn taken at the Enlightenment, she argues: "The Enlightenment challenged the epistemic status of Christian claims. Concomitantly, historical criticism also obscured pastoral aspirations of theological texts. Scholarly attention to the debates and circumstances surrounding the formation of Christian doctrines crowds out the implications of texts for Christian living."[13]

Interestingly, Charry's constructive argument proceeds by way of close reading of patristic, medieval, and Reformation theological texts demonstrating that in each era theological reflection on doctrines like the Trinity paid a great deal of attention to the formation of communities and individuals into a particular kind of life. Her constructive proposals based on this interpretation of the "fall" aim to retrieve insights from pre-modern

10. Pannenberg, *Theology and the Philosophy of Science,* pp. 229ff.

11. Ellen Charry, *By the Renewing of Your Minds: The Pastoral Function of Doctrine* (New York: Oxford University Press, 1997), p. 19.

12. Charry, *By the Renewing of Your Minds,* p. 5.

13. Charry, *By the Renewing of Your Minds,* p. 16.

thinkers for the purpose of reclaiming the practical dimensions of theological reflection upon such doctrines as the Trinity in a late modern or postmodern situation. While she recognizes the impossibility of ignoring or jumping back over the Enlightenment, she intends to correct some of the distortions of theological reflection brought about by the Enlightenment by bringing several pre-modern voices into contemporary theological conversations.[14] The shape of her argument lends itself quite favorably to consideration of the practical and pedagogical character of doctrine. Inasmuch as this is the case, my own constructive proposals in the final chapter should be seen as a complement to and in dialogue with Charry's proposals.

Something further must be said about Charry's view before moving on. Charry rightly highlights the significance and magnitude of the seismic shifts in thought associated with the Enlightenment. Something significant and not altogether salutary for the practical or pedagogical aspects of doctrine did take place during the Enlightenment. I have a great deal of sympathy for her effort to bring pre-modern voices into contemporary trinitarian conversation. I think there is much to learn about contemporary practical trinitarianism by bringing Cappadocian and Reformation voices into the mix.

I want to build upon and make a bit more complex Charry's view of the Enlightenment. While I agree with much of her critique at this point, I also want to lift up the potential value for practical trinitarianism of such unlikely Enlightenment figures as Immanuel Kant and his erstwhile disciple J. G. Fichte. I do so, not because I think that Kant or Fichte has the right answers to the questions about practical trinitarianism that Charry and I pose, but because their attempts at a practical approach to the doctrine of the Trinity help us to think about our task today more in terms of critical engagement with the Enlightenment than outright rejection of it.

In the Enlightenment the single greatest critic of unfettered theological speculation was Immanuel Kant (1724-1804). He aimed to deal a devastating blow to all flights of theological speculation in his watershed book, *The Critique of Pure Reason.*[15] Indeed, Kant set out to solve the problem of metaphysics once and for all. He did so by turning to a careful consider-

---

14. Charry, *By the Renewing of Your Minds,* p. 239.

15. Immanuel Kant, *Critique of Pure Reason,* trans. Norman Kemp Smith (New York: St. Martin's, 1965), p. 30.

ation of the functioning and limits of reason. Kant argued that most of the claims of metaphysics had no reliable basis in the way the human mind actually functions as it produces knowledge. In Kant's view, we cannot have reliable and certain knowledge of God on the basis of pure reason alone.

This does not mean, however, that Kant had no place for theology or for theological reflection about God. Kant had a great deal to say about God, even if his critical philosophy moved God to the margins of discourse.[16] He argued on the basis of practical reason that even though we can know very little about the nature of God, we can at least come to rationally defensible postulates of the existence of God, freedom, and the immortality of the soul.[17]

More to the point for our purposes, Kant acknowledged that the notion of God as Trinity might well be a matter of revelation. If so, it would be solely as a matter of faith within the context of the church. It would not be available to human knowledge on the basis of either pure or practical reason:

> But if this very faith (in a divine tri-unity) were to be regarded as not merely as a representation of a practical idea but as a faith which is to describe what God is in Himself, it would be a mystery transcending all human concepts, and hence a mystery of revelation, unsuited to man's powers of comprehension; in this account, therefore, we can declare it to be such. Faith in it, regarded as an extension of the theoretical knowledge of the divine nature, would be merely the acknowledgement of a symbol of ecclesiastical faith which is quite incomprehensible to men or which, if they think they can understand it, would be anthropomorphic, and therefore nothing whatever would be accomplished for moral betterment. Only that which, in a practical context, can be thoroughly understood and comprehended, but which, taken theologically (for the deter-

16. Immanuel Kant, *Religion within the Limits of Reason Alone,* trans. Theodore M. Greene and Hoyt H. Hudson (New York: Harper & Row, 1960), p. 47.

17. "Freedom, however, among all the Ideas of speculative reason is the only one whose possibility we know a priori. We do not understand it, but we know it as the condition of the moral law which we know. The Ideas of God and immortality are, on the contrary, not conditions of the moral law, but only conditions of the necessary object of a will which is determined by this law. . . . Thus, through the concept of freedom, the Ideas of God and immortality gain objective reality and legitimacy and indeed subjective necessity (as a need of pure reason)." Immanuel Kant, *The Critique of Practical Reason,* trans. Lewis White Beck, 3rd ed., Library of Liberal Arts (New York: Macmillan, 1993), p. 4.

mining of the nature of the object in itself), transcends all our concepts, is a mystery [in one respect] and can yet (in another) be revealed.[18]

Thus, while Kant did not rule out the possibility of God as Trinity as an article of faith, he did ridicule the notion that God should be thought of in rational terms as "an old man, a young man, and a bird (the dove)."[19] Along these lines, Kant claimed that such traditional language for the Trinity should not be thought of as in any way definitive; rather, such language should be treated as symbolic.[20]

Kant did, however, assign some very limited value to interpreting the doctrine of the Trinity in terms of practical reason. Since we simply cannot know God as God might happen to be in Godself, we must concern ourselves with "what He is for us as moral beings."[21] The traditional language related to the doctrine of the Trinity might convey some meaning if properly interpreted in terms of morality and the moral law. For Kant, this worked out into a kind of modalistic moralism in which "God wills to be served under three specifically different aspects."[22] By this, he meant that we should think of the One God as the Creator, Preserver, and Judge of the moral law.[23] On this basis, Kant provided a moral interpretation of the doctrine of the Trinity that closely parallels the separation of powers in American democracy: God as the originator of law (legislative branch), God as the upholder of the moral law (executive branch), and God as the arbiter of the moral law (judicial branch).[24] To be sure, Kant's interpretation of the doctrine of God as Trinity left a lot to be desired from the point of view of the churches and traditional Christian doctrine. Nevertheless, his attempt to make sense out of the doctrine in terms of the moral and political dimensions of human life remains fascinating and potentially generative for thinking about a contemporary trinitarian practical theology in relation to the public dimension of contemporary democracy in American society.

---

18. Kant, *Religion within the Limits of Reason Alone*, p. 133.

19. Immanuel Kant, *Anthropology from a Pragmatic Point of View*, trans. Victor Lyle Dowdell, rev. and ed. Hans H. Rudnick (Carbondale and Edwardsville: Southern Illinois University Press, 1978), p. 62.

20. Kant, *Anthropology from a Pragmatic Point of View*, p. 62.

21. Kant, *Religion within the Limits of Reason Alone*, p. 130.

22. Kant, *Religion within the Limits of Reason Alone*, p. 132.

23. Kant, *Religion within the Limits of Reason Alone*, p. 131.

24. Kant, *Religion within the Limits of Reason Alone*, pp. 130-31.

Kant's attempt to reinterpret the doctrine of the Trinity in relation to the fundamental concerns of morality and social practice was further developed by one of Kant's most famous, if controversial, disciples, Johann Gottlieb Fichte (1762-1814). Fichte's overall program aimed to resolve a number of outstanding problems in Kant's philosophy in such a way that it would both secure Kant's monumental discoveries and further develop his insights. That is to say, Fichte attempted to account for the dynamics of human subjectivity (as well as everything that exists) in terms of the single principle of freedom, which had been the capstone holding together each of Kant's three critiques and his critique of religion. Kant never accounted for the appearance of this spontaneity at the core of human subjectivity, nor did he fully account for its appearance in such political upheavals as the French Revolution. Kant had merely asserted the appearance of freedom within the individual and in certain social movements. In his *Science of Knowledge (Wischenschaftslehre)* of 1794, Fichte attempted to unify Kantian epistemology and ethics by means of a highly detailed reflection on the oppositional and self-positing dynamics of consciousness per se as the manifestation of freedom in practical reason.[25] The "I" and the "not-I" interact dialectically in such a way as to give rise to particular figurations of consciousness through time. For Fichte, the manifestation of freedom in the world and in human consciousness drives the entire process. Fichte believed that God himself shines through this manifestation of freedom. The resultant speculative metaphysic arising from his description of the self-positing and figurative nature of the self, born out of Fichte's reinterpretation of Kantian epistemology, made it possible for him to develop a thoroughly practical approach to the doctrine of the Trinity.

In his work, *The Way Towards the Blessed Life; or, The Doctrine of Religion,* Fichte interpreted the doctrine of the Trinity in terms of his figurational and self-positing view of human subjectivity in reference to human freedom and love.[26] The ultimate ground and source of the manifestation of freedom in both human consciousness and in society came from God. This Triune God was constituted by the same three elements that made up human subjectivity: primary, undifferentiated immediate consciousness;

25. Johann Gottlieb Fichte, *The Science of Knowledge,* ed. and trans. Peter Heath and John Lachs (Cambridge: Cambridge University Press, 1982; n.p.: Meredith Corporation, 1970).

26. Johann Gottlieb Fichte, *The Way Towards the Blessed Life; or, The Doctrine of Religion,* trans. William Smith (London: John Chapman, 1849).

self-positing reflection in determinateness; and a dynamic and vital interrelation between the two. For Fichte, these irreducible elements constituting the reality of God were *Sein, Dasein,* and *Liebe,* or Being, Determinate Being (Reflection), and Love.[27] In fact, human beings are what they are precisely because they participate in the self-positing activity of the divine in history.

The brilliance of Fichte's move lay in his reinterpretation of traditional Augustinian trinitarianism through the lens of Kantian epistemology in service to a radical social program of democratic freedom. Fichte attempted to close the gap between theory and practice in trinitarian doctrine in terms of the dynamics of the Johannine nexus of divine reality and human subjectivity depicted in John 1:3-4, "What has come into being in him was life, and the life was the light of all people" (NRSV). In Fichte, we see a modern attempt to develop a trinitarian practical theology of formation out of categories and terms provided by investigations into the dynamics of human subjectivity.

Georg Wilhelm Friedrich Hegel (1770-1831) further developed Fichte's project into his massive and all-encompassing system, which attempted to account for all of reality on the basis of the dynamics of the Fichtean dialectic applied to God's becoming in history.[28] Hegel's left-wing followers eventually laid bare serious problems with this trinitarian speculative metaphysic. The chief objection shared by left-wing Hegelians like Ludwig Feuerbach (1804-1872) and Karl Marx (1818-1883) had pertained to the abstract, inhuman, and highly speculative character of Hegel's system. Both Feuerbach and Marx sought to humanize and concretize Hegel's vision by relating it to concrete human facts and communal practices.

Feuerbach attempted to interpret the doctrine of the Trinity in strictly anthropological terms. He wrote,

> Man's consciousness of himself in his totality is the consciousness of the Trinity. The Trinity knits together the qualities or powers which were

27. Fichte, *The Way Towards the Blessed Life,* pp. 186-90.

28. A treatment of the way in which Hegel further developed the reflectivity of the Absolute Subject into a full-blown trinitarian system goes well beyond the scope of the present study. A separate study would be required to fully explore the expansive and highly speculative way in which Hegel further develops the trinitarian assays of Kant and Fichte. Though it may seem counterintuitive, it may not be completely wrong to say that Hegel's entire project can be seen as an effort to develop a trinitarian practical theology in a highly speculative form.

before regarded separately into unity, and thereby reduces the universal being of the understanding, *i.e.,* God as God, to a special being, a special faculty. . . . The triune God has a substantial meaning only where there is an abstraction from the substance of real life. The more empty life is, the fuller, the more concrete is God. The impoverishing of the real world and the enriching of God is one act. Only the poor man has a rich God. God springs out of the feeling of a want; what man is in need of, whether this be a definite and therefore conscious, or an unconscious need, — that is God. Thus the disconsolate feeling of a void, of loneliness, needed a God in whom there is society, a union of beings fervently loving each other. Here we have the true explanation of the fact that the Trinity has in modern times lost first its practical, and ultimately its theoretical significance.[29]

Karl Marx then went further. He wrote in his fourth thesis on Feuerbach:

Feuerbach starts out from the fact of religious self-alienation, of the duplication of the world into a religious, imaginary world and a real one. His work consists in resolving the religious world into its secular basis. He overlooks the fact that after completing this work, the chief thing still remains to be done. For the fact that the secular basis detaches itself from itself and establishes itself in the clouds as an independent realm can only be explained by the cleavage and self-contradictions within this secular basis. The latter must itself, therefore, first be understood in its contradiction and then, by the removal of the contradiction, revolutionized in practice. Thus, for instance, after the earthly family is discovered to be the secret of the holy family, the former must then itself be criticised in theory and revolutionised in practice.[30]

F. D. E. Schleiermacher's (1768-1834) appropriation of the Kantian revolution led him to ground his theological project in the dynamics of human consciousness. This project resulted in a restatement of the whole range of Christian doctrines. In his *Christian Faith*, Schleiermacher treated the doctrine of the Trinity only in the final pages. There, however, he de-

---

29. Ludwig Feuerbach, *The Essence of Christianity*, trans. George Eliot (Amherst, N.Y.: Prometheus, 1989), pp. 65 and 73.

30. Karl Marx, "Theses on Feuerbach," in *The Marx-Engels Reader*, 2nd ed., ed. Robert C. Tucker (New York: W. W. Norton, 1978 and 1972), p. 142.

scribed the doctrine as "the coping-stone of Christian doctrine" to the extent that it encoded the union of human nature with the divine essence itself.[31] He attempted to rethink the doctrine on the basis of "our Christian consciousness."[32] To the extent that Schleiermacher's overture toward a practical doctrine of the Trinity sought to ground the endeavor in the contours of human subjective experience, it, too, can be seen as a modern effort in practical trinitarianism. Schleiermacher saw his observations about the Trinity as only the beginning steps toward a reconstructed doctrine of the Trinity "corresponding to the present condition of other related doctrines."[33] He saw the project of a reconstructed doctrine of the Trinity in relation to the facts of human consciousness as a project that would take him beyond the landscape of his *Christian Faith.*

The trenchant critique by left-wing Hegelians concerning both the Hegelian speculative and the Schleiermacherian subjective projects with regard to the doctrine of the Trinity came to fullest expression in the thought of Swiss Reformed theologian Karl Barth (1886-1968). Barth argued in his early and widely influential commentary on Paul's Epistle to the Romans that all conceptions of "religion," whether speculative or anthropological in character, were simply idolatrous: "Such is our relation to God apart from and without Christ, on this side [of the] resurrection, and before we are called to order. God Himself is not acknowledged as God and what is called 'God' is in fact Man."[34] As the creations of humanity, they had nothing to do with the reality of the living God who engages in revelation to sinful humanity. Building on his trenchant critique of all those who sought to reconstruct the doctrine of the Trinity along the lines initially laid out by Kant, Barth's vision depended on the dynamics of divine revelation, particularly as manifested in the in-breaking of Jesus Christ into human history. On the basis of the dynamics of divine revelation, Barth claimed that the doctrine of the Trinity should function as the foundation of all ecclesial reflection on matters theological.

In the devastating aftermath of World War I, Barth sought to refound theology on the basis of the in-breaking and radically disruptive encounter

---

31. Friedrich Schleiermacher, *The Christian Faith,* ed. H. R. Mackintosh and J. S. Stewart (Edinburgh: T&T Clark, 1989, reprint), p. 739.

32. Schleiermacher, *The Christian Faith,* p. 750.

33. Schleiermacher, *The Christian Faith,* p. 749.

34. Karl Barth, *The Epistle to the Romans,* trans. from the 6th ed. by Edwyn C. Hoskyns (New York: Oxford University Press, 1933; paperback, 1968), pp. 44, 236.

of revelation. Barth's radical move upended and reframed the entire conversation about what can be known about God from Kant to his own day. In effect, Barth argued that by reframing the doctrine of God in terms of human experience, the modern religious voices of Kant, Fichte, Hegel, Schleiermacher, and others like them had simply established another historical instance of "religion" in the pejorative sense.[35] As with all human "religion," this modern form was idolatrous and had little if anything to do with the real Triune God who came in Jesus Christ to disrupt all human efforts to reach and comprehend the divine. Once Barth had cleared the intellectual ground with the critical bombshell of the revelation of Jesus Christ, he began his massive work of rearticulating Christian self-understanding on the basis of Scripture as the authoritative witness to the revelation of Jesus Christ. Barth argued that the deep structure of the scriptural witness was thoroughly and inescapably trinitarian.[36] Thus, Barth set about the project of reforming the church's self-understanding in terms of the most central affirmation of that revelation: the doctrine of God as Trinity.[37] By locating his trinitarian dogmatic project squarely in and for the life of the church, Barth led the way on the Protestant side to the recovery of the practical dimensions of the doctrine of the Trinity.[38] No longer would the doctrine of the Trinity be viewed as an ancillary holdover from a previous intellectual era; now it would form the foundation for the entirety of theological reflection and it would have a decidedly practical character inasmuch as the revelation of the Triune God is always "a concrete relation to concrete man."[39]

Spurred on by Barth's bold move, dramatic developments in the doctrine of the Trinity occurred in the latter half of the twentieth century. The recent radical reformulations of doctrine have opened the door to new construals of the theory-practice relationship and to reconceptualization of the doctrine of the Trinity as thoroughly practical. In many ways Jürgen Moltmann has functioned as the leader of the second generation of trinitarian theologians in the Reformed tradition — influenced primarily by Barth and secondarily by Karl Rahner — who seek to formulate the doc-

---

35. Barth, *The Epistle to the Romans*, pp. 40 and 240-79.

36. Karl Barth, *Church Dogmatics*, 1/1, *The Doctrine of the Word of God*, 2nd ed., trans. G. W. Bromiley, ed. G. W. Bromiley and T. F. Torrance (Edinburgh: T&T Clark, 1975), p. 333.

37. Barth, *Church Dogmatics*, 1/1, pp. 295-489.

38. Karl Rahner provided a similar service for the Roman Catholic community.

39. Barth, *Church Dogmatics*, 1/1, p. 325.

trine in a way that elucidates its far-reaching practical implications. Trinitarian theologian Joy McDougall observes:

> Although Karl Barth and Karl Rahner pioneered this return to trinitarian doctrine in the twentieth-century, it has been German Reformed theologian Jürgen Moltmann who more than any other contemporary theologian has spearheaded and creatively sustained the revival of trinitarian theology of love during the last thirty years. As early as 1972 Moltmann diagnosed the theological signs of contemporary times — what he termed Christianity's crises of relevance and identity — as stemming from the eclipse of its distinctive *trinitarian* understanding of God. Criticizing the dispassionate God of Enlightenment theism as incommensurate with the specific biblical witness to the God who is love, Moltmann issued a clarion call for "revolution in the concept of God," a revolution which would retrieve trinitarian belief as the hermeneutical key to unlocking the reconciling passion and liberating hope of divine love.[40]

Moltmann has made many seminal contributions to the still emerging discussion about practical trinitarianism. Drawing upon the insights of Barth and Rahner, Moltmann promulgates a Cappadocian-inspired social doctrine of the Trinity in which the three divine Persons exist in perichoretic equality. This, in turn, serves as the paradigm for all right relatedness in creation, church, and society. Moltmann has articulated a vision for the transformation and reordering of the inner life of the church in radically equalitarian relational terms. For Moltmann, the Trinity is not the self-positing or presiding Absolute Subject of either classical Greek philosophy or of classical German critical and idealist philosophies; rather, the mystery of God is a dynamic fellowship of equal Persons opening out to the life of the world.[41] This trinitarian opening to the world finds its highest and fullest expression in the cross and resurrection of Jesus Christ, the Son of God. For Moltmann, the cross is an event in the inner life of the Trinity as much as it is a determinative event for human beings.[42] The Triune God

---

40. Joy Ann McDougall, "The Pilgrimage of Love: The Trinitarian Theology of Jürgen Moltmann" (Ph.D. diss., University of Chicago, 1998), p. 9.

41. Jürgen Moltmann, *The Trinity and the Kingdom: The Doctrine of God,* trans. Margaret Kohl (San Francisco: Harper & Row, 1981), pp. 13-16.

42. Moltmann, *The Trinity and the Kingdom,* pp. 81-83; see also Jürgen Moltmann, *The*

expresses love for humanity in solidarity and suffering. The cry of dereliction on the cross discloses the rupture with the Trinity for the sake of radical love. He writes of the relationship between the Trinity and the cross:

> As Schleiermacher rightly said, any new version of the doctrine of the Trinity must be a "transformation which goes right back to its first beginnings." The place of the doctrine of the Trinity is not the "thinking of thought," but the cross of Jesus. "Concepts without perception are empty" (Kant). The perception of the trinitarian concept of God is the cross of Jesus. "Perceptions without concepts are blind" (Kant). The theological concept for the perception of the crucified Christ is the doctrine of the Trinity. The material principle of the doctrine of the Trinity is the cross of Christ. The formal principle of knowledge of the cross is the doctrine of the Trinity. . . . [T]he theology of the cross must be the doctrine of the Trinity and the doctrine of the Trinity must be the theology of the cross.[43]

For Moltmann the interplay and deep interconnectedness of the Trinity and the cross disclose the radicality of divine love. This disclosure, above all, makes the doctrine of the Trinity radically practical in character. He maintains further that "theology in action and theology in doxology belong together. There must be no theology of liberation without the glorification of God and no glorification of God without the liberation of the oppressed."[44] In short, according to Moltmann, the doctrine of the Trinity is the theological doctrine of human freedom.[45] In this, Moltmann brings together both the radical reformulation of the doctrine by Barth and draws out the radical political preoccupations of classical German philosophy — especially as articulated by Kant, Fichte, and Hegel — with respect to human freedom. Moltmann thus points further along the way to what might be called a trinitarian practical theology.

The argument advanced in this study owes a deep debt to Moltmann in his attempt to recover the practical dimensions of the doctrine of the Trinity. At the same time, it seeks to address a nagging difficulty with

---

Crucified God: The Cross of Christ as the Foundation and Criticism of Christian Theology, trans. R. A. Wilson and John Bowden (San Francisco: Harper & Row, 1974), pp. 240-49.

43. Moltmann, *The Crucified God,* pp. 240-49.

44. Moltmann, *Trinity and Kingdom,* p. 8.

45. Moltmann, *Trinity and Kingdom,* pp. 212-22.

Moltmann's account. Simply stated, the problem concerns the overly optimistic and largely tacit belief that getting one's thoughts properly ordered about the Trinity will actually lead to the hoped for changes in ecclesial and political practice. The problem here revolves around the tricky dynamics of moving from theory to practice. To know the good does not necessarily equate to doing the good. Great ideas — even trinitarian ones — do not necessarily lead to great actions. Moltmann's practical trinitarianism requires greater attentiveness to the complex interplay of theory and practice in order to make good his bold claims about the utter practicality of the doctrine of the Trinity for church and society. The revitalized conceptions of the doctrine of the Trinity in practical terms need grounding in the concrete, local, bodily life of the church and its members in order to realize their promise of a way of life more conducive to the praise of God and the flourishing of humanity. Talk of Triune love must have a local address.

The point of view promulgated in this study will aim, in part, to further Moltmann's approach to practical trinitarianism by arguing that a particularly effective way to make good on the promise of trinitarian practical theology begins and ends with the concrete, communal, and embodied rite of baptism.[46] One way that the current discussions about practical trinitarianism can advance entails paying sustained attention to the complex formational and transformational processes of Christian individuals and communities associated with the sacrament of baptism. To take things one step further, this means that the next phase in the revitalization of the doctrine of the Trinity must involve not only an assessment of the interplay between the Trinity and the ecclesial and personal concretion implied by the sacrament of baptism, but also an assessment of the way in which

---

46. Moltmann deals with baptism only in passing in most of his works. His most sustained discussion of baptism occurs in the final book of his earlier collection, *The Church in the Power of the Spirit*, which immediately preceded his, in a sense, starting all over again at the beginning with the doctrine of the Trinity. Though Moltmann argues that baptism places baptizands "in the Trinitarian history of God" (p. 226), this theme is underdeveloped. Most of Moltmann's discussion of baptism takes its cues from Barth and focuses on the need to move away from infant baptism and toward believer's baptism in order to address the deep ethical and political problems associated with cultural Christianity (and the state church). For Moltmann's discussion of baptism, see his *The Church in the Power of the Spirit: A Contribution to Messianic Ecclesiology*, trans. Margaret Kohl (New York: Harper & Row, 1975), pp. 226-42.

the doctrine of the Trinity and baptism point toward the dynamics of ecclesial pedagogy.

To linger just a bit longer with the case of Moltmann, it is important to affirm the way in which he points to the practical implications of the doctrine of the Trinity for reform of church and society in terms of power relations. His overture toward a genuinely egalitarian vision of an eschatologically conditioned future holds much promise for reform of church and society. Yet, his practical trinitiarian vision seems too abstract; even when addressing real social problems. Moltmann's vision provides a trinitarian practical ideal without the pedagogical sensitivity or agility to help bring it about. The characteristics of the vision he articulates seem to call for the most mature levels of personhood and faith if they are to be appropriated in any meaningful way.[47] Moltmann's vision of the doctrine of the Trinity calls for a level of faith and sophistication beyond the maturity of most church members. If his vision has promise for influencing more than a theologically educated elite, it will have to pay serious attention to practices of ecclesial pedagogy. To simplify my critique of Moltmann's vision of the practical dimensions of the doctrine of the Trinity, to know the good is not necessarily to do or be the good. Articulating an ideal vision of Trinity-inspired justice and equality may not be sufficient to precipitate the kind of widespread change of behavior in the church that would be required for such a vision to have any impact on the complexities of real life in the church. To bring this about would minimally require deep-level interface with disciplines that focus on the dynamics of formation and transformation in individual and social life. In other words, Moltmann's theological vision requires in-depth engagement with practical theology — particularly the practical theological subdiscipline of Christian education — if it is to realize its promise for transformative change in church and society. This stands as a project for an endeavor subsequent to the current one.

---

47. Moltmann's vision comports well with the most advanced stage — Stage 6 — of James W. Fowler's developmental schema. Fowler writes of this stage, "Heedless of the threats to the self, to primary groups, and to the institutional arrangements of the present order that are involved, Stage 6 becomes a disciplined, activist *incarnation* — making real and tangible — of the imperatives of absolute love and justice of which Stage 5 has partial apprehensions. The self at Stage 6 engages in spending and being spent for the transformation of present reality in the direction of a transcendent actuality." James W. Fowler, *Stages of Faith: The Psychology of Human Development and the Quest for Meaning* (San Francisco: Harper & Row, 1981), p. 200.

Here, I will attempt only to lay out the intellectual scaffolding for the type of strategy needed to advance Moltmann's practical trinitarian project and others like it.

Depth Soundings in Christian Education

The Doctrine of the Trinity in Christian Education

Works in Christian education over the past century that adopt an explicit and pervasive trinitarian framework have been few and far between, though many have operated with implicitly trinitarian commitments. To be sure, not every contribution of value to the field of Christian education has to have had a trinitarian framework in either the foreground or the background. Let me highlight a few works in Christian education that have utilized an explicitly trinitarian framework.

In the modern history of the field of Christian education one book stands out with regard to the interface between the doctrine of the Trinity and Christian education. Written as the result of the 1953 Robert F. Jones Lectures in Christian Education at Austin Theological Seminary, James Smart's *The Teaching Ministry of the Church: An Examination of the Basic Principles of Christian Education* attempted to rethink the entirety of the church's educational ministry on the basis of the doctrine of the Trinity.[48] In the foreword to the book, Smart laid out his vision:

> I have made it my aim to consider, not the theological bases of Presbyterian education, but rather the theological bases of Christian education in the most comprehensive sense. For that reason I have taken the doctrine of the Trinity, to which all Christian Churches, Protestant and Roman Catholic, give adherence, as my essential starting point, and have tried simply to show the character of the educational program that results when that doctrine is allowed to have its full force in our thinking and in our practices. It is my hope therefore that this book may have significance in forwarding a more ecumenical approach to the problems of Christian education.[49]

48. James D. Smart, *The Teaching Ministry of the Church: An Examination of the Basic Principles of Christian Education* (Philadelphia: Westminster, 1954).
49. Smart, *The Teaching Ministry of the Church*, p. 10.

Smart's approach to the Trinity and Christian education had a heavily Barthian cast to it. He was one of a number of Christian educators who in the postwar period attempted to bring new developments in theology to bear on the enterprise of Christian education. Among the leading Christian educators of the 1950s and 1960s, Smart stands out for having explicitly followed Barth's lead in making the doctrine of the Trinity the basis for the entire effort.

Smart's efforts were worthy and make for interesting reading. But we cannot simply return to Smart's program for two reasons. First, his approach to the doctrine of the Trinity in Christian education lacked substantial grounding in the practices of congregations. It functioned only as the master idea, or organizer, for the content of Christian teaching. It did not provide an effective grammar for the whole range of beliefs and actions associated with living the Christian life. His approach to the doctrine of the Trinity lacked moorage in baptism and the processes of Christian initiation.

Second, we cannot simply return to Smart's vision because much has taken place in discussions about the doctrine of the Trinity, about the nature and purpose of Christian education, and about the challenges faced by the churches since the 1953 Jones Lectures and the subsequent book. Some of the changes in discussions about the doctrine of the Trinity have been discussed above. The mainline Protestant churches — particularly the PC(USA) — have declined markedly in numbers and status over these years. The membership patterns of these churches have also changed in terms of denominational loyalty during this period.[50] Increasingly, members of churches belong to families containing more than one religious tradition. The list of changes could go on; suffice it to say that the situation of the churches in America has changed dramatically over the course of these decades.

Several creative approaches to educational ministry have emerged on the scene since Smart's trinitarian efforts in the mid-1950s and continue to enjoy some measure of currency among Christian educators. For instance, C. Ellis Nelson, John Westerhoff, and Charles Foster have helped Christian educators to think more carefully and deeply about the ways in which the congregation as a whole forms people into Christian faith and life.[51]

---

50. For a fuller discussion of these changes, see Robert Wuthnow, *The Restructuring of American Religion: Society and Faith Since World War II* (Princeton: Princeton University Press, 1988).

51. See C. Ellis Nelson, *Where Faith Begins* (Richmond: John Knox, 1967); John H. Wes-

Thomas Groome and Charles Foster have emphasized the need to put critical reflection on social location at the very center of the church's educational task.[52] Developmental theorists like James W. Fowler have stimulated thought about the ways in which faith changes, grows, and is transformed across the lifecycle.[53] Maria Harris contributed greatly to creative thinking about the aesthetic and spiritual dimensions of curriculum in particular and educational ministry more generally.[54] James Loder articulated a powerful model for thinking about the dynamics of transformation by the strange logic of the Holy Spirit.[55] Recently, Craig Dykstra and Dorothy Bass have enriched the field by lifting up the critical role that participation in religious practices has in fostering lively and robust faith.[56] This list certainly does not pretend to exhaust the major developments in the field in the decades since Smart wrote his work on the Trinity and Christian education; it only illustrates that the field has developed and expanded considerably since the mid-1950s.

In order to advance the effort to think about Christian education in reference to the doctrine of the Trinity, we must both affirm and go beyond Smart's fundamental insight. Smart may well have been on the right track, but his project remains unfinished and its promise unfulfilled. I maintain that one of the chief reasons for this has to do with the lack of orientation and mooring that could only be provided by the sacrament of baptism.

Three recent books on Christian education have placed the doctrine of the Trinity in the foreground. I have already discussed Richard Osmer's work *The Teaching Ministry of Congregations* with its profound engagement with Moltmann's practical trinitarianism. As the deepest of the three recent works on the Trinity and Christian education, it promises to play a significant role in this trajectory for some time into the future. Osmer's

terhoff, *Will Our Children Have Faith?* (New York: Seabury, 1976); and Charles R. Foster, *Educating Congregations: The Future of Christian Education* (Nashville: Abingdon, 1994).

52. Thomas H. Groome, *Christian Religious Education: Sharing our Story and Vision* (San Francisco: Harper & Row, 1980); and Foster, *Educating Congregations*.

53. Fowler, *Stages of Faith*.

54. Maria Harris, *Teaching and Religious Imagination: An Essay in the Theology of Teaching* (San Francisco: Harper & Row, 1987).

55. James E. Loder, *The Logic of the Spirit: Human Development in Theological Perspective* (San Francisco: Jossey-Bass, 1998).

56. Craig R. Dykstra, *Growing in the Life of Faith: Education and Christian Practices* (Louisville: Geneva, 1999). Dorothy C. Bass, ed., *Practicing Our Faith: A Way of Life for a Searching People,* Practicing Our Faith series (San Francisco: Jossey-Bass, 1997).

impressive interdisciplinary work involving thick description of three congregations and a lively trinitarian framework also provides a notable contribution to practical theological research in the mode of pedagogy. The work undertaken here has many points of contact and overlap with Osmer's trinitarian perspectives in ecclesial pedagogy.

Debra Dean Murphy's recent work, *Teaching that Transforms: Worship as the Heart of Christian Education*, brings together an explicit trinitarian framework and a strong emphasis on liturgical practices — with special focus on the linkage between baptism and Christian education. She offers her trinitarian and liturgical views as an antidote to the projects of modern religious education articulated by Roman Catholic educators Gabriel Moran, Thomas Groome, and Mary Boys. She takes each of these distinguished contributors to the field of Christian education to task for sacrificing the particularities of Christian beliefs and practices for the sake of wide engagement with other religions and the public. She intends to reject the modernity she sees at work in ecclesial pedagogy and replace it with emphases on the Trinity and liturgy.

My project stands at key points in marked contrast to Murphy's. While I will return to this theme in more detail in the final chapter, I want to emphasize here the similarities and differences between this project and that of Murphy. On the one hand, she rightly points to the lack of an explicit trinitarian framework and the overlooking of the significance of liturgy for ecclesial pedagogy as a contributing factor to the struggle for the effectiveness of Christian education in the modern period. As with practical theology, the diminishment of themes related to the historic Christian faith of the churches, like the doctrine of the Trinity, and the overlooking of liturgical practices, like baptism, have widened the gap between patterns of ecclesial pedagogy in local churches and the academic discipline of Christian education.

On the other hand, Murphy badly misses the mark in her project by rejecting modernity outright and by writing off the important contributions of figures like Moran, Groome, and Boys. Even if anyone really wanted to go back behind modernity to some earlier period, such a move simply cannot be carried out. Western civilization cannot and should not reject modernity wholesale. A better course of action involves affirming the positive gains of modernity and working to address its disfiguring problems. In terms of Christian education, this means Christian educators ought to celebrate and learn from the work of Moran, Groome, and Boys;

they should also find ways to build bridges between their work and a contemporary practical trinitarianism and distinctly ecclesial practices. In this sense, we will aim at building bridges rather than burning them.

Robert Pazmiño's book of 2001, *God our Teacher: Theological Basics in Christian Education,* also privileges the doctrine of the Trinity.[57] In this book, he seeks to further the work of James Smart by developing a "trinitarian grammar and imagination" in relation to ecclesial pedagogy.[58] He lays out his agenda early in the book:

> The Christian faith claims that God is most wonderfully revealed in Jesus Christ and in the continuing revelation of the Holy Spirit. Therefore, God's revelation is the starting point for our learning. We begin in chapter 1 with a discussion of the core distinctive of Christianity — the Trinity. The Trinity discloses a communion as God the Father, Son, and Spirit reveal for humanity and for all of creation the essence of life in its fullness. A further claim advanced in this work is that the Trinity is an organizing theological theme for the theory and practice of Christian education. The vitality of Christian education depends on the theological roots of the Trinity. These roots require thoughtful consideration and application to teaching practice.[59]

Pazmiño explores the doctrine of the Trinity in terms of both the organizational principle for the content of Christian education and the components and processes related to ecclesial pedagogy. He finds several triadic relations at the heart of pedagogy itself. He finds possibilities for thinking about the doctrine of the Trinity in relation to the processes and themes of Christian education in various pedagogical triads provided by Susanne Johnson (praxis, instruction, and teaching), Marianne Sawicki (celebration, care, and call), Lois LeBar (proclamation, edification, and mission), James Michael Lee (shape, flow, and content of religious instruction), and Peter Hodgson (critical thinking, heightened imagination, and liberating practice).[60] He highlights his own triad of content, persons, and context and relates each of these elements to one of the Persons of the Trinity: Father, as the source of all

---

57. Robert W. Pazmiño, *God Our Teacher: Theological Basics in Christian Education* (Grand Rapids: Baker Academic, 2001).

58. Pazmiño, *God Our Teacher,* p. 29.

59. Pazmiño, *God Our Teacher,* p. 9.

60. Pazmiño, *God Our Teacher,* pp. 32-34.

content; Son, as the exemplary master teacher; and Holy Spirit, as tutor who sustains the context for ecclesial pedagogy.[61] Further, Pazmiño sees great possibilities for addressing many themes and hungers associated with postmodernism in terms of the dynamic interplay of persons, content, and context developed in relation to his treatment of perichoretic love as the dominant theme of the doctrine of the Trinity in ecclesial education.[62] This leads to an affirmation of the need for "educational efforts that affirm both Christian identity and openness to the other."[63] With Pazmiño, the theme of "identity and openness" will play a very significant role in the constructive final chapter of this project. Though I came to the term independently of Pazmiño, I strongly resonate with this aspect of his work.

Pazmiño's helpful articulation of a vision of Christian education in relation to the doctrine of the Trinity has some limitations. First, he shares with Smart a tendency to treat the doctrine of the Trinity as the master idea that organizes the content of Christian teaching. To be sure, he does more than this; nonetheless, his work does sometimes veer in this direction. Related to this, the second point of concern has to do with the lack of grounding for his treatment of the doctrine of the Trinity in concrete practice. More particularly, the work does not connect the doctrine of the Trinity and ecclesial pedagogy with baptism as the practice of and paradigm for the Christian life. Such a concrete grounding in the local, the bodily, the personal, and the communal realities associated with baptism would further develop and nuance his argument. Third, Pazmiño's identification of each Person of the Trinity with a particular aspect of teaching (that is, Father = content, Son = person, and Holy Spirit = context) seems a bit reductionist. After all, doesn't the Trinity as a whole provide the matrix or context within which ecclesial pedagogy takes place? Similarly, the Triune God as a whole generates the content of ecclesial pedagogy. We might want to raise similar objections about the personal dimensions of ecclesial pedagogy. In other words, all three Persons engage in every aspect of the pedagogical enterprise. To assign parts in the way in which Pazmiño has may not provide the most helpful way to think about the role of the Trinity in the processes of ecclesial pedagogy.

By highlighting the recent work of Osmer, Murphy, and Pazmiño in re-

---

61. Pazmiño, *God Our Teacher,* pp. 32-33.

62. Pazmiño, *God Our Teacher,* pp. 164ff.

63. Pazmiño, *God Our Teacher,* p. 167. For this concept, Pazmiño credits Eastern Orthodox Christian educator Constance Tarasar; see p. 187, n. 11.

lation to the doctrine of the Trinity and ecclesial pedagogy, I do not mean to argue that every Christian educator today needs to adopt a trinitarian framework in order to contribute meaningfully to the field. I only wish to point out that these educators have begun to address a lacuna in the field. Further, I want to suggest that continuing to address this lack would make possible some critical advances in the field of Christian education.

Baptism and Christian Education

It is not only the doctrine of the Trinity that has been neglected in the modern history of Protestant Christian education. With some notable exceptions, baptism does not often play a crucial role in recent articulations of Christian education. One rarely finds explicit linkages in the literature of Christian education to the rite of baptism, except as one of a multitude of curricular content areas to be covered.[64] Almost never does one find an approach to Christian education built around baptism in all its fullness, as was the case during the period of the catechumenate in the early church.[65] In some ways, this is deeply ironic given the fact that ecclesial pedagogy originally emerged in relation to the sacrament of baptism and the processes of Christian initiation. As we will see later, close ties between baptism and ecclesial pedagogy can be seen in both the early church and in the period of the Protestant Reformation.

To be sure, one can find some notable exceptions to this predominant pattern. In his work *Sharing Faith*, Roman Catholic religious educator Thomas Groome has written helpfully on the linkage between liturgy and pedagogy.[66] Yet, Groome focuses mainly on the Eucharist and only touches briefly on baptism.[67]

More helpful in this regard, the book by Robert Browning and Roy Reed

64. For example, see Maria Harris, *Fashion Me a People: Curriculum in the Church* (Louisville: Westminster John Knox, 1989).

65. For an example of a vision of ecclesial pedagogy completely organized around baptismal initiation in the early church, see Edward Yarnold, *Cyril of Jerusalem*, The Early Church Fathers series, ed. Carol Harrison (New York: Routledge, 2000).

66. Thomas H. Groome, *Sharing Faith: A Comprehensive Approach to Religious Education and Pastoral Ministry* (New York: HarperSanFrancisco, 1991). See chapter 12, "Liturgy and Preaching," pp. 337-78.

67. Groome, *Sharing Faith*, chapter 12.

entitled *The Sacraments in Religious Education and Liturgy: An Ecumenical Model* provides a sustained attempt to articulate an approach to the educational ministry of the churches in reference to baptism and the Eucharist.[68] They assert that "religious education should express a sense of unity with the wider liturgical and action life of the community while, at the same time, preserving the needed critical and constructive roles, to keep the vision of God's love for all creation strong and to seek to renew the liturgical life of the community so that it is indeed open and growing in harmony with that vision."[69] Browning and Reed explore the relationship between baptism and Christian education in relation to the children of church members as well as to adult converts.[70] Tellingly, throughout their discussion of the interface between baptism and education, they only occasionally touch on the doctrine of the Trinity and when they do so, they fail to explore with any depth the contours of the deep trinitarian substructure of this interface.

Presbyterian Christian educator Elizabeth Francis Caldwell, in her book *Come Unto Me: Rethinking the Sacraments for Children*, provides a more helpful treatment of the central role of baptism in relation to ecclesial pedagogy. At the outset of her work, she issues a call to action to Christian educators:

> Like termites on a wood porch, we need to eat away at the long-held ecclesiological, theological, and educational traditions and practices that do not affirm the relationship between the holy and the daily, between the visions and the reality of God's dominion in the world. It is essential that we integrate worship and education, and more particularly the sacraments and the life of the people in the household of faith.[71]

Caldwell devotes fully one-third of her book to the close connections between baptism and ecclesial pedagogy.[72] She argues that this relation should receive significant attention in the life and work of the local congregation.

68. Robert L. Browning and Roy A. Reed, *The Sacraments in Religious Education and Liturgy: An Ecumenical Model* (Birmingham, Ala.: Religious Education Press, 1985).

69. Browning and Reed, *The Sacraments in Religious Education and Liturgy*, pp. 22-23.

70. Browning and Reed, *The Sacraments in Religious Education and Liturgy*, chapter 8, "Infant Baptism: Initiation," pp. 138-67, and chapter 13, "Adult Baptism: The Sacrament of Evangelization," pp. 239-53.

71. Elizabeth Francis Caldwell, *Come Unto Me: Rethinking the Sacraments for Children* (Cleveland: Pilgrim, 1996), p. 5.

72. Caldwell, *Come Unto Me*, pp. 11-53.

Inasmuch as her book aims to address church educators, pastors, and thoughtful laity, it tends to focus on practical strategies for developing the interplay between baptism and ecclesial pedagogy. While on a promising path, the perspective she offers requires deepening and thickening in order to fully establish her case.

Mary Elizabeth Mullino Moore in her recent work, *Teaching as a Sacramental Act,* does a great deal with the connections between baptism and pedagogy.[73] She does not reduce her exploration of sacramental teaching to the sacraments per se; rather, she holds that the sacraments of baptism and the Eucharist disclose the sacramental character of all of human life.[74] In her key claim, she affirms that *"the heart of sacramental teaching is mediating the grace of God through the concrete stuff of creation for the sanctification of human communities and the well-being of all God's creation.* My purpose in this book is to cast a bright light on the sacramental nature of religious education in mediating the Holy for human sanctification and creation's good."[75] Moore explores baptism as a rite of initiation that links together liturgy and ecclesial pedagogy.[76] Further, she adeptly brings out the character of sacramental living in relation to the following generative themes: expecting the unexpected, remembering the disremembered, seeking reversals, giving thanks, nourishing life, and reconstructing community and repairing the world.[77] In so doing, Moore has done more than any other current Christian educator to emphasize the interconnections between baptism, ecclesial pedagogy, and living a life of faith, love, and hope in the midst of contemporary society.

Moore's perspective, however, does not connect directly with the revitalized doctrine of the Trinity discussed above. It does afford several points of contact with discussions about practical trinitarianism. In particular, her work offers an important vision for connecting liturgy with life through vital ecclesial pedagogy. Conversely, her work would ensure that discussions of the Trinity, baptism, and pedagogy avoid a narrow ecclesiocentrism and maintain a broad and generous perspective on all of human life.

Clearly, not all Christian education contributions need to focus on

73. For example, see Mary Elizabeth Mullino Moore, *Teaching as a Sacramental Act* (Cleveland: Pilgrim, 2004), pp. 22-23, 30, 47-50, 72-73, 97-99, 161-62, and 197-98.
74. Moore, *Teaching,* pp. 5-10 and 217.
75. Moore, *Teaching,* p. 10; emphasis in the original.
76. Moore, *Teaching,* p. 30.
77. Moore, *Teaching,* pp. 30-38 and chapters 3-8.

baptism and the processes of initiation. At least some should. In so doing, the field of Christian education can advance because it can connect discourse about ecclesial pedagogy to the primary forming practices of churches — the worship work of the people ("liturgy"). It can also provide a highly effective means for teaching the baptized about the mystery of the Triune God and patterns of life in society consonant with such a belief.

One wonders how much recent trinitarian visions for life in church and society will actually affect the masses of the baptized in the way they live together in church and society. Conversations about the practical dimensions of the doctrine of the Trinity must have a well-developed and explicitly integrated pedagogical dimension if they are to realize their great promise for transformation of individuals and groups in the church and for the good of society. Practices of formation simply cannot be treated as a footnote in these conversations. If they are, then they will go unheeded by all except a small cadre of academic professionals. Similarly, practices of ecclesial pedagogy — particularly when closely tied to baptism as a process of initiation into a trinitarian pattern of life — have the potential to function as a generative source of systematic and practical theological knowledge. Inasmuch as ecclesial pedagogy rooted in baptism plays an absolutely crucial role in forming individuals and communities into a trinitarian pattern of life, it should be seen as a generative contributor to the ongoing development of both trinitarian theology and Christian education.

Toward a Trinitarian Practical Theology of Education and Formation for Discipleship

Where do these soundings in the fields of contemporary trinitarian theology and Christian education leave us? Taken as a whole, they point to the conclusion that conditions are ripe today for attempts to bring together the elements of the newly revitalized doctrine of God as Trinity, the rite of baptism, and the pedagogical practices of the churches. I will argue that this multivalent interdisciplinary conversation can best proceed by focusing on the rite of baptism as initiation into a whole way of life. By proceeding from the concrete and corporate locus provided by the baptismal rite, I will explore the necessarily interrelated vectors of trinitarian doctrine and practices of ecclesial faith formation, which likely would be missed if one were to simply focus on the features of the doctrine of the Trinity abstracted from actual ecclesial contexts and divorced from the lives of real human beings. I intend to define the effective zone of intersection between systematic theology concerned with the doctrine of the Trinity and Christian education by privileging the baptismal rite in the discourse.

In brief, I contend that renewed attention to the sacrament of baptism and the whole process of initiation will provide the crucial element in the development of effective strategies for furthering the vision James Smart first articulated by grounding trinitarian reflection in a concrete, bodily practice necessarily associated with the formation of Christian beliefs and practices. Contemporary rethinking about the educational ministry of the churches in relation to the doctrine of the Trinity will need to treat the sacrament of baptism as the starting point and orienting center for dynamic conversations about the faith formation of individuals and communities in relation to local church practitioners, systematic theologians, practical theologians, and Christian educators for at least three reasons.

First, the sacrament of baptism is a core, constituting practice of the Christian life. Baptism affords entrance into the church through an ongoing process of dying and rising with Jesus Christ into newness of life. In this sense, baptism provides *the* paradigm for the entirety of the Christian life. Baptism confers Christian identity and defines Christian vocation. Through baptism, the Triune God calls women and men, young people and people of mature years, to lives of grateful and obedient service to God and neighbor in the many arenas of life.

Second, and growing out of the first reason, baptism in all its fullness is inescapably trinitarian in character. At the epicenter of the rite stands the economic doctrine of the Trinity in epitomized form. To explain baptism — both the rite itself and its paradigmatic significance for the Christian life — requires the use of a dynamic trinitarian grammar. Some of the Christian traditions' most insightful and creative minds have plumbed the depths of the relation between baptism, the Trinity, and ecclesial pedagogy. Privileging the baptismal rite makes possible a way of holding together in dynamic tension the doctrine of the Trinity and Christian education. One simply cannot adequately explain the meaning of the baptismal rite without referring simultaneously to the doctrine of the Trinity and to practices of ecclesial pedagogy.

Third, baptism necessarily has to do with the body, the local, and the contextual. The practice of baptism inescapably involves the body and it always takes place at a particular time and in a specific place. There is no such thing as abstract or disembodied baptism. Baptism involves applying something as earthy and elemental as water to particular human bodies. It is as concrete as a handful of water applied to the fuzzy head of a squirming baby. Since baptism belongs to the church, it is not only bodily and concrete; it is also intensely ecclesial. Baptism has to do with the life and character of the church. If it is true that the doctrine of the Trinity — properly conceived — is a thoroughly practical doctrine, then it must relate in some real and significant way to the embodiment of our lives. If the doctrine of the Trinity is truly practical with radical implications for the Christian life, then it needs in some meaningful way to come down to the level of water dripping off of fussing babies.

CHAPTER 3

Baptism, Trinity, and Ecclesial Pedagogy in the Work of Gregory of Nyssa

What beyond this do they who remain attached to paganism bring forward in disparagement of our creed? Do not they too make the majesty of the sacred Names, in which the faith is ratified, an occasion of laughter? Do not they deride the sacramental tokens and the customs which are observed by the initiated? And of whom is it so much a distinguishing peculiarity as of the pagans, to think that piety should consist of doctrines only?

Gregory of Nyssa, *Against Eunomius*

I have elected to engage Gregory of Nyssa (c. 330–c. 395) and John Calvin (1509-1564) as dialogue partners in this study because they each play an important role in contemporary discussions about the doctrine of the Trinity, particularly in the Reformed tradition, and because they made important contributions to the doctrine of the Trinity in their respective eras. Recent Reformed trinitarian theologians such as Jürgen Moltmann, Colin Gunton, and T. F. Torrance have drawn from theological resources within the Reformed tradition and from the Cappadocian fathers for new and creative insight into the doctrine of the Trinity.[1] This recent "turn to the

---

1. For example, see Jürgen Moltmann, *The Trinity and the Kingdom: The Doctrine of God,* trans. Margaret Kohl (San Francisco: Harper & Row, 1981); Colin Gunton, *The Promise of Trinitarian Theology* (Edinburgh: T&T Clark, 1991; paperback ed., 1993); and Thomas F. Tor-

Cappadocians" by many Calvinist theologians carries with it varying degrees of criticism toward the traditional Reformed appropriation of the Augustinian inheritance on the doctrine of the Trinity. The credibility of this move has been funded, in part, by both Calvin and Karl Barth. They drew upon both Augustine and the Cappadocians in constructing their respective approaches to the doctrine of the Trinity.[2]

While not every Reformed trinitarian theologian today would use the Cappadocians as normative sources over and against Augustine, a definite trend along these lines within Reformed circles has developed. Gunton went so far as to argue that trinitarian theology in the West had gone off the rails ever since Augustine. He proposed a move away from Augustine in favor of the Cappadocians as the remedy to the ills of abstract Western trinitarianism.[3] A more moderate and judicious view would perhaps argue that the perspectives of both the Cappadocians and Augustine have significant contributions to make toward a contemporary practical trinitarianism and that neither source holds all the answers. Even though the current project focuses on the Cappadocian contribution, it does not intend to support the rejectionist views of Gunton. In this chapter, I aim only to make a contribution to recent Reformed conversations about the practical

---

rance, *The Trinitarian Faith: The Evangelical Theology of the Ancient Catholic Church* (Edinburgh: T&T Clark, 1988; paperback ed., 1993) and *Trinitarian Perspectives: Toward Doctrinal Agreement* (Edinburgh: T&T Clark, 1994).

2. Calvin particularly favored a key statement from Gregory Nazianzen's oration *On Holy Baptism* (oration 40.41, in A Select Library of Nicene and Post-Nicene Fathers of the Christian Church, 2nd series [hereafter NPNF²] [Grand Rapids: Eerdmans, reprint, 1994], 7.375), when he wrote about the mystery of the Trinity. See John Calvin, *Institutes of the Christian Religion*, ed. J. T. McNeill, trans. Ford Lewis Battles, 2 vols., Library of Religious Classics, vols. 20 and 21 (Philadelphia: Westminster, 1960), 1.13.17. See also John Calvin, *Commentary on the Gospel According to John*, vol. 1, trans. William Pringle (Grand Rapids: Eerdmans, 1949), p. 29. Karl Barth drew upon the Cappadocians at various points in his discussion of the doctrine of the Trinity; Karl Barth, *Church Dogmatics*, 1/1, *The Doctrine of the Word of God*, trans. G. W. Bromiley, ed. G. W. Bromiley and T. F. Torrance (Edinburgh: T&T Clark, 1936; 2nd ed., 1975), pp. 364-65, 369, 411, 413, 474, 477, and 482.

3. Colin Gunton put the matter too strongly when he wrote, "Augustine either did not understand the Trinitarian theology of his predecessors, both East and West, or looked at their work with spectacles so strongly tinted with Neoplatonic assumptions that they have distorted his work. The tragedy is that Augustine's work is so brilliant that it blinded generations of theologians to its damaging weaknesses." Gunton, *The Promise of Trinitarian Theology*, pp. 38-39.

character of the doctrine of the Trinity by pointing out something crucial that has been missing from current study of the Cappadocians.

A treatment of each of the Cappadocian bishop-theologians on the crucial nexus with which we are concerned would require a lengthy study in its own right. Instead, the current study will focus only on one of the Cappadocian pastor-theologians: Gregory of Nyssa. He made explicit the interplay between baptism and doctrine in his teachings. In addition to his theological profundity and startling insights about baptism and the doctrine of the Trinity, Gregory of Nyssa alone among the Cappadocians developed catechetical materials. Neither Basil nor the other Gregory produced anything like Gregory of Nyssa's guidelines for clerical catechists in his *Catechetical Oration*.[4] Inasmuch as this study seeks to consider not only the relation between baptism and the doctrine of the Trinity, but also the pedagogical vector arising from that relation, Gregory of Nyssa merits special treatment among the Cappadocians.

Further rationale for a focus on Gregory of Nyssa arises from the fact that standard accounts of ecclesial pedagogy in the church in the late fourth and early fifth centuries invariably focus on Cyril of Jerusalem (c. 315-386), Ambrose of Milan (c. 339-397), Theodore of Mopsuestia (c. 350-428), Augustine of Hippo (354-430), and John Chrysostom (c. 347-407).[5] If treated at all, Gregory's contribution to ecclesial pedagogy often is relegated to a brief footnote.[6] In the current climate of renewed interest in the practical and formational dimensions of trinitarian theology, Gregory of Nyssa's way of holding together the rite of baptism, the doctrine of the Trinity, and ecclesial pedagogy — especially in, but not limited to, his *Catechetical Oration* — offers something potentially very significant. His contribution to ecclesial pedagogy during the golden age of the catechumenate may offer helpful insight for contemporary efforts to de-

---

4. Gregorii Nysseni, *Oratio Catechetica*, Opera Dogmatica Minora, pars IV, ed. Ekkehardus Mühlenberg, *Gregoryii Nysseni Opera*, ed. Wernerus Jaeger, Hermannus Langerbeck, and Henricus Dörrie, vol. III, part IV (Leiden: E. J. Brill, 1996) (hereafter, Jaeger, *Oratio Catechetica*). English translations include *The Great Catechism*, trans. William Moore, *Select Writings and Letters of Gregory, Bishop of Nyssa*, NPNF[2,] 5.473-509 and *The Catechetical Oration of St. Gregory of Nyssa*, trans. J. H. Srawley (London: Society for Promoting Christian Knowledge, 1917) (hereafter, *Catechetical Oration*).

5. For example, see the study by Edward Yarnold, *The Awe-Inspiring Rites of Initiation: The Origins of the R.C.I.A.*, 2nd ed. (Collegeville, Minn.: Liturgical, 1994).

6. Yarnold, *The Awe-Inspiring Rites of Initiation*, pp. 189-90.

velop a thoroughgoing practical trinitarianism that focuses on the formation of faith in individuals and communities.

I will argue in this chapter that when contemporary theologians read Gregory of Nyssa's trinitarian theology apart from its inherent connections with baptism and pedagogy, crucial dimensions of what he tried to convey in his doctrine of the Trinity are too easily overlooked. If I can persuade contemporary practical theologians and Christian educators to read Gregory of Nyssa at all, I will count my effort as a success. I argue here that a highly effective way to access the full complexity of his trinitarianism begins not with a treatment of the notional content of his trinitarian teachings but with a consideration of the role of baptism in his thought. While one can read Gregory of Nyssa in a variety of ways, I have found that interpreting his work through the lens of baptism affords richness and complexity often missed by other approaches. By beginning with baptism, we can see the complex interplay between ecclesial practice, theological reflection, and pedagogy.

Background and Context

One of the most creative and fertile minds the Christian religion ever produced, Gregory of Nyssa forged a deeply insightful approach to the doctrine of the Trinity. He — along with Basil and Gregory Nazianzen — made several very important contributions to the cause of Nicene orthodoxy over and against the ongoing threat posed by Neo-Arianism and the emerging challenges of Pneumatomachianism and Appolinarianism. Thomas M. Finn, scholar of Christian initiation in the early church, refers to Gregory of Nyssa as "the architect of Eastern Christian spirituality."[7] Gregory of Nyssa developed apophatic, or negative, theology in particularly compelling forms. Alluding to mystical encounters with the Trinity, he introduced memorable phrases like "illuminated darkness," "sober inebriation," and "watchful sleeping" into Christian mystical vocabulary.[8] His thought influenced such thinkers as Pseudo-Dionysius (c. 500), Maximus

---

7. Thomas M. Earl Finn, *Early Christian Baptism and the Catechumenate: West and East Syria*, Message of the Church Fathers series, vol. 5 (Collegeville, Minn.: Liturgical, 1992), p. 61.

8. See Jean Daniélou, *From Glory to Glory: Texts from Gregory of Nyssa's Mystical Writings*, trans. and ed. Herbert Musurillo (New York: Scribner's Sons, 1961; reprint, Crestwood, N.Y.: St. Vladimir's Seminary Press, 2001). For "illuminated darkness," see pp. 23-35 and 118. On "sober inebriation," see pp. 33-46 and 238-40. Concerning "watchful sleeping," see pp. 240-42.

Confessor (c. 580-662), John Damascene (c. 675–c. 749), Gregory Palamas (c. 1296-1359), and even John Scotus Eriugena (c. 810–c. 877).[9]

Gregory of Nyssa hailed from the Roman province of Pontus in Asia Minor and spent most of his adult life in the neighboring district of Cappadocia.[10] His family belonged to the local aristocracy. His father, Basil the Elder, owned vast tracts of land and held a widely respected reputation as both a teacher and a legal advocate.[11] In a letter written while bishop of Nyssa, Gregory mentioned in passing that he himself owned an entire village in Pontus![12] The family apparently owned several estates in the region.[13] Though wealthy, the family had a reputation for generosity toward the local peasantry.[14]

That Gregory of Nyssa had intended to become a teacher of rhetoric and ended up as a priest and a bishop indicates something significant about the status of his family in fourth-century Asia Minor. The sons of aristocrats often aspired to positions in the imperial administration. Raymond Van Dam, historian of fourth-century Cappadocia, observes that several other respectable options also presented themselves during this period:

> Notables from Cappadocia, as well as other provincial aristocrats, could also choose other options for maintaining and enhancing their prestige and authority. Ownership of land and control over its resources obviously still conferred great influence, and men could still serve as municipal magistrates or decurions in their native cities. They also had increasingly more opportunities to serve in the ecclesiastical hierarchy. In the later Roman empire the ecclesiastical hierarchy expanded in size probably even more rapidly than did the imperial administration. . . .

---

9. On Gregory's influence on later thinkers, see Anthony Meredith, *Gregory of Nyssa*, The Early Church Fathers series (London and New York: Routledge, 1999), pp. 138-39; see also David L. Balás's entry "Gregory of Nyssa," in *Encyclopedia of Early Christianity*, 2nd ed., ed. Everett Ferguson, vol. 1839 in Garland Reference Library of the Humanities (New York: Garland, 1999), p. 497.

10. See Raymond Van Dam, *Families and Friends in Late Roman Cappadocia* (Philadelphia: University of Pennsylvania Press, 2003), pp. 18 and 29 for information on Gregory's early family life in Pontus.

11. Van Dam, *Families and Friends in Late Roman Cappadocia*, p. 18.

12. Van Dam, *Families and Friends in Late Roman Cappadocia*, p. 103.

13. Raymond Van Dam, *Kingdom of Snow: Roman Rule and Greek Culture in Cappadocia* (Philadelphia: University of Pennsylvania Press, 2002), p. 21.

14. Van Dam, *Kingdom of Snow*, p. 114.

For local landowners and educated provincials, service in the clergy had become an option and might be more attractive than service in the imperial administration.[15]

Though Gregory's older brother, Basil, could well have taken a post in the imperial administration on the basis of his family's standing and his outstanding higher education in Athens, he opted for clerical service.

Some brief observations about the status of Christianity in northeastern Asia Minor during the fourth century will further develop the background for understanding Gregory's life and work. While Jews from Pontus and Cappadocia had witnessed the birth of the Christian church on the Day of Pentecost (Acts 2:9), Christianity became firmly established in the region probably in the third century.[16] Another famous Gregory a century earlier had also come from this region. Gregory Thaumaturgus (c. 213–c. 270) had converted to Christianity in the third century and had received catechetical instruction from Origen of Alexandria (c. 185-254). Upon return to his homeland, Gregory Thaumaturgus left a lasting impression on the inhabitants of the region, particularly on Gregory of Nyssa's family. Gregory of Nyssa's grandmother apparently had memorized and passed down some of the teachings of the "wonder-worker."[17] Gregory may have been named in honor of his earlier namesake.[18]

The family from which Gregory of Nyssa came also had strong ties to the Cult of Forty Martyrs. The family had kept alive the memory of a group of forty soldiers from Sebasteia in Pontus who chose death by hypothermic exposure on a frozen lake over apostasy. When Gregory's parents and older sister died, they were buried in a tomb that contained relics of the martyrs. Gregory also appears to have financed a shrine to the martyrs' memory in Nyssa.[19] Describing the character of Gregory of Nyssa's family as a complex mixture of wealth and piety, Raymond Van Dam writes:

> Basil the Elder [Gregory's father] had become a local teacher at Neocaesarea, and his family owned many estates in the region. The fam-

---

15. Van Dam, *Kingdom of Snow*, pp. 61-62.

16. Raymond Van Dam, *Becoming Christian: The Conversion of Roman Cappadocia* (Philadelphia: University of Pennsylvania Press, 2003), p. 1.

17. Van Dam, *Becoming Christian*, p. 78.

18. Van Dam, *Families and Friends in Late Roman Cappadocia*, p. 123.

19. Van Dam, *Becoming Christian*, p. 78, and *Families*, p. 112.

ily had hence become wealthy under Roman rule and had flourished because of Basil the Elder's familiarity with Greek culture.

Yet Basil [Gregory's brother] and Gregory of Nyssa preferred to tell a different story of their family. In their version, the defining event had been the suffering of their ancestors during the persecutions of Christians at the beginning of the fourth century. Their maternal grandfather had been executed, and their paternal grandparents had spent seven years hiding in the mountains of Pontus to escape the persecutions of the emperors Diocletian, Galerius, and in particular, Maximinus. Two generations later Basil and his siblings were able to find a sense of pride in the horrors their grandparents had experienced. The mementos of those final persecutions were always with them. . . . In order to emphasize the continuity of their lives and careers they preferred to situate the history of their family in a longer tradition of martyrdom and hostility to Roman rule, of withdrawal and uneasiness about classical culture, and of clerical service. For this sort of family history neither Roman rule nor Greek culture was necessary. Their prominence was a consequence of the suffering of their ancestors in the name of Christianity.[20]

Thus, even though their standing in the region probably had a great deal to do with the fact that they were prominent members of the landed aristocracy, Gregory's family preferred to emphasize their Christian credentials. This complex mixing of temporal and spiritual power marked Basil's episcopacy, and to a lesser extent, that of Gregory's as well.

Gregory's family had a number of other features that left an impact on his ministry and thought. He was one of the middle children in a family of nine or ten children. There is every indication that his father was a notable of some importance in the region as a teacher and as a lawyer.[21] He apparently died while Gregory was a young boy.[22] Gregory was raised by his mother and, perhaps even more influentially, by his older sister Macrina. Later in life, he credited the latter as one of his main theological teachers.[23] Gregory's brother Basil — his other primary theological instructor — had been sent abroad to Athens to receive the best and most prestigious *paideia*

20. Van Dam, *Becoming Christian*, pp. 77-78.
21. Van Dam, *Families and Friends in Late Roman Cappadocia*, p. 18.
22. Van Dam, *Families and Friends in Late Roman Cappadocia*, p. 68.
23. Van Dam, *Families and Friends in Late Roman Cappadocia*, p. 69.

available to the sons of wealthy notables of the day.[24] Unlike his more pasto-
rally minded brother, Gregory originally intended to become a rhetor or a
teacher of *paideia* who would mold future generations of the rich and powerful sons of the upper crust.[25] His elder siblings Macrina and Basil per-
suaded him to drop his rhetorical ambitions in favor of a life of service to
God and the church as a priest. Later, as a calculated political move, Basil
would establish Gregory as bishop in the newly formed diocese of Nyssa.

In his hagiographical *Life of Saint Macrina*, Gregory recounted the development of a remarkable monastic community on the grounds of the
family estate headed by his mother Emmelia and his elder sister Macrina
sometime after the death of his father.[26] Susanna Elm notes that Gregory's
portrait of his sister represents the very first literary depiction of "the perfect Christian woman" in history.[27] Gregory not only memorialized his sister in his account of her life, but also he used her as a kind of Christian
Socrates in his treatise *On the Soul and the Resurrection*.[28] Referring to her
as "the teacher," he credited her with providing the theological instruction
and inspiration that decisively shaped the pastoral work of three of her
younger brothers, each of whom became a bishop.[29]

The other great teacher in Gregory's life was his older brother Basil.
Drawing upon his own first-rate classical education in Athens, Basil taught
his younger brother the discipline of rhetoric.[30] To counter the political influence of the Neo-Arians, Basil, as bishop of Caesarea, created several additional dioceses in surrounding regions. Basil then promptly installed his
best friend and fellow student, Gregory Nazianzen, and his younger
brother Gregory as bishops over these newly minted dioceses. Gregory
Nazianzen expressed intense objection to Basil's political machinations

24. Peter Brown, *Power and Persuasion in Late Antiquity: Towards a Christian Empire*
(Madison: University of Wisconsin Press, 1992), pp. 35-70 (see esp. pp. 37-41).

25. Van Dam, *Families and Friends in Late Roman Cappadocia*, pp. 69-70.

26. Gregory of Nyssa, *The Life of Saint Macrina*, trans. Kevin Corrigan (Toronto:
Peregrina, 1997), pp. 25-29.

27. Susanna Elm, *Virgins of God: The Making of Asceticism in Late Antiquity*, Oxford
Classical Monographs (New York: Oxford University Press, 1994; New York: Clarendon Paperbacks, 1996), p. 39.

28. *On the Soul and the Resurrection*, NPNF[2], 5.430-68.

29. Gregory of Nyssa, *The Life of Saint Macrina*, pp. 24-25 and 28-30. See also *On the
Soul and the Resurrection*, 5.430.

30. On Basil's instruction of Gregory, see Van Dam, *Families and Friends in Late Roman
Cappadocia*, pp. 68-69.

and never actually showed up for episcopal duty in the little diocese of Sasima.[31] In contrast, Gregory of Nyssa did show up for duty in the humble little episcopal see of Nyssa and faithfully executed the office of bishop. Eventually, Gregory's pastoral ministry came to mean a great deal to the people of his little diocese, as evidenced by their turnout along the streets when he returned from a brief period of exile.[32]

Gregory's younger brother Peter, the baby of the family, eventually became bishop of Sebasteia in Pontus.[33] Earlier, while in exile from his see in Nyssa, Gregory had been invited to assist in selecting a new bishop. During the selection process, the other bishops involved decided to elect their consultant as the new bishop. Gregory served as the bishop of Sebasteia for a brief period.[34] Several years later, his younger brother Peter was elected to that very same episcopal throne.

Gregory left some clues in his writings that indicate he may have been married for a brief period early in his adult life. The details of his marriage, his wife, and end of their marriage remain matters of some debate.[35] If he was married, it does not appear that any children came from the union. Whatever the case may have been with regard to a marriage in his early adult years, he later embraced celibacy as a priest for the duration of his adult life. Early in his pastoral ministry, he helped Basil establish a monastic movement in Cappadocia through the powerful and articulate arguments for ascetic celibacy in his earliest known work entitled *On Virginity*.[36]

In addition to the context of his family and his clerical vocation, Gregory of Nyssa's life should be seen in reference to the larger currents of conflict and change that marked the Roman Empire during the period in which he lived. Van Dam notes:

> Basil and Gregory of Nazianzus were born at about the time Constantine was dedicating his new capital of Constantinople, and Gregory of Nyssa at about the time of Constantine's death. All three Cappadocian Fathers were students of Greek literature and philosophy. All three

---

31. Van Dam, *Families and Friends in Late Roman Cappadocia*, p. 51.

32. Daniélou, *From Glory to Glory*, p. 4.

33. Van Dam, *Families and Friends in Late Roman Cappadocia*, p. 72.

34. Van Dam, *Becoming Christian*, p. 56.

35. Van Dam, *Families and Friends in Late Roman Cappadocia*, pp. 116 and 207-8. See also Elm, *Virgins of God*, pp. 157-58.

36. *On Virginity*, NPNF², 5.343-71.

served as bishops of Cappadocia. All three contributed extensively to the development of Christian theology. Basil died a few years before the Council of Constantinople in 381 reaffirmed the orthodoxy of Nicene Christianity. By the time Gregory of Nazianzus and Gregory of Nyssa died, the emperor Theodosius [346/7-395] had declared orthodox Christianity the sole legitimate religion of the empire.

The renewal of the Roman empire, conversion, orthodoxy and heresy, Christianity and classical culture, the foundation of Constantinople as New Rome, the evolution of cities, the rise of bishops: the Cappadocian Fathers were participants in all these grand transformations, and the reigns of Constantine and Theodosius were the parentheses that enclosed their careers.[37]

Gregory's life and ministry spanned an extraordinarily important period of change within the Roman Empire in late antiquity. He lived through and contributed to the period in which the Roman Empire metamorphosed from a classical pagan orientation into the era of Christendom.

In many ways, the pivotal and dominating figure of the Roman Empire during the period of late antiquity was the emperor Constantine I (c. 285-337). He brought about massive changes in the Roman religious situation first through the Edict of Milan (313), which granted imperial tolerance to Christianity and to all other religions. As he gave increasing prominence to Christian symbols and institutions, Constantine consolidated his hold on the empire partly on the basis of this relatively new religious movement that had emerged from the eastern end of the Mediterranean.[38] Constantine himself had called and presided over the decisive first ecumenical council in 325. He had even supplied the crucial term in the debate — *homoousios* — for describing the relationship between the first two Persons of the Trinity.

Constantine's embrace of Christianity — particularly in its Nicene form — wrought many changes to the Roman Empire. Peter Brown, historian of Late Antiquity, provides insight into the effect of Constantine's absorption of Christianity into his reign:

Constantine's condemnation of [pagan] sacrifice and the closing and

---

37. Van Dam, *Families and Friends in Late Roman Cappadocia*, pp. 1-2.

38. "Edict of Milan," in *The Concise Oxford Dictionary of the Christian Church*, ed. E. A. Livingstone (Oxford: Oxford University Press, 1977), p. 337.

spoliation of many temples further undermined the cultural autonomy of the cities. The local notables found themselves denied the right to resort to precisely those religious ceremonies that had once enabled each city to give public expression to its own sense of identity. It was no longer considered advisable to sacrifice, to visit temples, or to celebrate one's city as the dwelling place of particular gods bound to the civic community by particular, local rites. Instead, the Christian court offered a new, empire-wide patriotism. This was centered on the person and mission of a God-given, universal ruler, whose vast and profoundly abstract care for the empire as a whole made the older loyalties to individual cities, that had been wholeheartedly expressed in the old, polytheistic system, seem parochial and trivial.[39]

In the new era of state-tolerated — and eventually state-sponsored — Christianity, the elite class of wealthy citizens was increasingly displaced by Christian bishops. Many of the bishops, often beneficiaries of *paideia* themselves, had come from notable families or had been notables prior to taking up holy office.[40] Van Dam notes that

> despite the repeated emphasis on the importance of spiritual qualities, local aristocrats, especially those with family connections, consistently had the best chance of becoming clerics and bishops. In fact, in Cappadocia during the fourth century all the known bishops with known backgrounds were wealthy enough to have otherwise become decurions, members of their municipal councils.[41]

Rather than deriving legitimacy from the public displays of polytheistic cult observance, the bishops solidified their position among residents of town and country by their embrace of the poor and disenfranchised in the name of the preexistent, incarnate, crucified, and risen Christ.[42] Gregory of Nyssa's desire to teach rhetoric and his subsequent role as bishop must be seen in this light. He put his training in *paideia* to work as a kind of theological rhetor in service both to the church and to the effort at religious consolidation of the empire along Orthodox Nicene lines.

---

39. Brown, *Power and Persuasion in Late Antiquity*, p. 19.
40. Brown, *Power and Persuasion in Late Antiquity*, p. 119.
41. Van Dam, *Becoming Christian*, p. 58.
42. Van Dam, *Becoming Christian*, pp. 71-117.

Adherents to Greco-Roman religious traditions and their long-established social functioning continued to exist during this period. They offered significant resistance to the Christianization of the empire. One of the strongest challenges came from the emperor Julian (332-363), a fellow Cappadocian and a classmate of Basil and Gregory Nazianzen in Athens. The so-called Apostate attempted during his brief reign (360-363) to brush away the "atheist" nightmare of Christian rule during the past two generations and to restore the empire to its classical and polytheistic identity.[43] This pitched cultural and political struggle between the old ways of classical civilization with its pervasive polytheism and the new ways of the Christian church with its Nicene proclamation of the One God in Three Persons formed an important feature of the backdrop of Gregory's life and work.

Significant conflicts within the church during this period abounded. As the church grappled with the need to hold on to both the Jewish inheritance of radical monotheism and claims about the divinity of Jesus Christ arising from traditional Christian practice and apostolic-era writings, several conflicts arose, the chief of which focused on the divinity of Christ. Two major parties emerged in this struggle. On the one hand, we find the followers of the Alexandrian presbyter, Arius, who asserted that Christ was divine, but not ontologically equal with the Creator. On the other hand, we find those who followed another Alexandrian, Athanasius; this party held to the conviction that Christ's divinity shared the same essence as that of the Creator. While the homoousins won the first major round, the matter was far from settled in 325. The battle between the pro-Nicene Orthodox party and the Arian party raged for much of the rest of the fourth century. Those who attempted to stake out a middle position — the homoiousins — added further complications to the field of conflict by attempting to stake out theological middle ground. Gregory Nazianzen, Basil, and Gregory of Nyssa together took up the pro-Nicene mantle upon the death of Athanasius. The Cappadocians waged unrelenting battle against Neo-Arians like fellow Cappadocian Eunomius (c. 325–c. 395) throughout the course of their public ministries. Much of Gregory's work, therefore, has a polemical cast to it.

It was not until Basil died in 379 that Gregory stepped out from be-

---

43. Peter Brown, "The Last Pagan Emperor: Robert Browning's *The Emperor Julian*," in *Society and the Holy in Late Antiquity* (Berkeley: University of California Press, 1982), pp. 83-102.

hind his brother's shadow and entered visibly into the fray. Prior to Basil's death, Gregory had supported Basil from behind the scenes. He quite deliberately assumed his brother's mantle and sought to carry forward his unfinished polemical work. While continuing Basil's fight against Eunomius, Gregory came into his own as an imaginative and capable theologian of the first order. Through his many occasional and polemical writings, he distinguished himself as a profound trinitarian theologian as he argued with subtlety, precision, and consistency for the doctrine of the One God in Three equal and distinct Persons.

He wrote weighty refutations of the thought of the Neo-Arian Eunomius. By one account, both Gregory Nazianzen and Jerome listened with strong approval to a private reading of an early draft of his work against Eunomius that took place at some point during the meeting of the so-called second ecumenical council in Constantinople (381).[44] He also wrote against the Pneumatomachoi[45] (who argued against the full *homoousian* divinity of the Holy Spirit), the Apollinarians[46] (who denied the full humanity of Christ), and assorted others.

Much more was at stake in these theological controversies than merely proving the rectitude of one's scriptural exegesis or the proper performance of the liturgy. Too often, ending up on the wrong side of a theological dispute meant imperial persecution or exile. The leading figures in these controversies fought both for the correctness of their cause and for political and economic favor from the emperor. The three Cappadocian defenders of Nicea fell on hard times during the short reign of the Christian-turned-pagan Julian (332-363) as he attempted to de-Christianize the empire and to forbid Christians from teaching the classics of Greco-Roman culture.[47] The Arian emperor Valens (c. 328-378) ban-

---

44. Jerome (c. 342-420), the great scholar of Scripture and correspondent of Augustine, recounts that he sat together with Gregory Nazianzen and listened with approval to Gregory of Nyssa read aloud a draft text of what may well have been an early version of his *Contra Eunomius*. Jerome wrote, "Gregory bishop of Nyssa, the brother of Basil of Caesarea, a few years since read to Gregory Nazianzan and myself a work against Eunomius. He is said to have also written many other works, and to be still writing." Jerome, *Lives of Illustrious Men*, NPNF[2], 3.383.

45. *On the Holy Spirit*, NPNF[2], 5.315-25.

46. Anthony Meredith, *The Cappadocians* (Crestwood, N.Y.: St. Vladimir's Seminary Press, 1995), p. 113.

47. For a treatment of Julian's rejection of Christianity and embrace of classical paganism, see Van Dam, *Kingdom of Snow*, pp. 163-80; for Basil's response, see pp. 181-88.

ished several pro-Nicene bishops including Gregory of Nyssa, but later allowed them to return.[48] Relative prosperity for the Nicene party returned under the reign of the Orthodox emperor Theodosius I. As an eventual sign of his status in the eyes of this Orthodox emperor who reigned from the year Basil died (379) until the year Gregory of Nyssa died (395), Gregory was designated a teacher of authentic Christian doctrine in 381 by imperial decree.[49] He also called upon Gregory to preside and preach at the funerals of the empress Aelia Flacilla (d. 383) and the imperial princess Pulcheria (d. 385).[50] Gregory appears to have served for some time in his mature years as something of a royal theologian and a court chaplain. Jean Daniélou noted:

> During these years Gregory enjoyed the favor of the imperial court. In 385 he was chosen to deliver the funeral eulogies in honor of the departed empress Flacilla and her daughter Pulcheria. At Constantinople, too, Gregory enjoyed the friendship of Olympias, one of the most outstanding women of the age. This was the lady to whom St. John Chrysostom was to address so many letters during his exile. And it was to her, some years later, that Gregory would dedicate his *Commentary on the Canticle of Canticles* about the year 389.[51]

That Gregory was given such an honored position attests to his effectiveness as a defender of orthodox Nicenism, his considerable rhetorical abilities, and the social standing of his family.

Gregory also wrote a series of profound works of ascetic and mystical theology in which he depicted the perpetual ascent of the baptized into deeper apprehension of the Triune mystery. Some of his most compelling work focused on the exemplary biblical figures of Moses and Solomon.

As mentioned above, Catholic and Protestant educational theologians have largely overlooked Gregory's contributions to ecclesial pedagogy.[52] Books dealing with the history of the church's educational ministry tend to focus on the pedagogical contributions to the catechumenate of figures like Ambrose (c. 339-397), Cyril of Jerusalem (c. 315-386), Augustine (354-

---

48. Van Dam, *Kingdom of Snow*, pp. 129 and 137.
49. Van Dam, *Becoming Christian*, p. 144.
50. Meredith, *The Cappadocians*, p. 53.
51. Daniélou, *From Glory to Glory*, p. 8.
52. For example, see Yarnold, *The Awe-Inspiring Rites of Initiation*.

430), Theodore of Mopsuestia (c. 350-428), and John Chrysostom (c. 347-407). If treated at all, such studies cover Gregory's pedagogical contributions only very briefly. Given the contemporary ferment and creativity concerning the practical dimensions of the doctrine of the Trinity, a closer look at his work in general and his pedagogical contribution in particular may yield useful insights for a contemporary practical trinitarian approach to faith formation. We now turn to this task as we examine how Gregory of Nyssa understood baptism in relation to the doctrine of the Trinity and ecclesial pedagogy.

The Baptismal Rite

Like his brother Basil and their common friend Gregory Nazianzen, Gregory of Nyssa did not produce new liturgical materials for the baptismal rite. Instead, he worked within the predominant liturgical framework of his time and place.[53] His unique contributions to the complex rites of Christian initiation came in the form of insightful interpretations of the meaning of baptism. His insights into the meaning of the Christian initiation rite contributed to the development of his doctrine of God as Trinity and laid bare the inherently pedagogical character of the Christian life. In this section, I will provide a likely sketch of the key features of the baptismal rite Gregory used based both on liturgical studies of the fourth century and on clues he provided in his own writings.

With antecedents stretching back probably into the first century, clearly identifiable linguistic and cultural distinctions marked significant differences between Greek-speaking Eastern and Latin-speaking Western Christian liturgical traditions.[54] E. C. Whitaker summarized the major features of these overarching differences with respect to the baptismal rite in the following manner:

The Eastern Rite
Renunciation
1 *apotaxis* (renunciation, facing west)
2 *syntaxis* (act of adherence, facing east)

---

53. Finn, *Early Christian Baptism and the Catechumenate*, p. 62.
54. E. C. Whitaker, *The Baptismal Liturgy*, 2nd ed. (London: SPCK, 1981), pp. 22-28.

Pre-baptismal anointing
  1 by the minister to the forehead
  2 by some other person to the whole body
Baptism accompanied by the form "I baptize you in the name . . ."

The Western Rite
Renunciation without *syntaxis*
Baptism accompanied by triple interrogation of the faith
  (but no form "I baptize you in the name . . .")
Post-baptismal ceremonies
  prayer for the Holy Spirit
  anointing of forehead
  imposition of the hands.[55]

A comparison of the two large-scale groupings of early baptismal traditions indicates that the East had more fully developed pre-baptismal practices than the West. In general terms, the baptismal rite in the East contained three major sections: renunciation, pre-baptismal anointing, and baptism.[56] The renunciation portion of the rite contained two subsections. First, the baptizand would face the west (where light dies) and renounce all allegiances to the devil, sin, and the ways of darkness *(apotaxis)*. Next, the baptismal candidate would turn to the east (where light arises) in order to profess adherence to the Triune God *(syntaxis)*. After this dual action of renunciation and profession, the liturgical leader would then anoint the baptizand with oil. The final phase of the Eastern rite called for the application of water to the baptizand with the formula "I baptize you in the name of the Father, and the Son, and the Holy Spirit."[57]

In the West, the pre-baptismal phase only called for a renunciation of ties to spiritual realities in opposition to the Triune God. The water phase of the rite did not require the formulaic utterance of the Triune Name. The

---

55. Whitaker, *The Baptismal Liturgy*, p. 23.

56. Whitaker, *The Baptismal Liturgy*, p. 23.

57. This formula later changed under the influence of another outstanding leader in the West Syrian liturgical tradition, John Chrysostom. His formula ran "You *are* baptized in the name of the Father, and of the Son, and of the Holy Spirit"; see E. C. Whitaker, *Documents of the Baptismal Liturgy* (London: SPCK, 1960; 2nd ed., 1970; paperback ed., 1977), p. 36; emphasis added. Chrysostom's approach emphasized the work of the Triune God in baptism and deemphasized the role of the presiding cleric.

post-baptismal phase was more elaborate than in the East and involved conferral of the Holy Spirit by means of anointing and the imposition of hands.

Within these larger divisions, further differentiation emerged. Whitaker documented the key differences among early Christian liturgical traditions in terms of several major regional groupings. Among the many distinctive patterns of Christian initiation that arose under the larger umbrella of the Greek-speaking East, we find the Syrian (Eastern and Western versions), Armenian, Byzantine, and Egyptian traditions.[58] Gregory and his Cappadocian comrades operated within the larger Syrian pattern of the Greek East. Thomas Finn helps us further to locate Gregory in the West Syrian variant of the larger Syrian liturgical family:

> Although there is a discernible unity to Syrian baptismal tradition and a good deal of bilingualism, the Hellenized Greek-speaking Syrian Christians and the Semitic Syriac-speakers differed not only in language but in patterns of thought, literary genius, and historical circumstances. The former, for instance, lived within the shifting eastern borders of the Roman Empire, were oriented to the Mediterranean world, and spoke its language, primarily Greek. The latter lived beyond Rome's borders in the land of ancient Sumer, were oriented toward Persia, and spoke Syriac, a dialect of the Aramaic that Jesus used. West Syrian baptismal instruction tends to be analytic and expository; the Eastern tradition tends to be symbolic and poetic. These differing patterns of thought and modes of expression will be immediately apparent to the reader.
>
> For our purposes "West Syrian" denotes the predominantly Hellenized Greek-speaking Christianity of Asia Minor, Syria, and Palestine, whose principal center of influence was Antioch and then Constantinople (Istanbul, Turkey). "East Syria" . . . refers to the predominantly Semitic, Syriac-speaking Christianity east of Palestine as far as Mesopotamia, whose principal centers were Edessa and Nisibis.[59]

Inasmuch as Gregory of Nyssa was located in Asia Minor, spoke Greek, and was oriented toward the Greco-Roman cultural world — particularly

---

58. Whitaker, *Documents of the Baptismal Liturgy,* pp. 21-98. See also Maxwell E. Johnson, *The Rites of Christian Initiation: Their Evolution and Interpretation* (Collegeville, Minn.: Liturgical [A Pueblo Book], 1999), pp. 89-124.

59. Finn, *Early Christian Baptism and the Catechumenate,* pp. 29-30.

Alexandria — we can safely conclude that he was part of the West Syrian liturgical tradition.[60]

In his treatment of patterns of Christian initiation in the East during the fourth century, Maxwell Johnson provides even more detail than does Whitaker as to the elements of the West Syrian baptismal rite. With regard to the post-Nicene West Syrian tradition in which Gregory lived and carried out his pastoral ministry Johnson observes that

1. the final preparation of catechumens for baptism now takes place during the forty days of Lent and appears to have included not only daily catechesis but daily exorcism as well;

2. the Easter vigil has become in the East the prime time for the rites of initiation themselves, and that the central paradigm for interpreting baptism is now Romans 6 (participation in the death and burial of Christ), although the earlier emphasis on the "new birth" theology of John 3 still operates to some extent;

3. the pre-baptismal rites have been transformed from a pneumatic to an exorcistic emphasis with the pre-baptismal anointing(s) gradually becoming related to preparation for athletic and even military-like contests with evil; and

4. the explicit reference to the gift of the Holy Spirit gradually shifts from a pre-baptismal or baptismal (Chrysostom) location to a post-baptismal one (Theodore and Cyril), and becomes associated with the addition of a post-baptismal anointing (Cyril).[61]

It should be noted here that in mid-fourth-century Cappadocia, distinctive Western elements of the baptismal rite — like the triple interrogation and post-baptismal anointing and imposition of hands — were not yet present.[62] Eastern church baptismal liturgies incorporated such features as described in (4) at a date subsequent to the ministry of Gregory of Nyssa.

Johnson compares in some detail three West Syrian baptismal liturgies

60. Finn, *Early Christian Baptism and the Catechumenate*, pp. 60-70.

61. Johnson, *The Rites of Christian Initiation*, p. 107.

62. There is some reason to believe that pilgrims from western parts of the empire may have influenced the baptismal liturgy as it was practiced in Jerusalem during Cyril's ministry. Western church traditions like the post-baptismal anointing (confirmation) were incorporated into Eastern patterns in the fifth and sixth centuries. For a fuller discussion of this, see Johnson, *The Rites of Christian Initiation*, p. 112.

from the time in which Gregory carried out his ministry: Cyril of Jerusalem, John Chrysostom, and Theodore of Mopsuestia.[63] We can infer the most likely elements of Gregory's own baptismal practice from Johnson's comparison of this particular collection of baptismal patterns. Cyril, Chrysostom, and Theodore all used the following pattern for the pre-baptismal phase: renunciation, *syntaxis* (pledge of allegiance), anointing of the head, stripping of clothes, and anointing of the body. During the water phase, Chrysostom and Theodore employed the Triune formula from Matthew 28:19; Cyril did not provide evidence that he used the Triune formula during the immersions. In the post-baptismal phase, Cyril and Chrysostom indicate that the baptizand was clothed in a new garment; Theodore lacks this detail. Cyril includes anointing with chrism; neither Chrysostom nor Theodore includes this element. Theodore refers to the kiss of peace immediately after the baptizand emerges from the baptismal waters, while Chrysostom places it immediately prior to the celebration of the Eucharist; Cyril omits it entirely. All three include the Eucharist as the final act of the post-baptismal phase of the initiation rite.[64]

What can we infer about Gregory's practice of baptism? He would have engaged in intense catechetical instruction during the forty-day period of Lent. Lenten preparation would likely have involved not only daily instruction in the basic beliefs of Christian faith, but also daily exorcisms. He would most likely have administered baptism during the Easter vigil.[65] The baptismal rite would have had three phases. The pre-baptismal phase would have included an act of renunciation facing the west, an act of adherence to Jesus Christ while facing east, an anointing of the head, the removal of clothing, and an anointing of the whole body. Baptism per se would have involved threefold immersion while the Triune formula from Matthew 28:19 was invoked.[66] Finally, the post-baptismal phase may have involved

63. Johnson, *The Rites of Christian Initiation*, p. 122. Johnson does not analyze Gregory's own baptismal practice because Gregory did not provide direct commentary on the baptismal liturgy per se in his writings.

64. Johnson, *The Rites of Christian Initiation*, p. 122.

65. It remains a possibility that Gregory administered baptism on Epiphany, January 6, but this seems less certain. See Finn, *Early Christian Baptism and the Catechumenate*, pp. 61-62.

66. We can decide in favor of the practices of Chrysostom and Theodore against Cyril on this point because Gregory makes reference to the fact that baptizands are baptized into the One Name That Is Three. See Finn, *Early Christian Baptism and the Catechumenate*, p. 66. See also *Against Eunomius*, NPNF[2], 5.103.

one or more of the following elements — anointing, clothing with a new garment, signing, and a kiss — and the celebration of the Eucharist.

When we turn to Gregory's writings, we can find details that corroborate this reconstruction of the salient features of his celebration of the baptismal rite. For example, due to the great stress that he placed on baptism as a mystical dying and rising with Christ culminating in the Eucharist, it seems that the Easter vigil would have been his preferred occasion for the administration of the rite.[67] Confession of faith, prayer, invocation of the Triune God, anointing with oil, threefold immersion in water, and admittance to the Eucharist can all be found in his various treatments of baptism.[68]

Gregory maintained that human beings are a compound of body and soul.[69] Whereas baptism addresses the body and its need for transformation, the Eucharist heals the soul.[70] For him, baptism and the Eucharist made up a complex rite through which the Triune God addressed and transformed both body and soul.[71] Baptism and Eucharist may be differentiated, but not separated. The Triune God gave the sacramental mysteries together in order to transform both the inner and the outer lives of human beings. These mysteries function in a complementary fashion and are indissolubly joined. Baptism culminates in partaking of the Eucharist; inversely, celebration of the Eucharist rests upon baptismal foundations. Taken together, these sacramental mysteries catalyze the participation of the whole person in Christ's death and resurrection.

Who would have been baptized by Gregory? With a fairly high degree of certitude, we can affirm that he would have baptized mostly adult converts from paganism, Judaism, or non-Nicene sects of Christianity. He directed fellow catechetical instructors to highlight different aspects of Christian teaching depending upon the religious background of the cate-

---

67. For the culmination of catechetical instruction in baptism and the Eucharist, see *Catechetical Oration,* 97-120. See also Jaeger, *Oratio Catechetica,* pp. 82-106.

68. For the act of confession of faith, see Finn, *Early Christian Baptism and the Catechumenate,* p. 69; for invocation of the Triune Name, see p. 66. With regard to anointing, see *On the Holy Spirit,* NPNF², 5.321. On three immersions, see Finn, *Early Christian Baptism and the Catechumenate,* pp. 65-66. For the close connection between baptism and the Eucharist, see *Catechetical Oration,* pp. 107-12.

69. *Catechetical Oration,* p. 107.

70. *Catechetical Oration,* pp. 107-12.

71. *Catechetical Oration,* p. 108.

chumens who happened to be present.[72] Gregory made no references to the preparation of children and youth for baptism. This makes sense in light of the fact that it was only during the period of his pastoral ministry that the movement toward baptism of infants gained momentum. That Gregory emphasized the need for authentic faith on the part of baptizands to ensure the efficacy of baptism lends support to the claim that he baptized only adult converts to Nicene Christianity.[73]

Stepping Back from the Baptismal Gestalt

The Meaning of Baptism

Even if he did not offer a new liturgy or detailed commentary on each liturgical moment of the rite, Gregory of Nyssa had quite a number of things to say about the meaning and significance of baptism. While his baptismal liturgy clearly fits in the West Syrian liturgical tradition, his way of interpreting the rite had a distinctively Alexandrian tone to it. Gregory tended to emphasize the allegorical and symbolic meanings of both the rite and the sacred texts upon which it was based. Theologically, he drew a great deal from Alexandrian sources. Philo (c. 20 BCE–50 CE), Origen (c. 185–c. 254), and Athanasius (c. 297-373) all influenced his theological vision and likely influenced the way he interpreted the meaning of baptism.[74]

Gregory interpreted the meaning of baptism in a number of interrelated ways. His overarching interpretation followed the pattern of the prebaptismal phase of the rite in which baptismal candidates renounce allegiance to sin and the devil *(apotaxis)* and turn toward the Triune God

---

72. *Catechetical Oration,* p. 23.

73. We might have expected Gregory to address the question of paidobaptism in his pastoral treatise on the death of infants. That he did not suggests rather strongly that this was not a live issue for him. See *On Infants' Early Deaths,* NPNF², 5.372-81. Finn's argument that children were baptized in the West Syrian tradition during this period does not seem compelling in Gregory's case based on evidence from his writings. See Finn, *Early Christian Baptism and the Catechumenate,* pp. 14-15.

74. Gregory's penchant for Alexandrian perspectives comes through, for instance, in his use of Philo of Alexandria's *De Vita Mosis.* See Philo, *De Vita Mosis,* in *Philo: An English Translation in Ten Volumes,* trans. F. H. Colson, vol. 6, The Loeb Classical Library (Cambridge, Mass.: Harvard University Press, 1935), pp. 274-595. For the influence of Origen and Athanasius on Gregory's thought, see Meredith, *The Cappadocians,* pp. 4, 54-62, 86, and 90.

through faith in Jesus Christ *(syntaxis)*. On the one hand, Gregory depicted the significance of baptism as cleansing "from every defilement both of body and spirit."[75] He also described it as "release from bondage" to the powers of sin and the devil.[76] In this sense, baptism signifies a decisive move away from human participation in or intermingling with that which has "no existence of its own and is not found to possess any substance of being."[77] It is also a rupture or a break in the individual's participation in evil.[78] Baptism, then, signifies the death of death in the baptizand.

The turn away from nonbeing and evil tells only half of the story. This mystical washing also signified for Gregory the beginning of spiritual illumination and the process of regeneration. Baptism marks the turn from darkness to light:

> Although we were darkened through sin, God made us bright and loving through his resplendent grace. When everything is shrouded by the prevailing gloom of night, even if things happen to be light by nature, with the coming of light, the comparison to darkness does not apply to things previously obscured by gloom. The soul is thus led over from error to truth, and the dark form of its life is changed to resplendent grace. . . . Paul . . . says that Christ entered the world to enlighten those who were dark.[79]

Gregory described the old life with its conceptions of self, world, and God apart from grace as darkness; the enlightened life in which things are seen in their true character begins with the grace bestowed in baptism. In his recent study of Gregory of Nyssa's conception of faith, Martin Laird traces the theme of light in Gregory's teachings on creation and the incarnation and offers the following observation on the illuminating character of baptism:

---

75. *Commentary on the Song of Songs*, trans. Casimir McCambley, vol. 12, The Archbishop of Iakovos Library of Ecclesiastical and Historical Sources, ed. N. M. Vaporis (Brookline, Mass.: Hellenic College Press, 1987), p. 151, and also pp. 61, 78. See also Finn, *Early Christian Baptism and the Catechumenate*, pp. 62-63.

76. Finn, *Early Christian Baptism and the Catechumenate*, p. 62.

77. *Catechetical Oration*, p. 44.

78. *Catechetical Oration*, p. 103.

79. *Commentary on the Song of Songs*, p. 63.

On the basis of these texts on creation and incarnation it is obvious enough that by the designation of that enlightenment consequent upon the incarnation Gregory does not envisage simply a movement out of darkness; it is more fundamentally a return to and an intensification of that luminous state which characterized the human condition before it was obscured by sin. Baptism returns one to this and is likewise described in the language of bathing and light. The bath of rebirth makes those darkened by sin "to shine like the stars of heaven." When Gregory says that the Ethiopians washed off their darkness "in the mystical water," the luminous quality they knew was but a return to the luminous state of God's original, creative intention.[80]

Thus, illumination characterizes the positive side of baptism. Moving away from darkness leads into the light of divine grace through which the baptizand comes to self, world, and God in their true light.

Illumination does not, however, exhaust Gregory's interpretation of baptism. He also interpreted it as regeneration. Human beings, as part of the creation, were brought into being by the Triune God out of love and for the purpose of knowing and participating in the Triune glory.[81] The Trinity acted to bring into being a creature that would be able to see the light of Triune splendor and serve as witness to it.[82] Humanity, then, was created specifically for the purpose of recognizing, sharing in, and enjoying the goodness and love that is God.

Recognizing and participating in the glorious life of the Triune God required a certain affinity between God and human beings. Differentiating himself from the Platonic tradition from which he drew a great deal, Greg-

---

80. Martin Laird, *Gregory of Nyssa and the Grasp of Faith: Union, Knowledge and Divine Presence* (New York: Oxford University Press, 2004), p. 185. The illumination of baptism should not be confused with entering into the "illuminated darkness" of mystical contemplation. Gregory seems to have two different aspects of the encounter with God in mind when he uses the terms *light* and *darkness* for crucial dimensions of the Christian life. He used the metaphor of light when describing authentic insight into God, self, and the world resultant from the transforming power of grace. He used the metaphors of cloud and darkness when describing the way in which faith can grasp what discursive reason cannot at the summit of contemplation. For a fuller discussion of the ways in which Gregory used light and darkness as descriptive metaphors for aspects of the Christian life, see the entirety of Laird's chapter 7, "The Luminous Dark Revisited," pp. 174-204.

81. *Catechetical Oration*, p. 35.

82. *Catechetical Oration*, p. 35.

ory argued that resonance of being does not amount to continuity of being; God and human beings have fundamentally different kinds of being. In discussing the status of theological language in relation to the reality of the divine itself, he tended to emphasize the breadth of the gulf between the divine and the human:

> Wide indeed, is the interval in all else that divides the human from the divine; experience cannot point here below to anything at all resembling in amount what we may guess at and imagine there. So likewise, as regards the meaning of our terms, though there may be, so far as words go, some likeness between [humanity] and the Eternal, yet the gulf between these two worlds is the real measure of the separation of meanings.[83]

Yet he did not stress the discontinuity between humanity and God too far. Inasmuch as human beings were created in the image of God, they do have a certain created aptitude for the divine. Gregory maintained that for human beings to participate in the goodness and beauty of the Trinity they had necessarily to be "framed of such a kind as to be adapted to the participation of such good."[84] He understood this distinctive human capacity for participation in divine beauty as reason or intellection.[85] While asserting that human beings are composite creatures of the earthly and the ethereal, Gregory clearly emphasized the spiritual and intellectual dimensions of human existence.[86] The Triune God thus constituted human beings for "enjoyment of Divine good."[87] For Gregory, one finds a strong desire for the beauty and goodness of the Trinity at the core of what it means to be human.

Enjoyment of divine beauty meant something more for Gregory than abstract contemplation or speculation. Knowledge of the divine for him entailed deep and pervasive personal engagement with the Trinity. This primal condition of humanity he described in terms of participation (*metousia*).[88] In his *Catechetical Oration* he wrote:

---

83. *Against Eunomius,* 5.93.

84. *Catechetical Oration,* p. 35.

85. *On the Making of Man,* 5.395.

86. *On the Making of Man,* 5.403. See also *Commentary on the Song of Songs,* p. 207, and *On the Making of Man,* 5.405-6.

87. *Catechetical Oration,* p. 35.

88. *Catechetical Oration,* p. 35. See also Jaeger, *Oratio Catechetica,* p. 19.

Now that alone is unchangeable in its nature which does not come into being through creation, whereas whatever the uncreated nature has brought into being out of a state of non-existence, as soon as it has begun to exist as the result of a transformation, is continually passing through a state of change; such change, if the creature acts in accordance with nature, being always in the better direction, whereas, if it is perverted from the right path, a movement in the opposite direction awaits it.

Such was the state of man, the changeable part of whose nature had lapsed in the contrary direction. And when once the withdrawal from good had taken place, its consequence was the introduction of every form of evil, so that as a result of the withdrawal of life death was introduced instead; on the privation of light there followed darkness; and in the absence of virtue wickedness took its place, and for every kind of good there was substituted the list of opposite evils.[89]

While the essential nature of the Trinity is unchanging, human beings are subject to change by the very nature of their existence as creatures.[90] The original purpose for humankind entailed not a static awareness of Triune perfection, but perpetual growth and transformation toward the infinite. The fall away from participation in divine beauty and goodness resulted in an inevitable movement toward death:

Now change is a kind of movement always proceeding from the state in which a thing is to a different state, and such a movement takes two forms. The one is always in the direction of the good, and in this the advance cannot be arrested, because there is no limit to that which is explored. The other is in the contrary direction, and its essence consists in having no existence. For the contrast with the good, as we have said previously, implies something of the same idea of opposition as is implied when we say that that which exists is logically opposed to that which does not exist and existence to non-existence. Now in the tendency and movement towards variation and change it is not possible for the nature to remain wholly independent and unmoved, but the will tends wholly in some one direction, because its desire for that which is good impels it naturally into movement.[91]

---

89. *Catechetical Oration*, p. 51.
90. *On the Making of Man*, 5.406, and *Catechetical Oration*, p. 41.
91. *Catechetical Oration*, pp. 71-72.

Human beings, while created to focus on and move toward the infinite source of life, have chosen to focus on and move increasingly toward non-existence, or death. Now utterly caught up in death and servitude to the devil, human beings need divine intervention in order to reconnect with and move ever more toward the Triune Source of Life.[92]

One further dimension of Gregory's account of the human situation prior to the choice to fall away from divine goodness needs brief attention before we can grasp the full sense of what he understood by baptismal regeneration. According to Gregory's eschatological reading of the Genesis creation accounts, God created human beings in two stages. The first stage lacked gender differentiation.[93] In anticipation of the exercise of human freedom to turn away from God into living death, the Triune Creator brought about gender differentiation and sexual reproduction as a means of preventing humanity from completely succumbing to the power of death. In this second stage of the creation of humanity, God gave gender differentiation and sexual reproduction as an affirmation of life over and against the yawning abyss of death. This stopgap measure — fueled by the distorting power of disordered desire that is closely tied to the irrational and animalistic dimensions of the complex compound that constituted human nature — did not diminish the rational capabilities of either gender.[94]

When Gregory interpreted baptism as regeneration, then, what did he mean? Essentially, he understood baptismal regeneration as a recovery of the original blessedness and beauty intended by God in the creation of humanity. Regeneration as restoration of original blessedness entailed enjoyment and rational contemplation of divine beauty, participation in the Triune God, and the relativization and transcending of gender differentiation. The eschatological future made present through the rite of baptism is for Gregory the recovery and restoration of that which was lost *(apokatastasis)* in the fall away from participation in Triune beauty, goodness, life, and love.[95] The process of "the reconstitution of our nature in its original form," which comes to completion in the general resurrection, has

---

92. *Catechetical Oration*, p. 72. See also *Against Eunomius*, 5.126-27.

93. Gregory's warrant for this comes from Luke 20:35-36 in which he interprets future resurrection as a recovery of the original condition of humanity. See *On the Making of Man*, 5.407.

94. *On the Making of Man*, 5.405.

95. *Catechetical Oration*, p. 105. See also Jaeger, *Oratio Catechetica*, p. 91.

its beginning in baptism.[96] In the midst of an exegetical discussion of Christology in the first chapter of Colossians, Gregory described three births of human beings:

> [Jesus Christ] is the first-born from the dead, Who first himself loosed the pains of death, that He might also make that birth of the resurrection a way for all men. Again, He becomes "the first-born among many brethren," Who is born before us by the new birth of regeneration in water, for the travail whereof the hovering of the Dove was the midwife, whereby He makes those who share with Him in the like birth to be His own brothers, and becomes the first-born of those who after Him are born of water and of the Spirit: and to speak briefly, as there are in us three births, whereby human nature is quickened, one of the body, another in the sacrament of regeneration, another by that resurrection of the dead for which we look, He is the first-born in all three: of the twofold regeneration which is wrought by the two (by baptism and by resurrection), by being Himself the leader in each of them; while in the flesh He is first-born, as having first and alone devised in His own case that birth unknown to nature which no one in the many generations of men had originated.[97]

Baptismal regeneration comes as a twofold event: the administration of the sacrament and its fulfillment eschatologically in the resurrection from the dead. For those who die unbaptized and unconverted, Gregory envisioned a different route to regeneration; the unbaptized will have to endure a period of post-resurrection purgation.[98] Eventually, though, all things and all people will be transformed by the Triune love. Ultimately, no one will exist as unregenerate.

Stepping back from the overarching interpretation of baptism as a complex double movement of renunciation and adherence, we can see that Gregory epitomized these teachings in his juxtaposition of the passion of Jesus Christ with baptism in his *Catechetical Oration.* Out of compassion for enslaved and dying humanity, the Triune God intervened to mitigate, and finally, to overcome the deadly effects of the intermingling of nonbeing

---

96. *Catechetical Oration*, p. 105. See also Jaeger, *Oratio Catechetica*, p. 91. See also *On the Soul and the Resurrection*, 5.464.

97. *Against Eunomius*, 5.158; emendations mine.

98. *Catechetical Oration*, pp. 105-6. See also *On the Soul and the Resurrection*, 5.444.

with the original human nature through the incarnation, death, and resurrection of Jesus Christ. The economy of Triune salvation culminated in the death and resurrection of Jesus Christ. Gregory taught that since Jesus Christ was perfect in every way, the devil greatly desired to possess him.[99] The humanity of Jesus served as the bait used to lure the devil to the fishhook of the cross.[100] In and through his death, the devil was justly captured and overthrown. The Triune God defeated death by means of death. Through the resurrection of Jesus Christ, the possibility of genuine life and vitality was restored to humanity. In place of participation in and inevitable movement toward death, human beings now have the possibility of participation in the life that is true life: participation in the Trinity.[101]

In his directions to catechists, Gregory taught that climactic event of the death and resurrection of Jesus Christ should lead immediately into a discussion of baptism and the Eucharist.[102] This juxtaposition signals that while the passion of Christ functions as the objective, historical, and definitive moment in the Triune plan of salvation, baptism provides the subjective, contemporaneous, and concrete counterpart. Having taken his cues here from Romans 6, Gregory communicated that baptism provides the concrete, material, and corporate means by which the transforming power of God's work in history may be appropriated by human beings.[103]

How did Gregory describe the power of baptism? To deal with this question requires a consideration of the interplay between his interpretation of baptism and his understanding of the doctrine of the Trinity. He articulated his deepest understanding of the meaning of baptism in all its

---

99. *Catechetical Oration,* p. 75.

100. *Catechetical Oration,* p. 78.

101. *Against Eunomius,* 5.210, and *On Infants' Early Deaths,* 5.376.

102. *Catechetical Oration,* pp. 92-99.

103. Along these lines, Gregory interpreted the three immersions in the water not in reference to the three divine Persons of the Godhead, but as an identification with and participation in the three days Christ spent in the grave. In so doing, Gregory further cemented the deep connection between the death and resurrection of Jesus Christ and the baptismally determined life of the Christian. Based on his understanding of the four elements that make up the cosmos — air, fire, water, and earth — Gregory held that affinities exist between air and fire on the one hand and water and earth on the other. Jesus Christ was buried in the earth; believers are buried in earth's elemental cognate, water. Christ was resurrected from the dead out of the earth and lives now eternally with a new quality of incorruptible life; the baptized emerge from the waters having died to their previous life and having been raised to new and incorruptible life. See *Catechetical Oration,* pp. 101-3.

fullness in practical trinitarian terms. Examination of this interplay between baptism and Trinity will lay bare the distinctive and necessary pedagogical vector in Gregory's thought.

On Practices and Doctrines

As preface to a consideration of the relationship between baptism and the doctrine of the Trinity in Gregory's thought, we must take account of the way in which he understood the connection between liturgical practices and doctrine. He was no crypto-Gnostic for whom esoteric and mystical ideas were divorced from concrete, bodily practices. While arguing against the views of Eunomius in *Against Eunomius*, he made the following emblematic statement:

> What beyond this do they who remain attached to paganism bring forward in disparagement of our creed? Do not they too make the majesty of the sacred Names, in which the faith is ratified [that is, in baptism], an occasion of laughter? Do not they deride the sacramental tokens and the customs which are observed by the initiated? *And of whom is it so much a distinguishing peculiarity as of the pagans, to think that piety should consist of doctrines only?*[104]

Only pagan philosophers, in other words, would put forward doctrines about God disconnected from concrete, bodily practices. To Gregory's way of thinking, theological reflection or abstract theory disconnected from concrete ecclesial practice proved the error of their whole approach. He assumed, instead, that sacraments and doctrines function reciprocally together.

While Gregory alluded to the relationship between baptism and the doctrine of the Trinity in the statement above from *Against Eunomius*, he laid out explicitly his understanding of the relationship between baptism and trinitarian doctrine quite clearly in two of his letters. In them he spelled out the way in which he saw the interrelation of baptism, the dogmatic teaching of faith, and the church's practice of doxological worship. In his epistle to the church in Sebasteia, he wrote:

104. *Against Eunomius*, 5.238; emphasis added.

We confess the doctrine of the Lord, which He taught His disciples, when He delivered to them the mystery of godliness, is the foundation and root of all right and sound faith, nor do we believe that there is aught else loftier or safer than that tradition. Now the doctrine of the Lord is this: "Go," He said, "teach all nations, baptizing them in the name of the Father, and of the Son, and of the Holy Ghost." Since, then, in the case of those who are regenerate from death to eternal life, it is through the Holy Trinity that the life-giving power is bestowed on those who with faith are deemed worthy of the grace, and in like manner the grace is imperfect, if any one, whichever it may be, of the names of the Holy Trinity be omitted in saving baptism — for the sacrament of regeneration is not completed in the Son and the Father alone without the Spirit: nor is the perfect boon of life imparted to Baptism in the Father and the Spirit, if the name of the Son be suppressed: nor is the grace of that Resurrection accomplished in the Father and the Son, if the Spirit be left out: — for this reason we rest all our hope, and the persuasion of the salvation of our souls upon the three Persons, recognized by these names; and we believe in the Father of our Lord Jesus Christ, Who is the Fountain of life, and in the Only-begotten Son of the Father, Who is the Author of life, as saith the Apostle, and in the Holy Spirit of God, concerning Whom the Lord hath spoken, "It is the Spirit that quickeneth." And since on us who have been redeemed from death the grace of immortality is bestowed, as we have said, through faith in the Father, and the Son, and the Holy Spirit, guided by these we believe that nothing servile, nothing created, nothing unworthy of the majesty of the Father is to be associated in thought with the Holy Trinity; since, I say, our life is one which comes to us by faith in the Holy Trinity, taking its rise from the God of all, flowing through the Son, and working in us by the Holy Spirit. *Having, then, this full assurance, we are baptized as we were commanded, and we believe as we are baptized, and we hold as we believe: so that with one accord our baptism, our faith, and our ascription of praise are to the Father, and to the Son, and to the Holy Ghost.*[105]

Gregory continued from this point to demonstrate the distortions of Nicene trinitarian doctrine as promulgated by polytheism and Arianism. The Triune formula at the center of the baptismal rite provided the substrate out of which Gregory's doctrine of the Trinity developed. Likewise,

---

105. *Letter 11: To the City of Sebasteia*, NPNF[2], 5.528; emphasis added.

the baptismal rite lay behind his doctrinal polemics against non-Nicene theologians.

In another of his epistles, Gregory laid out the same relationship between baptism and the doctrine of the Trinity in more compact form. He wrote: "We baptize, then, as we received it: into Father and Son and Holy Spirit. And we believe as we were baptized — for the faith shall correspond with our confession. And we worship as we believe — for it is not natural for the faith to struggle against worship; what we believe, we also worship."[106] In Gregory's view, the logical sequence runs: revelation and scriptural teaching (that is, Jesus' command in the Great Commission [Matt. 28:19-20]); ecclesial practice of baptism and all that this implies for the Christian life; theological reflection resulting in the development of Nicene trinitarian doctrine; and the ongoing practice of doxological praise by the church. Thus, we see that for Gregory, trinitarian doctrine arose out of the church's obedient practice of baptism into the one name of Father, Son, and Holy Spirit. For him, each item in the sequence harmonizes with every other item. In his epistle to the Sebasteians, he indicated not only that trinitarian doctrine arose out of reflection upon baptism, but also that baptism, doctrine, and doxology "speak the same language" *(homophonos)* with regard to the Trinity.[107]

Jaroslav Pelikan in his recent work on the Cappadocians, *Christianity and Classical Culture: The Metamorphosis of Natural Theology in the Christian Encounter with Hellenism,* draws out the same point with reference to one of Basil's epistles, which uses identical language to that of Gregory's epistles:

> For the Cappadocians, baptism was in many ways the most cogent example of what Nazianzen called "the spirit of speaking mysteries and dogmas" — which meant both mysteries and dogmas, and ultimately neither dogmas without mysteries nor mysteries without dogmas. This can, then, be taken as an enunciation of the principle, "The rule of prayer determines the rule of faith [lex orandi lex credendi]," which in that Latin formulation was a Western principle, but which in its content was universal throughout patristic thought and was probably applied even more fully and more frequently in the Christian East than in

106. Jaeger, *Oratio Catechetica*, p. 77; translation mine.

107. *Sebasteia*, 5.528. See also Jaeger, *Oratio Catechetica*, p. 33. See also "Ὁμόφωνος," in G. H. W. Lampe, *A Patristic Greek Lexicon* (Oxford: Clarendon, 1961), p. 962.

the Christian West. "As we were baptized," Basil summarized the orthodox axiom, "so we profess our faith; and as we profess our faith, so also
we offer our praise [hōs baptizometha, houtō kai pisteuomen; hōs
pisteuomen, houtō kai doxologoumen]. As then baptism has been
given to us by the Savior in the name of the Father and of the Son and
of the Holy Spirit, so we make our confession of the creed in accordance with our baptism, and our doxology in turn in accordance with
our creed." The most nearly appropriate language for rational creatures
to use in acknowledging divine transcendence was not the language of
doctrine at all, not even that of orthodox Nicene doctrine, but the language of doxology and worship, and of silent worship at that, which
was how the orthodox Nicene doctrine of the Trinity was intended to
be read.[108]

Pelikan rightly draws attention to the deep reciprocity, or interplay, between baptism and trinitarian doctrine in Cappadocian thought. The linkage between baptism and the doctrine of the Trinity appears to open up a
window of insight into the practical character of Cappadocian thought as
a whole. Basil and the two Gregorys apparently did not think great and
deep thoughts about the Trinity in the abstract; rather, they developed
their profound trinitarian thought both out of and in service to the practice of the praise of God. For Gregory of Nyssa, doctrine aimed to distill
the meaning embedded in and arising from the liturgical practice of baptism. Further, his purpose for developing doctrine centered on fostering
the practice of ortho-doxology.

What did Gregory teach about the doctrine of the Trinity on the basis
of reflection upon the baptismal rite? To this subject we now turn. While
the following discussion does not provide an exhaustive exposition of his
trinitarian teaching, it will consider several key features of it.

The Doctrine of the Trinity

Gregory of Nyssa did not approach the doctrine of the Trinity as a philosophical puzzle, nor did he treat it as an abstraction divorced from ecclesial

108. Jaroslav Pelikan, *Christianity and Classical Culture: The Metamorphosis of Natural
Theology in the Christian Encounter with Hellenism,* Gifford Lectures at Aberdeen, 1992-93
(New Haven: Yale University Press, 1993), pp. 300-301.

practice. He took the baptismal formula at the heart of the rite with utmost seriousness and sought to explicate its doctrinal implications in order to guide the ongoing liturgical life of the church and the pattern of life for individual believers.

For Gregory, the central dynamics of the doctrine of the Trinity were conveyed implicitly in the central moment of the rite when the baptizand is baptized "in the name of the Father, the Son, and the Holy Spirit." He focused on the reciprocal interplay between the singular and the plural in the baptismal formula. He made much out of the interplay between the one name that comes as three: there is but one divine name, yet that name is constituted by three distinct divine Persons.[109] The baptismal formula itself carries the dynamic interchange of one and three with respect to the divine mystery. In his *Refutation of Eunomius's Confession*, Gregory rendered the doctrine of the Trinity on the basis of an exposition of the meaning and significance of the formula used at the core of the baptismal rite:

> For while there are many other names by which the Deity is indicated in the Historical Books, in the Prophets and in the Law, our Master Christ passes by all these and commits to us these titles as better able to bring us to the faith about the Self-Existent, declaring that it suffices us to cling to the title, "Father, Son, and Holy Ghost," in order to attain to the apprehension of Him Who is absolutely Existent, Who is one and yet not one. In regard to essence He is one, wherefore the Lord ordained that we should look to one Name: but in regard to the attributes indicative of the Persons, our belief in Him is distinguished into belief in the Father, the Son, and the Holy Ghost; He is divided without separation, and united without confusion. . . . [T]he mystery of godliness was committed in a form expressing at once union and distinction, — that we should believe on the Name of the Father, and of the Son, and of the Holy Ghost. For the differentiation of the subsistences makes the distinction of Persons clear and free from confusion, while the one Name standing in the forefront of the declaration of the Faith clearly expounds to us the unity of essence of the Persons Whom the Faith declares, — I mean, of the Father, and of the Son, and of the Holy Spirit. For by these appellations we are taught not a difference of nature, but only the special attributes that mark the subsistences, so that we may know that neither is the Father the Son, nor the Son the Father, nor the

109. *Against Eunomius*, 5.101-2.

Holy Spirit either the Father or the Son, and recognize each by the distinctive mark of His Personal subsistence in illimitable perfection, at once contemplated by Himself and not divided from that with which He is connected.[110]

By "the mystery of godliness" Gregory refers to the baptismal rite. For him the doctrine of the Trinity explicates and makes explicit the formula at the core of the baptismal rite. By implication, trinitarian doctrine runs the risk of losing its proper interpretive and normative framework if divorced from the baptismal rite. Speaking of Gregory's doctrine of the Trinity apart from the lens and orientation provided by baptism leads only to that severance of doctrine and practice that he railed against.[111]

As if to stress the practical character of the doctrine of the Trinity that developed out of reflection upon the baptismal rite, Gregory described the work of human transformation as a common work of the three divine Persons. The life-giving power of baptism does not arise from the water itself; rather, it comes from the three Persons working in concert. In arguing his case for the full divinity of the Holy Spirit against those who would deny it in his treatise, *On the Holy Spirit*, Gregory wrote:

> What then? Is that life-giving power in the water itself which is employed to convey the grace of Baptism? Or is it not rather clear to every one that this element is only employed as a means in the external ministry, and of itself contributes nothing towards the sanctification unless it be first transformed itself by the sanctification; and that what gives life to the baptized is the Spirit: as our Lord Himself says in respect to Him with His own lips, "It is the Spirit that giveth life"; but for the completion of this grace He alone, received by faith, does not give life, but belief in our Lord must precede, in order that the lively gift may come upon the believer, as our Lord has spoken, "He giveth life to whom He willeth." But further still, seeing that this grace administered through the Son is dependent on the Ungenerate Source of all, Scripture accord-

110. *Against Eunomius*, 5.102-3.

111. *Refutation of Eunomius' Confession*, NPNF², 5.238. Lewis Ayres points out the mislabeling of this document in NPNF² as "Book II" of *Against Eunomius*. See Lewis Ayres, "On Not Three People: The Fundamental Themes of Gregory of Nyssa's Trinitarian Theology as Seen in *To Ablabius: On Not Three Gods*," in *Re-Thinking Gregory of Nyssa*, ed. Sarah Coakley (Malden, Mass.: Blackwell, 2003), p. 43.

ingly teaches us that belief in the Father Who engendereth all things is to come first; so that this life-giving grace should be completed, for those fit to receive it, after starting from that Source as from a spring pouring life abundantly, through the Only-begotten Who is the True life, by the operation of the Holy Spirit. If then, life comes in baptism, and baptism receives its completion in the name Father, Son, and Spirit, what do these men mean who count this Minister of life as nothing?[112]

Here Gregory conveyed two key insights about the Trinity. First, inasmuch as the efficacy of baptism comes from the work of each of the Persons in concert with that of the other two, the three Persons work in a differentiated unity on behalf of human regeneration. Second, we also find a non-temporal logic of causation in which the First Person of the Trinity functions as the ultimate source of all, including the Second and Third Persons.[113] This second point requires brief further discussion.

At several key points in his work, Gregory argued for a nontemporal logic of causation in which the Father is the Source of the divine life. In this vein, he held that while each of the Persons shared equally in the essence of divinity, there were important differences with respect to cause. With regard to the differentiation of Persons with respect to the logic of causation, Gregory wrote near the end of his treatise *On "Not Three Gods"*:

While we confess the invariable character of the nature, we do not deny the differences in respect of cause, and that which is caused, by which alone we apprehend that one Person is distinguished from another; — by our belief, that is, that one is the Cause, and another is of the Cause; and again in that which is of the Cause we recognize another distinction. For one is directly from the first Cause, and another by that which is directly from the first Cause; so that the attribute of being Only-begotten abides without doubt in the Son, and the interposition of the Son, while it guards His attribute of being Only-begotten, does not shut out the Spirit from His relation by way of the nature to the Father.

But in speaking of "cause," and of "the cause," we do not by these

112. *On the Holy Spirit*, NPNF[2], 5.322.

113. For a discussion of the revolutionary character of the personalism of Cappadocian trinitarian ontology, see John D. Zizioulas, *Being as Communion: Studies in Personhood and the Church*, vol. 4, *Contemporary Greek Theologians* (Crestwood, N.Y.: St Vladimir's Seminary Press, 1993), pp. 40-42.

words denote nature (for no one would give the same definition of "cause" and of "nature") but we indicate the difference in manner of existence. . . . Thus, since on the one hand the idea of cause differentiates the Persons of the Holy Trinity, declaring that one exists without a Cause, and another is of the Cause; and since on the one hand the Divine nature is apprehended by every conception as unchangeable and undivided, for these reasons we properly declare the Godhead to be one, and God to be one, and employ in the singular all other names which express Divine attributes.[114]

Gregory's logic of nontemporal causation depended upon the metaphor of a stream or a river.[115] The transforming grace administered in baptism flows down like a stream from the Father through the Son and the Spirit to baptizands. To disparage the Holy Spirit as fully divine has the effect of denying the divinity of the entire Trinity.

Gregory offered another theme, however, as counterpoint to his logic of causation argument. Toward the end of his treatise on the Holy Spirit, he articulated a more radically egalitarian understanding of the interplay of the three divine Persons found at the pivot point of the baptismal rite. At this later point, he brought into bold relief the conviction that the three Persons are equal and open toward one another. He reflected:

You see the revolving circle of glory moving from Like to Like. The Son is glorified by the Spirit; and the Father is glorified by the Son; again the Son has His glory from the Father; and the Only-Begotten thus becomes the glory of the Spirit. For with what shall the Father be glorified, but with the true glory of the Son: and with what shall the Son be glorified, but with the majesty of the Spirit? In like manner again, Faith completes the circle, and glorifies the Son by means of the Spirit, and the Father by means of the Son.[116]

The baptismal formula and the experience of transforming grace in the baptismal rite disclose a dynamic circularity of doxological glory at the heart of the mystery of the Triune God. Here Gregory emphasized the rad-

---

114. *On "Not Three Gods,"* NPNF[2], 5.336.

115. *On the Holy Spirit,* 5.323.

116. *On the Holy Spirit,* 5.324. See also *Against Eunomius,* 5.203, for a statement of the co-causation of Father and Son in relation to creation.

ically open and ecstatic character of each of the divine Persons. Each one gives and receives glory in reference to the other two. Further, in and through the baptismal rite this eternal *pas de trios* of glory, to coin a phrase, opens out to the baptized. By participation in this relational dynamism at the core of the divine mystery, the Holy Trinity leads the baptized from inexorable movement toward death to a life of transformation from one degree of glory to another (2 Cor. 3:18).[117]

Gregory taught that the three divine Persons who perpetually glorify one another supersede gender. Reflection upon baptism carried implications not only for the relativization of human gender, but also for the way in which we think about gender in relation to the Trinity.[118] For example, he described the work of the Holy Spirit in baptism as that of a midwife who helps to bring transforming faith in Jesus Christ to birth.[119] Likewise, those newly reborn through baptism need to feed regularly at the breasts of the teaching provided by the Son, or Word.[120] God as the "first cause of our being" can properly be called "Mother."[121] Speaking of the Triune essence, Gregory could say:

> No one can adequately grasp the terms pertaining to God. For example, "mother" is mentioned (in the Song) in place of "father." Both terms mean the same, because there is neither male nor female in God (for how can anything transitory like this be attributed to God?). . . . Therefore, every name equally indicates God's ineffable nature; neither can "male" nor "female" defile God's pure nature.[122]

---

117. *Catechetical Oration,* p. 114.

118. In his work on theological anthropology, *On the Making of Man,* Gregory taught that human beings were first created without gender differentiation in the image of the Trinity (5.405). Foreseeing the human turn away from grace, the Trinity acted a second time in the creation of humanity to provide a means for maintaining the existence of the race in the face of the yawning abyss of death. Picking up on Paul's eschatological teaching about baptism in the third chapter of Galatians and on Luke's eschatological teaching about the resurrection (Luke 20:27-40), Gregory argued that baptism relativized gender distinctions. In his *Commentary on the Song of Songs* (p. 145), Gregory wrote, "But when we are one in Christ, we are divested of the signs of this difference along with the old man."

119. *Against Eunomius,* 5.158.

120. *Commentary on the Song of Songs,* p. 55.

121. *Commentary on the Song of Songs,* p. 131.

122. *Commentary on the Song of Songs,* pp. 145-46.

Gregory taught the appropriateness of both male and female metaphors for the Trinity and for the particular Persons. Lucian Turcescu, Gregory of Nyssa scholar, notes, however, that even though Gregory affirmed the possibility of using both genders to refer to the Trinity, he tended to stick with "Father, Son, and Holy Spirit" language because they had been "revealed by the Lord himself."[123] Though he articulated an inclusive approach to God language, he tended to use traditional masculine language in his nonmystical writings. He seems to have habitually employed more masculine language in practice on the basis of his respect for scriptural disclosure and ecclesial tradition.

It should not be thought that the baptismal formula leads to full disclosure of the mystery of the Triune God. Gregory of Nyssa stands out among the company of theologians in the history of Christianity for his careful and compelling articulation of the limits of what can be known about this mystery. While transformed human reason can know something about the particular attributes and functions of each particular Person *pro nobis* and something of the character of their harmonious relations with each other, the shared essence of the Trinity cannot be known. Gregory maintained that the meaning of the One Name That Is Three into which persons are baptized remains unknown to human reason:

> The uncreated Nature alone, which we acknowledge in the Father, and in the Son, and in the Holy Spirit, surpasses all significance of names. For this cause the Word, when He spoke of "the name" in delivering the Faith, did not add what it is, — for how could a name be found for that which is above every name? — but gave authority that whatever name our intelligence by pious effort be enabled to discover to indicate the transcendent Nature, that name should be applied alike to Father, Son, and Holy Ghost, whether it be "the Good" or "the Incorruptible," whatever name each may think proper to be employed to indicate the undefiled Nature of the Godhead. And by this deliverance the Word seems to me to lay down for us this law, that we are to be persuaded that the Divine Essence is ineffable and incomprehensible: for it is plain that the title of Father does not present to us the Essence, but only indicates the relation to the Son. . . . [T]he knowledge [of the divine Essence] is be-

---

123. Lucian Turcescu, *Gregory of Nyssa and the Concept of Divine Persons*, American Academy of Religion Academy series, ed. Carole Myscofski (New York: Oxford University Press, 2005), p. 103.

yond our capacity, as we have in the profession of faith [in baptism] the doctrine delivered to us what suffices for our salvation.[124]

What has been disclosed is *that* the tri-relational God is one, not *the way in which* that is the case. Knowledge of the inner essence of the Trinity has not been and will not ever be revealed to humanity or to any other creature. Such knowledge belongs only to God.

Gregory developed this argument partly by analogy to human nature. It is not possible, he maintained, for human beings to comprehend fully the nature of their existence. He wrote:

> "Who hath known the mind of the Lord?" the apostle asks; and I ask further, who has understood his own mind? Let those who tell us to consider the nature of God to be within their comprehension, whether they understand themselves — if they know the nature of their own mind. "It is manifold and much compounded." How can that which is intelligible be composite? Or what is the mode of mixture of things that differ in kind? Or, "It is simple, and incomposite." How then is it dispersed into the manifold divisions of the senses? How is there diversity in unity? How is unity maintained in diversity?
>
> But I find the solution of these difficulties by recourse to the very utterance of God; for He says, "Let us make man in our image, after our likeness." The image is properly an image so long as it fails in none of those attributes which we perceive in the archetype; but where it falls from its resemblance to the prototype it ceases in that respect to be an image; therefore, since one of the attributes we contemplate in the Divine nature is incomprehensibility of essence, it is clearly necessary that in this point the image should be able to show its imitation of the archetype . . . but since the nature of our mind, which is the likeness of the Creator, evades our knowledge, it has an accurate resemblance to the superior nature, figuring by its own unknowableness the incomprehensible Nature [*ousia*].[125]

Thus for Gregory, possessing an unknowable essence comprised a crucial dimension of making the claim that human beings have been made in the image of the Triune God. Even though human beings are formed and will

---

124. *Against Eunomius*, 5.103.
125. *On the Making of Man*, 5.397.

be transformed over time and through eternity, that which is at the very core of human existence remains an unknown and unknowable mystery. If such is the case with human self-knowledge, how can anyone dare to claim to know the hidden essence of the Triune God?

Gregory did not treat the limits of reason in relation to the Triune God as a barrier to intimate encounter with that mystery. In his *Life of Moses*, he taught that what discursive knowledge of the Trinity is possible for us comes only after long athletic struggle on the intertwined fronts of virtue and contemplation. On the principle that "like can be known only be like," Gregory called for intense effort in virtue to become like that which is contemplated. Only on the basis of the combined discipline of contemplation and the striving for moral purity is clear and mature knowledge of the Trinity possible.[126] Many people will not be up to the challenge and will remain below at the base of Mount Sinai.[127] A few will dare to make the long ascent to greater knowledge of the relational mystery at the heart of all things.[128] Yet even they will reach a point at which discursive reason can take them no further.[129]

Discursive reason reaches its limit upon entering the cloud at the peak of Sinai. It is in this unknowing and unseeing, this "illuminated darkness,"[130] that one enters most deeply into encounter with the mystery. In his insightful study of Gregory of Nyssa's understanding of faith, Martin Laird argues that Gregory's discussions of the limitations of discursive reason *(dianoia)* must be kept together with his rich sense of the role of faith in the mystical encounter with the Triune mystery:

> Hence, both *dianoia* and *pistis* can mediate the same graced encounter. However, this is not to say that the two are synonymous. While the two can at times overlap, when Gregory wants to be quite specific and emphasize the experience of union, he will employ *pistis*. Herein lies the difference: both *dianoia* and exalted *pistis* can enter the Holy of Holies, the darkness wherein God dwells, but in this non-discursive sanctuary *dianoia* is purely receptive; it cannot perform its characteristic grasp of

---

126. Gregory of Nyssa, *Life of Moses*, trans. Abraham J. Malherbe and Everett Ferguson, The Classics of Western Spirituality: A Library of the Great Spiritual Masters series, ed. Richard J. Payne (New York: Paulist, 1978), p. 93.

127. *Life of Moses*, p. 94.

128. *Life of Moses*, p. 94.

129. *Life of Moses*, pp. 95-96.

130. *Life of Moses*, p. 95.

comprehension. *Pistis*, by contrast, can yet grasp; not a cognitive grasp of comprehension but a grasp of union beyond images and concepts. The bride [in the Song of Songs] herself has stated it perhaps the most succinctly: "when I let go of every sort of comprehension, I found the Beloved . . . by the grasp of faith." Hence, while both terms can be used to mediate divine indwelling, Gregory can also be more specific and indicate the difference between exalted *pistis* and *dianoia*. *Pistis* can do what *dianoia* cannot do; grasp the Beloved. Having grasped the Beloved it can pass on to *dianoia* something of what it has grasped of the Beloved. Between *dianoia* and *pistis*, then, there is as much rapport as rupture.[131]

The encounter with the mystery of the Triune God is beyond the limits of discursive reason, yet it remains a kind of knowing or conscious awareness. It is not irrational; rather, it is supra-rational. It is intuitive and existential knowing. In this cloud of unknowing, which only a very few reach after years of ascetic discipline, one encounters the Triune mystery in this way. It is possible in the illuminated darkness at the peak of the ascetic mountain to, like Moses, "be known by God and to become his friend."[132] This mystical encounter between those who have become more and more like the Trinity remains beyond the grasp of human reason and language. Because the experience cannot be put into words, Gregory employed paradoxical terminology like "sober inebriation" and "wakeful sleep" to allude to this encounter.[133] This deep-level personal encounter with the Trinity precipitates a profound transformation of inner motives and outward practice. Subsequent to this experience, according to Gregory, one acts in such a way as not so much to avoid divine punishment or to attain divine rewards, but to preserve this special friendship with the Triune God.[134]

Gregory warned that scriptural language and concepts should not be reified. We should take them, however, with great seriousness as God-given pointers to the Triune reality. He wrote of the teachings of Scripture about the divine mystery:

> Every teaching concerning the ineffable nature of God, even if it seems to reveal the best and highest possible understanding, is the likeness of

---

131. Laird, *Gregory of Nyssa and the Grasp of Faith*, p. 208.
132. *Life of Moses*, p. 137.
133. *Commentary on the Song of Songs*, pp. 193-95.
134. *Life of Moses*, p. 137.

gold, not gold itself, for the good transcending the human mind cannot be accurately represented. Even if someone like St. Paul was initiated into the ineffable mysteries of paradise and heard words not to be spoken [2 Cor. 12:4], any understanding of God remains unutterable. Paul himself says that such conceptions are ineffable. Those persons, therefore, who offer us any good thoughts about these mysteries, are unable to state anything regarding the divine nature. Rather, they speak of the splendor of God's glory, the stamp of his nature [Heb. 1:3], the form of God, the Word in the beginning, the Word being God [1 John 1:1]. All these expressions seem to us who have not seen the divine nature as gold from that treasure. But for those capable of looking on the truth, they are likenesses of gold and not gold shining in the delicate studs of silver. Silver is the meaning of these words as scripture says: "The tongue of the just is a fire-tried silver" [Prov. 10:20].

The revelation presented here says that the divine nature transcends every conception which tries to grasp it. Our understanding of the divine nature resembles what we seek. It does not show its form which no one has seen or can see, but through a mirror and a riddle [1 Cor. 13:12] it provides a reflection of the thing sought, that is, a reflection present in the soul by a certain likeness. Every word signifying these conceptions is like a point lacking extension (στιγμή) since it cannot show what is present in the mind. Thus every thought falls short of the comprehension of God. Every word which tries to explain God seems to be a little dot *(stigme)* incapable of being coextensive with the breadth of the conception. Thus the soul led through such conceptions to comprehend what cannot be laid hold of except by faith must establish in itself a nature transcending every intelligence.[135]

Thus, the Trinity does not disclose complete knowledge to human beings. Nevertheless, the Trinity has disclosed healing grace through Scripture and liturgical rites such as baptism and the Eucharist; furthermore, such healing grace can be appropriated through faith, even if such faith outstrips reason's capacity to grasp it in full measure. The weight of scriptural revelation, authoritative ecclesial tradition, and the personal experience of transformation by means of baptism singly and collectively call believers to a sober acknowledgment of the limits of their rational capacities with respect to the Triune mystery of grace.

135. *Commentary on the Song of Songs,* p. 82.

Knowledge of the activities and character of the three Persons — though not their shared essence — is available to human beings on the basis of participation in the rite of baptism. Even though the way in which the three are one is beyond human comprehension, for Gregory reliable knowledge about the work of the Triune God in and for creation has been disclosed. God has revealed the knowledge necessary for salvation, healing, and restoration of the human family. The Bible recounts the effects of Triune *philanthropia*.[136] The Triune God makes known precisely that which is necessary for human healing and transformation:

> We account for God's willingness to admit men to communion with Himself by His love towards mankind. But since that which is by nature finite cannot rise above its prescribed limits, or lay hold of the superior nature of the Most High, on this account He, bringing His power, so full of love for humanity, down to the level of human weakness, so far as it was possible for us to receive it, bestowed on us this helpful gift of grace. For as by Divine dispensation the sun, tempering the intensity of his full beams with the intervening air, pours down light as well as heat on those who receive his rays, being himself unapproachable by reason of the weakness of our nature, so the Divine power, after the manner of the illustration I have used, though exalted far above our nature and inaccessible to all approach, like a tender mother who joins in the inarticulate utterances of her babe, gives to our human nature what it is capable of receiving; and thus in the various manifestations of God to man He both adapts Himself to man and speaks in human language and assumes wrath, and pity, and such-like emotions, so that through feelings corresponding to our own our infantile life might be led as by the hand, and lay hold of the words which His foresight has given. . . . God's providence helps our infirmity by using our own idioms of speech, so that such as are inclined to sin may be restrained, and that those who are overtaken by it may not despair of return by the way of repentance when they see God's mercy, while those who are walking uprightly and strictly may yet more adorn their own life with virtue, as knowing that by their own life they rejoice Him Whose eyes are over the righteous.[137]

---

136. *Catechetical Oration*, p. 59. See also Gregorius Pasquali, ed., *Gregorii Nysseni Epistulae*, vol. 8, part 2, in Gregorii Nysseni Opera, ed. Wernerus Jaeger (Leiden: E. J. Brill, 1959), p. 43.

137. *Against Eunomius*, 5.292.

As the ultimate teacher and healer, the Triune God takes the initiative to come to finite and fallen humanity. That which is disclosed to the human family in Scripture will lead to rescue and restoration. Revelation does not aim at solving intellectual puzzles; rather, it intends very concrete and practical effects in human life. Gregory understood that baptism provides the orientation for his practical trinitarianism.

If baptism supplies the orientation for his practical trinitarianism, ecclesial pedagogy provides the process of its realization in the lives of baptizands. Gregory did not view the healing and enlightenment initiated by baptism as a singular event or a static reality. The transformation associated with the work of the Triune God in baptism initiates a process of perpetual progress in and toward the Triune mystery. The interplay of baptism and Trinity gave rise to an inescapably pedagogical vector in Gregory's thought. To this subject we now turn.

Ecclesial Pedagogy

Gregory's whole theology as witnessed by the entire corpus of his writings had a fundamentally pedagogical bent to it. As ecclesial rhetor, Gregory aimed to form the baptized into a pattern of life marked by ever deeper engagement with the Triune God. Scholar of ancient Greek *paideia* and of Gregory of Nyssa, Werner Jaeger in his book *Early Christianity and Greek Paideia* noted the fundamentally pedagogical character of Gregory's thought:

> If paideia was the will of God and if Christianity was for the Christian what philosophy was for the philosopher, according to Plato — assimilation to God — the true fulfillment of the Christian ideal of life was one continuous and lifelong effort to achieve that end and to approach perfection, in so far as that was possible for man. As the Greek philosopher's whole life was a process of paideia through philosophical ascesis, so for Gregory Christianity was not a mere set of dogmas but the perfect life based on the *theoria* or contemplation of God and on ever more perfect union with him. It is *deification,* and paideia is the path, the divine anabasis. Basil had been the first to organize monastic life in Asia Minor and had drawn up his rule for it. In contrast to his brother, Gregory considered it his task to give that way of life its philosophy. He does so by in-

terpreting it as the attempt at the full realization of his ideal of Christian perfection. Not all would be able to go this way, but this idea ought to permeate the entire life of the church and of every Christian as far as possible.[138]

The one who had initially hoped to become a rhetor forming the elite youth of Asia Minor into high Greco-Roman culture became a doctor of the church whose entire theological vision forged a distinctive Christian *paideia*. In all of his writings, Gregory sought to facilitate the profound transformation into the mystery of the Trinity that baptism initiated and symbolized.

The work of the Trinity to liberate and to heal us culminates objectively in the cross and resurrection and subjectively in baptism and the Eucharist. This does not mean, however, that the work is fully accomplished in the event of the liturgy. A lifetime of living into the mystery initiated by baptism is required.[139] How one continues to live out one's baptism throughout the course of the rest of one's life is crucial. Baptism, in this sense, is much more than a one-time event; rather, it forms the thematic character of one's entire life from font to grave and beyond.

Baptism provides the paradigm for the perpetual process of growth in and toward the Trinity. In his *Commentary on the Song of Songs*, Gregory described the intensely pedagogical character of the life initiated by baptism:

> The person looking at the divine, invisible beauty will always discover it anew since he will see it as something newer and more wondrous in comparison to what he had already contemplated. He continues to wonder at God's continuous revelation; he never exhausts his desire to see more because what he awaits is always more magnificent and more divine than anything [he] has seen. Thus the bride wonders and is amazed at her knowledge. Despite this, she never ceases to long for further vision.[140]

Baptism forms the architectonic pattern for the entirety of the life of the church and those who are members of it. Each gestalt of understanding with regard to the Triune mystery must give way to another yet more won-

---

138. Werner Jaeger, *Early Christianity and Greek Paideia* (Cambridge, Mass.: Belknap Press of Harvard University Press, 1961), pp. 89-90.

139. *Commentary on the Song of Songs*, p. 163.

140. *Commentary on the Song of Songs*, pp. 201-2.

derful. In this sense, the entirety of the Christian life must be seen as a series of dyings and risings.[141] Early church and mysticism scholar Jean Daniélou captured this dynamic in Gregory's thought in the opening of his work *Platonisme et Théologie Mystique:* "The entirety of the spiritual life is for Gregory of Nyssa a mystery of death and resurrection. It is in this regard the realization of the mystery of baptism, even the baptism of which, according to the doctrine of Saint Paul, we die with Christ in order to be resurrected with him."[142] Daniélou rightly saw that baptism is the key to unlocking Gregory's teachings about the Christian life as a journey of perpetual discovery and growth in relation to the Triune God. The mystery of baptism expands in his thought to encompass the entire range of activities of believers in church and in society.

This baptismal life requires not only Triune activity in us and for us but also our active engagement in perpetual learning, discovery, striving, and growth toward the infinite Trinity. Since the Triune object of the doxological life is infinite, the pedagogical process of growth and transformation is also infinite.

Baptism for Gregory has to do with the pattern of dying and rising. Each configuration or apprehension of the glory of the Trinity must finally die or give way to make room for a fuller, more joyous, and ever more beguiling apprehension.[143] In his *Commentary on the Song of Songs,* Gregory wrote about the life of the baptized: "Neither can any measure of knowledge limit the comprehension of our objective and prevent us from moving further on. But the mind running on high through its understanding of transcendent reality should realize that all perfection of knowledge attainable by human nature is only the beginning of a desire for more lofty things."[144] A little later in the same work, he described further the perpetual process marked by discovery, desire for more, jettisoning previous con-

---

141. *Commentary on the Song of Songs,* pp. 223-24.

142. "La vie spirituelle tout entière est pour Grégoire de Nysse un mystère de mort et de résurrection. Elle est à cet égard la realization du mystère même du baptême qui, selon le doctrine de saint Paul, nous fait mourir avec le Christ pour ressuciter avec lui." Jean Daniélou, *Platonisme et Théologie Mystique: Doctrine Spirituelle de Saint Grégoire de Nysse.* Théologie: Études Publiées Sous la Direction de la Faculté de Théologie S.J. de Lyon-Fourvière, no. 2. Nouvelle edition, revue et augmenté (Aubier: Éditions Montaigne, 1944), p. 2.

143. *Against Eunomius,* 5.62.

144. *Commentary on the Song of Songs,* p. 130.

figurations of understanding, and further discovery in terms of the bride's longing for the bridegroom:

> Because her desire for her beloved is frustrated, her yearnings for his beauty cannot be fulfilled. But the veil of despair is removed when the bride learns that the true satisfaction of her desire consists in always progressing in her search and ascent: when her desire is fulfilled, it gives birth to a further desire for the transcendent. Thus the veil of her despair is removed and the bride will always see more of her beloved's incomprehensible beauty throughout all eternity.[145]

Gregory understood baptism to be the initiation of a process of transformation from one degree of glory to another (2 Cor. 3:18) that has no end. The Spirit-led and Christ-focused process of progress toward the infinite Trinity that baptism initiates continues throughout the course of one's life and into eternity. Writing about the full divinity of the Son in his polemic against Eunomius, Gregory argued that the quest of the baptized for the Triune infinity has no limit:

> The First Good is in its nature infinite, and so it follows of necessity that the participation in the enjoyment of it will be infinite also for more will always be grasped, and yet something beyond that which has been grasped will always be discovered, and this search will never overtake its Object, because its fund is inexhaustible as the growth of that which participates in it is ceaseless.[146]

While this growth in the doxological life has a definite beginning point in baptism, it does not have a terminus for the believer. Gregory maintained that even after death the baptized continue to yearn for and grow toward the infinite Trinity. Since the object toward which the baptized move is infinite (that is, the Trinity), so then is their progress. In this sense, Gregory's view of the character of the desire for the Trinity that arises out of baptism is asymptotic.[147] Any given level of understanding and insight will always give way to another ad infinitum.

---

145. *Commentary on the Song of Songs*, p. 225.

146. *Against Eunomius*, 5.62.

147. An asymptote is a "line which approaches nearer and nearer to a curve without meeting it." See "Asymptote," in *The Oxford Dictionary of English Etymology*, ed. C. T. Onions (Oxford: Oxford University Press, 1966), p. 58.

This process of growth or ascent toward the Trinity is inherently pedagogical in that it requires desire for knowledge and insight, expenditure of effort toward the goal of attaining greater understanding, the benefits of instruction, and the transformation of character. Gregory's understanding of the Christian life as desirous movement toward the Trinity initiated by baptism is a pedagogical summons from which one never finally graduates.

Gregory understood the curriculum that would guide this life of striving for ever greater insight into the Trinity as a kind of cognitive therapy for the person previously diseased by death. The "core curriculum" aimed at curing the diseased soul and helping it flourish in praise and wonder. Gregory recognized that while all human beings share in the terminal disease of adherence to nonbeing, the symptoms of the disease manifest themselves in a variety of ways. He made this point quite clearly when he advocated using approaches to subject matter that will most suit the existing intellectual framework of the learner:

> The method of recovery must be adapted to the form of the disease. You will not by the same means cure the polytheism of the Greek, and the unbelief of the Jew as to the Only-begotten God: nor as regards those who have wandered into heresy will you, by the same arguments in each case, upset their misleading romances as to the tenets of the Faith. No one could set Sabellius right by the same instruction as would benefit the Anomoean. The controversy with the Manichee is profitless against the Jew. It is necessary, therefore, as I have said, to regard the opinions which the persons have taken up, and to frame your argument in accordance with the error into which each has fallen, by advancing in each discussion certain principles and reasonable propositions, that thus, through what is agreed upon on both sides, the truth may conclusively be brought to light.[148]

He argued that one size does not fit all when it comes to forming people into a baptismally grounded Christian faith, at least in terms of apologetic content. Jews, Greco-Roman polytheists, and Christian heretics each require a different approach to the core content of Christian belief. Hence, differentiated pedagogical strategies were required to achieve the common end of regeneration as defined by ever more rapturous enjoyment of the

---

148. *Catechetical Oration,* p. 24.

Triune mystery. For Gregory, the Triune content of both pre- and post-baptismal teaching had a curative function for the soul in that it provided cognitive and moral orientation to Reality or Being as such. He thought that this therapeutic curriculum ought to bring people from diverse cultural and religious frames of meaning to the place where they personally encountered and baptismally appropriated the truth, which is the Triune mystery of God made known to us in Jesus Christ by the sanctifying power of the Holy Spirit.

While Christian instruction culminated in some sense with the baptismal rite, it did not conclude in that moment. The baptized needed a lifetime of instruction in order to grow ever more deeply into the Triune mystery. That instruction came from Scripture. Jaeger brought into clear focus the crucial importance of biblical instruction for the Christian life in Gregory's thought:

> But what in a Christian education corresponded to the highest level of Greek paideia, the study of philosophy? As Origen had taught his students to read all the Greek philosophers, so the Cappadocians went through a serious study of this part of the classical tradition, and Gregory of Nyssa, the most philosophical of them, no doubt thought it necessary for an educated Christian to follow that difficult path. But when he speaks of paideia he chiefly has in mind that which distinguishes its Christian form from the Greek. As the Greek paideia consisted of the entire corpus of Greek literature, so the Christian paideia is the Bible. Literature is paideia, in so far as it contains the highest norms of human life, which in it have taken on their lasting and most impressive form. It is the ideal picture of man, the great paradigm. Gregory clearly sees the analogy between this Greek concept of literature and the function of the Bible. He did not read the Bible as literature, as the modern tendency is. That would be a complete misunderstanding of his concept of literature, which was the Greek concept of literature as paideia. With it he had been brought up, and the application of this sort of reading to the Christian's relation to the Bible was for him, therefore, the most natural thing in the world. He never tires of impressing the basic idea of education on his readers. The formation of the Christian man, his *morphosis,* is the effect of his unceasing study of the Bible. The form is Christ. The paideia of the Christian is *imitation Christi:* Christ must take shape in him.[149]

149. Jaeger, *Early Christianity and Greek Paideia,* pp. 92-93.

Jaeger rightly points out here that for Gregory the inherently pedagogical character of the Christian life as progress in and toward the Trinity required a steady diet of scriptural instruction. The disclosure of therapeutic trinitarianism came through Scripture and through study of Scripture. Under the guidance of the Holy Spirit, the baptized hear the summons to climb ever higher toward the infinity of Triune beauty.

Gregory did not think that the pedagogical process of preparation for baptism entailed only attending lectures and getting one's theological perspective in line with ecclesial orthodoxy. He believed that the catechetical process also called for an intentional process of moral transformation. The goal of the transformational process involved not only greater insight into the Trinity, but also becoming like the Triune God in perfection of virtue. Thus, to become like the Triune God one had to become more and more virtuous, according to the archetype of virtue, Jesus Christ, and by the power of the Spirit of all true virtue.

The seriousness with which Gregory took the moral formation aspect of catechesis can be seen in the final chapter of his *Catechetical Oration*. It seems as though he was not quite satisfied with what he had said in the main body of his manual for catechists about baptism. At the culmination of his catechetical instructions, he circled back to baptism and the character of the Christian life at the point of moral reform. He seemed particularly bothered by the pastoral problem of baptized persons who lived morally reprehensible lives. In the final paragraphs of his catechetical instructions, he put into bold relief the implications of baptism for the Christian life:

> If the washing is applied to the body, while the soul does not wash away the stains of its passions, but the life after initiation is of the same character as the uninitiated life, even though it is a bold thing to say, yet I will say it and not draw back, in such cases the water is water, and the gift of the Holy Spirit nowhere appears in what takes place, whenever not only the deformity of anger dishonours the Divine image, or the passion of covetousness, and the uncontrolled and unseemly thought, and pride, envy, conceit, but also when a man retains in his possession the gains made by injustice, and the woman he has made his own by adultery continues to minister to his pleasures even after baptism. If these and the like vices mark the life of him who has been baptized after, no less than before, I cannot see how he has been changed; for I behold the same man as I formerly did. He who has suffered injustice, he who has

118

been falsely accused, he who has been thrust out of his own possessions, these, for their part, see no change in the man who has been washed. . . . If then, you have received God and become a child of God Who is in you, show in yourself Him who has begotten you. . . . If you share these characteristics [of God], you have in truth become a child of God. But if you persist in exhibiting the characteristics of vice, it is in vain for you to babble to yourself of your birth from above.[150]

Clearly, the whole catechetical process culminating in the grace of baptism should determine the course of the rest of one's life. If one has been baptized into participation in the mystery of the Trinity, then one must strive to live in a manner consistent with the character of that holy mystery.

The grace of the Triune God given in baptism must meet with human faith and a serious commitment to reform of life. Gregory seems to have had a kind of synergistic vision of the Christian's journey in and toward the Trinity as initiated and defined by baptism. The power of the Holy Spirit causes spiritual transformation, yet human agency is also required. Without the use of freedom in the service of virtue, baptism ceases to function as a transformative reality in the life of the believer.

Human agency, however, requires instruction and guidance in order to harmonize with baptismal grace. Gregory thought of the Triune God as the primary teacher of the baptized.[151] The Holy Spirit taught prophets and apostles the crucial things to know about the Triune mystery.[152] The Holy Spirit inspired the use of anthropomorphic figures of speech in Scripture for specifically pedagogical purposes.[153] Further, the Holy Spirit provides the necessary illumination for understanding the Scriptures.[154] On Gregory's convictions about the Holy Spirit as teacher, Jaeger observed:

The Spirit itself is conceived as the divine educational power that is ever present in the world and that has spoken through human beings who

---

150. *Catechetical Oration*, pp. 117-18. See also *On the Baptism of Christ*, NPNF², 5.523, and *Life of Moses*, pp. 83-85.

151. Martin Laird, "Under Solomon's Tutelage: The Education of Desire in the Homilies on The Song of Songs," in *Rethinking Gregory of Nyssa*, ed. Sarah Coakley (Malden, Mass.: Blackwell, 2003), pp. 81-83.

152. *Against Eunomius*, 5.117 and 193.

153. *Against Eunomius*, 5.204-5; see also *Answer to Eunomius' Second Book*, 5.274.

154. *Against Eunomius*, 5.139-40.

were its instruments. The way in which the Spirit speaks to the human race in the Scriptures is that of the wise educator who never forgets the narrow limits of the pupils' capacity. If they are unable to understand the truth by immediate approach to the divine mystery, He leads them by means of symbolic expression appropriate to the sensual and finite nature of man. The anthropomorphic language used in the Scriptures with relation to things divine serves only as a starting point for the process of a deeper understanding. Gregory here follows Origen's theory of the various levels of meaning that must be distinguished in the Bible. His exegesis leads from the direct literal sense to the historical sense of the biblical text, and from this second level it advances to the higher spiritual meaning. An insight into this methodical stratification of the process of interpretation implies the educational intention of the Holy Spirit itself. Only that man is a true interpreter of the sacred text who possesses the Spirit, that is to say, only the Holy Spirit is really capable of understanding itself.[155]

Further, the Holy Spirit functions as the spiritual midwife in baptism who brings about not only regeneration, but also enlightenment.[156] Indeed, only by means of the Holy Spirit is a profession of faith in Jesus Christ possible.[157]

Gregory also referred to Jesus Christ the Word as teacher. More specifically, he spoke of Jesus' teachings as the "divine breasts" that provide nourishment to those who are newly born in Christ. He wrote of John the beloved disciple at the Last Supper:

> John, who reclined upon the Lord's chest, loved the Word's breasts [John 13:25]; and having placed his heart like a sponge, as it were, beside the fountain of life, he was filled by an ineffable transmission of the mysteries hidden in the heart of the Lord. John offers us the teat filled by the Word and fills us with the good things he got from the fountain of goodness, loudly proclaiming the Word who exists eternally.[158]

Jesus Christ provides spiritual nourishment to the baptized and, in so doing, strengthens them for their ascent to the infinite Trinity. Jesus' breast milk for the newly (re)born comes through the mediation of the teats of

155. Jaeger, *Early Christianity and Greek Paideia*, pp. 93-94.
156. Jaeger, *Early Christianity and Greek Paideia*, p. 158, and *Commentary on the Song of Songs*, pp. 154-55.
157. *On the Holy Spirit*, 5.324.
158. *Commentary on the Song of Songs*, p. 55.

scriptural teaching like that found in the Gospel of John and the writings of the apostle Paul.

Gregory did not say a great deal about the Father as teacher. In his *Commentary on the Song of Songs,* however, he did describe the Father as the archer who shoots the arrow of Christ into the soul of the bride:

> The bride praises the bowman for his good marksmanship because he hits her with his arrow. The bride says, "I am wounded with love" [2:5]. These words indicate that the bridegroom's arrows have penetrated the depths of her heart. The archer of these arrows is love [1 John 4:8] who sends his own "chosen arrow" [Isa. 49:2], the only begotten Son, to those who are saved, dipping the triple-pointed tip of the arrow in the Spirit of life. The tip of the arrow is faith, and by it God introduces the archer into the heart along with the arrow. As the Lord says, "I and the Father (are one); we will come and make our home with him" [John 14:23].[159]

Here the "triple-pointed tip of the arrow" seems to refer to baptism and, more particularly, to the Triune Name used at the center of the rite. In baptism, then, the Father implants faith in the Triune Name and brings about the birth of Triune love within the heart of the baptizand. Likewise, the initiative of the Father evokes desire for the Trinity on the part of the newly reborn individual.

Summing up Gregory's teaching about the Trinity as teacher, Martin Laird succinctly lays out the pattern of divine pedagogy in the *Commentary on the Song of Songs:*

> For Gregory of Nyssa, Solomon's tutelage is from first to last Trinitarian. The erotic Beauty of the Word in Scripture attracts desire that is excited and inflamed by the Spirit. The divine Archer shoots the Spirit-moistened arrow of the Son. Penetrated by this arrow, she is ever moving repose and becomes a vehicle of presence for all to see. At rest in the Bridegroom's embrace, she is at the same time shot forth in mission for all the daughters of Jerusalem.[160]

The Trinity instructs and guides the Christian on the journey of ascents initiated and framed by baptism. In other places in the *Commentary on the*

---

159. *Commentary on the Song of Songs,* p. 103.
160. Laird, "Under Solomon's Tutelage," p. 90.

Songs of Songs, Gregory refers to the divine pedagogy as a fountain, as rain, or as drops of dew.[161] The divine pedagogy so permeates Gregory's thought that Laird can say with some justification that, for Gregory, "God is present to the soul as teaching."[162] Thus, the Trinity functioned for Gregory simultaneously as the aim, the teacher, and the curriculum of baptismal pedagogy.

Yet human teachers, too, play an important role in Gregory's pedagogical vision. Often he also drew upon the teachings of such secular teachers as Plato, Aristotle, the Stoics, and Plotinus.[163] Such teachers he compared to the "wealth of Egypt" that the Israelites plundered immediately prior to the Exodus.[164] In so doing, Gregory argued for a kind of Christian humanism:

> Those who follow the leader to virtue must, I think, not lack the wealth of Egypt or be deprived of the treasures of the foreigners, but having acquired all the property of their enemies, must have it for their own use. This is exactly what Moses then commanded the people to do. . . . It commands those participating through virtue in the free life also to equip themselves with the wealth of pagan learning by which foreigners to the faith beautify themselves. Our guide in virtue commands someone who "borrows" from the wealthy Egyptians to receive such things as moral and natural philosophy, geometry, astronomy, dialectic, and whatever else is sought by those outside the Church, since these things will be useful when in time the divine sanctuary of mystery must be beautified with the riches of reason. . . . For many bring to the Church of God their profane learning as a kind of gift: Such a man was the great Basil, who acquired the Egyptian wealth in every respect during his youth and dedicated this wealth to God for the adornment of the Church, the true tabernacle.[165]

---

161. *Commentary on the Song of Songs*, pp. 184, 235, and 238.

162. Laird, *Gregory of Nyssa and the Grasp of Faith*, p. 141.

163. For a discussion of the influences of Plato and Plotinus on Gregory's understanding of "power" in relation to the Trinity, see Michel René Barnes, *The Power of God: Δύναμις in Gregory of Nyssa's Trinitarian Theology* (Washington, D.C.: Catholic University of America Press, 2001), pp. 240-46. For the influence of Aristotle, see Laird, *Gregory of Nyssa and the Grasp of Faith*, p. 80, and for a nuanced discussion of parallels between Gregory and Plotinus, pp. 124-29. For a treatment of the ways in which Aristotle, Plotinus, Porphyry, Stoicism, Poseidonius, and Galen influenced Gregory's notion of the individual, see Turcescu, *Gregory of Nyssa and the Concept of Divine Persons*, pp. 25-46 and 115.

164. *Life of Moses*, pp. 80-81.

165. *Life of Moses*, pp. 80-81.

In terms of Christian teachers, Gregory claimed Macrina and Basil, two of his older siblings, as his own teachers in the mysteries of the Triune faith.[166] He also regularly drew upon human teachers of the past like the Alexandrian teachers Origen and Athanasius. The entirety of his teaching can be said to fall within the framework of the human formulation of the faith framed in 325 at the Council of Nicea. He said that such teachers can be compared to the teeth of the bride in the Song of Songs:

> The Song symbolically names "teeth" discerning and perceptive teachers who enable us to learn and profit from such teachings. For this reason, praise bestows loveliness upon teeth only if the praise of lips is joined to them: the lips cannot blossom in spiritual praise unless the teeth, by diligent care bestow grace upon these lips when they speak. . . . Persons reducing the divine mysteries into small fragments for a clearer interpretation of the text make spiritual food more easily accessible for the body of the church. They perform the function of teeth by receiving the thick, dense bread of the text in their mouths; by a more subtle contemplation, they make the food delectable.[167]

This "ministry of teeth" plays a crucial role in aiding the baptized to ascend to the infinite Trinity. In another place, Gregory refers to wise human teachers in the church as breasts who provide the "teat of the Word to those in need, thereby providing nourishing food to its children."[168] In this connection, we should also keep in mind that he likely saw himself as contributing to the "ministry of teeth," as he alone among the Cappadocians developed a manual for catechetical instruction for use by fellow priests and teachers in preparing candidates for baptism.

Obviously, Gregory was not a modern educator who paid a great deal of attention to participatory or active teaching methods. He utilized the teaching methods that were standard for his culture and ecclesial status; namely, lecture and inculcation of doctrine. He was a highly educated, upper-class nobleman who became a bishop. This meant that he was a person whose word carried enormous authority.[169] Learners were expected to sit at his feet and to listen attentively. They would be held accountable for

---

166. *On the Soul and the Resurrection*, 5.430, and *Against Eunomius*, 5.85.
167. *Commentary on the Song of Songs*, pp. 150-51.
168. *Commentary on the Song of Songs*, p. 157.
169. Brown, *Power and Persuasion*, p. 77.

their learning as the time for the baptismal rite approached. They would need to be able to echo back to an interrogator that which they had learned about the mystery of God as Trinity and the economy of salvation. They would also need to provide evidence that they understood the ways in which these beliefs connected to daily life.

Summary and Assessment

The Cappadocians have played a major role in the development of Eastern Christian theology. At various points, they also exerted significant influence on the development of Western Christian theology. There is credible evidence that Augustine's trinitarian theology was significantly influenced by Cappadocian thought, despite the fact that he did not read Greek well. As T. F. Torrance notes, "Augustine was said not to know much Greek but there is no doubt that his *De Trinitate,* surely one of the greatest works on theology ever written, is steeped in the teaching of the Greek fathers, which he got to know partly through Hilary who did have a good knowledge of Greek and was well versed in Athanasian and Cappadocian theology."[170] The evidence that Augustine was influenced by Cappadocian thought is strengthened by noting that Augustine was influenced by Ambrose (who was well-versed in Cappadocian theology) and Jerome (who translated many Greek theological works into Latin for Augustine's use and was present at the Second Ecumenical Council).[171] In the following chapter, we will see that Calvin was influenced by both Augustine and the Cappadocians in his trinitarian theology.

The Cappadocians collectively took up the mantle of Athanasius and

---

170. T. F. Torrance, *Trinitarian Perspectives: Toward Doctrinal Agreement* (Edinburgh: T&T Clark, 1994), p. 22. See also Edmund Hill in the introduction to his translation of Augustine's *De Trinitate: The Trinity in the Works of Saint Augustine: A Translation for the 21st Century, Part I — Books, vol. 5: The Trinity* (Brooklyn: New City, 1991). Hill writes, "it seems certain that Augustine had read the relevant writings of Gregory of Nazianzus and Didymus the Blind, possibly also of Basil the Great and Epiphanius of Salamis. In any case he had a general knowledge of the kind of problems, largely linguistic and metaphysical, that engaged their attention" (p. 38). Hill notes that Augustine's way of talking about the relationship between the divine Persons bears a distinctively Eastern stamp in terms of the logic or causation (p. 45).

171. See Van Dam, *Becoming Christian*, p. 34.

argued strongly and consistently for Nicene orthodoxy in the face of near constant and ever more sophisticated challenges from the Arian party. These three pastor-theologians laid the groundwork for much that followed in liturgy, spiritual practices, and theological reflection in the Eastern branches of Christianity. Increasingly today, they exert influence on efforts to develop a practical trinitarianism.

The most direct influence of Gregory of Nyssa on Western Christianity has been through the mystical traditions of monasticism, particularly with respect to the apophatic tradition as refracted through Pseudo-Dionysius. Gregory of Nyssa's influence on the development of doctrine in Western Christian traditions has largely been a fairly recent phenomenon. With growing interest in the possibilities of apophatic thought in some postmodern philosophical discussions, the influence of Gregory of Nyssa in Western theology will likely increase in coming years.

Contemporary trinitarian theologians who harvest insights from the trinitarian doctrine aspects of Gregory's thought may well miss or overlook the practical, pastoral, pedagogical dimensions of his trinitarian theology. This chapter has explored and elucidated the interconnections in his thought between the rite of baptism, the doctrine of God as Trinity, and ecclesial pedagogy. These components formed a dynamic and differentiated whole in his thought and practice. Because these elements are so interconnected, to consider one element in isolation from the others runs the risk of interpretive distortion. This means that the current tendency to harvest Gregory's trinitarian ideas abstracted and disembodied from the rite of baptism and practices by which people are formed into Christian faith would have puzzled Gregory. Further, to separate these elements from one another today may risk perpetuating the false notion that the doctrine of the Trinity can be treated adequately apart from its liturgical context and pedagogical dimensions.

While Gregory's world is not our world, our own efforts at trinitarian practical theology of formation for a contemporary situation stand to gain a great deal from considering the way that he held these components together. The key to his trinitarian theology and the closely correlated theological anthropology is, in many ways, the baptismal rite. Baptism served as the well from which he developed his profound insights into the mystery of God and the situation of humanity. Daniélou is right to assert that baptism is the substrate out of which all of Gregory's writings on the Christian life emerge. Baptism was not merely a punctiliar rite for him;

rather, it was the central determinate moment for a pattern of continual growth into ever deeper apprehension of the Triune mystery.

Among the many crucial insights into the relationship of baptism, the Trinity, and pedagogy afforded by a careful look at the work of Gregory of Nyssa, perhaps none may be more important than his conviction that doctrine ought not and cannot be separated from concrete ecclesial practices. His stark observation that only pagans believe that there can be doctrines without practices calls into question attempts to engage in systematic theological reflection abstracted from the concrete life of a given Christian church. This conviction would appear to be particularly relevant with respect to the doctrine of God.

One of the most fruitful and persuasive lines of argument used by Gregory in his writings against the Neo-Arian Eunomius began with exegesis of the baptismal liturgy. One of his chief warrants for the assertion that the One God exists in Three Persons of equal power and dignity came from the baptismal formula itself. He observed that Scripture teaching in Matthew 28:16-20 and the orthopractic baptismal practices of the church arising from it necessitate affirming that the One God is also Three. People are baptized into the One Name that is Father, Son, and Holy Spirit. For Gregory, the baptismal rite serves as perpetual compass and boundary for all theological reflection on the nature and activities of God that is distinctively Christian.

Gregory understood baptism to be the beginning of participation in the Trinity. Human participation in this joyously doxological circle of authentic Life must be seen asymptotically; that is, the baptized are perpetually transformed by stages and degrees into the likeness of the Triune God by the ongoing work of the Trinity within and upon them. Dying and rising with Christ in baptism sets them on an eternal journey of divinization in which they both participate in the Trinity and grow into ever deeper and more beautiful apprehensions of that mystery or mysteries. Learning, growth, and discovery about the mysterious riches of the Triune God are, therefore, endemic to the lives of Christians. Since it is of the very nature of human beings to change and to be in flux, this process of perpetual growth is not only for this life; rather, it continues into the afterlife as well.

Gregory's insistence that there are limits to human comprehension of the Triune mystery will also prove to be an invaluable resource for us. While it is true that most responsible theologians down through the centuries have articulated some sense of the limits of human reason when it comes to the knowledge of God, Gregory's apophatic sensitivity stands out as particularly profound and useful for today's context. Human thought simply cannot penetrate the inner mystery of the Triune God. This means that all conceptualizations of and all language in reference to this mystery must be held with intellectual humility. Our thinking and speaking about the Triune God must always be done within carefully circumscribed limits. Those limits run very close to the contours provided by the scriptural accounts of God's activity in creation and redemption. This also means that even when speaking about the mystery of the Triune God on the basis of what is given to us in and through Scripture, we must hold our conceptions in such a way as to avoid making them absolute. We must not make idols out of our conceptualizations of this mystery. Conviction must be balanced with respect for the loftiness of the supra-rational character of any knowledge of the Trinity. In Gregory's thought, then, we find an interesting interplay between what can and what cannot be known about the mystery of the Triune God. He taught that that which lies beyond human comprehension conditions and qualifies that which can be comprehended. That which cannot be known must condition that which we can know. The implication would seem to be that the baptized are entitled to hold distinctively Christian convictions about the mystery of the Trinity and the economy of salvation, but that they must hold these convictions with a certain measure of intellectual humility and generosity of spirit.

Finally in this vein, Gregory offers to us the suggestion that the experience of the Triune God gained through a life committed to contemplative prayer and the struggle for moral purity may well exceed our abilities to comprehend and to put into words the meaning of those experiences.

With regard to ecclesial pedagogy, Gregory provides several fruitful avenues for contemporary work. First, in light of his understanding of the nature of human beings as always in flux combined with his conviction of asymptotic perpetual progress into deeper participation in the Triune life of God, ecclesial education ought to be conceived as a lifelong pursuit. Living in faithfulness to the meaning and character of baptism implies that intentional ecclesial education must go beyond something offered to children and adolescents. Indeed, the essential character of the Christian life is inherently educational. More than that, Triune education ought to be seen as the ontological vocation of humanity.

There is much to be learned also from Gregory's conviction that ecclesial pedagogy is a form of cognitive therapy. The ongoing transformation initiated by the baptismal rite and characterized by ever deepening participation in the doxological mystery of the Triune God must aim to transform the whole person. Ideas that are held about the nature and activities of God exert enormous influence in our lives. Effective teaching about the work of the Triune God in the economy of salvation plays an essential role in the therapeutic process of moving from a life pattern caught up in the forces of death and destruction to the vivaciousness of growing in the doxological life. Gregory's vision calls for a robust and compelling program of engagement with not only the liturgical center of the church, but also with a well-developed program of para-liturgical pedagogy that aims to bridge the gap between liturgy and life.

We might also learn from Gregory that the content of ecclesial pedagogy must be modulated to speak to the framework of meaning that people bring to the process. It cannot be assumed that "one size fits all" in ecclesial pedagogy. Learners come from a variety of meaningful frameworks. While there ought to be a kind of "core curriculum" that guides the ecclesial enterprise of education, the religious needs and perspectives of the learners should determine the particular strategies utilized.

Not everything Gregory offers will prove to be useful for us in our contemporary situation. For example, his attentiveness to the ethical implications of baptism into participation in the mystery of the Triune God tends to be limited to personal morality. Gregory lacks any viable social critique. His aristocratic rearing and education combined with his role as sometime chaplain to the imperial family tended to limit his vision of the implications of the baptism-Trinity-pedagogy nexus for anything beyond personal moral conduct. Though it is true that he wrote compelling treatises advocating the culturally critical practice of monasticism, it is difficult to see Gregory's baptismal *paideia* as anything but sympathetic to Constantinianism with its close association of state and church. For all the potential that a Cappadocian social trinitarian may offer trinitarian thinkers like Moltmann who desire to transform oppressive hierarchies in church and state into egalitarian fellowship,[172] the Cappadocians themselves — Gregory of Nyssa included — tended not to see the potential for radical social critique inherent in the perichoretic vision of the relation of the divine Persons. One only need look at Gregory's contemporary, John Chrysostom, to find an example of someone who addressed such issues as

172. Moltmann, *The Trinity and the Kingdom*, pp. 191-222.

power and money in both baptismal and social terms.[173] Today, we do not have the luxury of avoiding or submerging the politically transformative dimensions of the nexus of baptism, the Trinity, and ecclesial pedagogy. To avoid the overtly political in this nexus is always and everywhere to support — however unwittingly — the status quo in both church and state.

Moreover, the sort of pedagogy utilized by Gregory are wholly inadequate today. Changes in the way authority is understood and in the way learners best appropriate content call for more diverse and creative teaching strategies than was the case in the fourth century. No longer can we assume that a cleric or a catechist can simply transmit content via lecture if effective learning is the goal. This is particularly true among well-educated members of mainline Protestant denominations in America. Effective ecclesial pedagogy must pay as much attention to the complex dynamics of the teaching-learning process as to the fine points of curricular content. Recent research into how people think and learn has yielded important insights that simply were unavailable to Gregory of Nyssa. To be sure, sensitivity to developmental appropriateness and trajectories along with judicious appropriations of multiple intelligence theory, for example, would perhaps enhance his pedagogical vision.[174] One might make the case that the use of such insights into the complexities of human subjectivity may complement and extend Gregory's notion of perpetual asymptotic spiritual growth. He certainly argued for a differentiated approach to the content of ecclesial pedagogy; surely a differentiated approach to the teaching-learning process would be more boon than bane to his pedagogical vision.

Finally, a note of caution might be sounded about Gregory's notion of participation. While he maintained that the creatureliness of human beings would never be compromised by participation in the Triune life of God, questions must be raised about the usefulness of the notion of participation precisely because it runs the risk of blurring the distinction be-

---

173. "The wonderful, unbelievable thing is that every difference and distinction of rank is missing here. If anyone happens to be in a position of worldly importance or conspicuous in wealth, if he boasts of his birth or the glory of this present life, he stands on just the same footing as the beggar in rags, the blind man or the lame. Nor does he complain at this since he knows that all such differences have been set aside in the life of the spirit; a grateful heart is the only requirement." John Chrysostom, "Baptismal Homily II," in Yarnold, *The Awe-Inspiring Rites of Initiation*, p. 156.

174. For Multiple Intelligence Theory, see Howard Gardner, *Intelligence Reframed: Multiple Intelligences for the 21st Century* (New York: Basic Books, 1999).

tween creature and Triune Creator. If he meant suffusion rather than absorption, fine. Gregory may well have intended a rather sophisticated notion of human boundaries such that our boundedness in time and space is definite and clear. He might also have advocated for a conception porous enough to allow for relational interpenetration or suffusion. Gregory's notion of participation may well require further investigation in order to serve as a useful concept in a contemporary late modern or postmodern context.

CHAPTER 4

Baptism, Trinity, and Ecclesial Pedagogy in the Work of John Calvin

For all the gifts of God proffered in baptism are found in Christ alone. Yet this cannot take place unless he who baptizes in Christ invokes also the names of the Father and the Spirit. For we are cleansed by his blood because our merciful Father, wishing to receive us into grace in accordance with his incomparable kindness, has set this Mediator among us to gain favor for us in his sight. But we obtain regeneration by Christ's death and resurrection only if we are sanctified by the Spirit and imbued with a new and spiritual nature. For this reason we obtain and, so to speak, clearly discern in the Father the cause, in the Son the matter, and in the Spirit the effect, of our purgation and our regeneration.

John Calvin, *Institutes of the Christian Religion*

The focus of the investigation shifts now from the West Syrian tradition of the Eastern church in the fourth century to the Latin Christian tradition's Protestant Reformed movement of the sixteenth century. In so doing, we shift our focus from a bishop-theologian embroiled in the defense of Neo-Nicene orthodoxy to a pastor-theologian whose efforts to promote evangelical transformation of church and society heralded the coming of modernity. While Gregory of Nyssa developed his thought in the context of the Christianization of imperial Rome in the fourth century, John Calvin worked in the transitional zone between medieval Latin Christendom and emerging modernity.[1]

Gregory's ideas were disseminated mainly by handwritten manuscript and by word of mouth; Calvin's well-reasoned arguments spread across the face of Europe by means of the printing press. Gregory participated in an ecclesial system that increasingly blurred the lines between ecclesial and civil powers; Calvin almost single-handedly developed a new form of church-state relations in which the ecclesial and civil authorities were differentiated, but not completely separated.[2] Gregory served as occasional chaplain to the Roman emperor; Calvin engaged in protracted battles with both religious and civil authorities. Gregory worked in his homeland and sought imperial support for his views; Calvin lived in permanent exile and sought to persuade, if not to undermine, the ruler of his homeland.[3] Gregory was appointed doctor of the true faith by Theodosius; Calvin sent clandestine waves of Protestant pastors into France in order to solidify and spread the Protestant faith over and against the wishes of the French monarch. While we might draw many more such contrasts, suffice it to say that these two pastor-theologians lived in markedly different historical, theological, and ecclesial contexts.

Their differences, however, ought not to obscure points of convergence. Gregory of Nyssa and John Calvin shared enough similarities on the matter under investigation that meaningful comparison is both possible and useful in service to developing overtures to a contemporary trinitarian practical theology of formation. Both were servants of the church and dedicated their lives to the defense and promotion of the Christian faith. Both possessed first-class theological minds and directed their intellectual resources to the upbuilding of the church through intentional pedagogy. More to the point, both Gregory of Nyssa and Calvin held together the sacrament of baptism, the doctrine of the Trinity, and the practices of ecclesial pedagogy in dynamic interplay. Given the differ-

1. Bernard Cottret, *Calvin: A Biography,* trans. M. Wallace McDonald (Grand Rapids: Eerdmans; Edinburgh: T&T Clark, 2000), p. ix.

2. John Calvin, *Institutes of the Christian Religion,* ed. J. T. McNeill, trans. Ford Lewis Battles, 2 vols., Library of Religious Classics, vols. 20 and 21 (Philadelphia: Westminster, 1960), 4.20.

3. Calvin, *Institutes,* "Prefatory Address to King Francis I of France," pp. 9-31. See also Carlos M. N. Eire, *War Against the Idols: The Reformation of Worship from Erasmus to Calvin* (Cambridge: Cambridge University Press, 1986; paperback reprint, 1997), pp. 234-75.

ences of ecclesial and cultural context that lie between them, we should expect that the particularities of this crucial nexus will look rather different from one another and will carry somewhat different freight. Both their differences and their similarities with regard to the triadic nexus with which we are concerned will prove valuable in the work of the final chapter. Before turning to the task of developing overtures toward a trinitarian practical theology of Christian formation, however, we must inquire as to the contours of the nexus of the sacrament of baptism, the doctrine of the Trinity, and practices of ecclesial pedagogy in the work of John Calvin.

Background and Context

The details of Calvin's life and ministry have been thoroughly traced in several biographical studies and do not, therefore, need rehearsal here in exhaustive detail.[4] Nonetheless, a brief biographical sketch will provide a concrete historical framework within which to interpret his manner of conceiving of the dynamic interplay of baptism, the Trinity, and pedagogy.

John Calvin was born and baptized on July 10, 1509, in Noyon, France.[5] He was the youngest of four boys.[6] When he was a school-age child, his mother died.[7] His father remarried and that union produced Calvin's two half-sisters.[8] The family seems to have been relatively well off and comfortable. For many years, Calvin's father provided legal services for the local ecclesiastical authorities.[9] Initially, his father's position with local church authorities yielded financial benefits that helped to defray the costs of Calvin's pre-clerical studies in Paris. Subsequently, Calvin was awarded a clerical beneficence at the age of twelve that provided enough money to sup-

---

4. There has been a resurgence of interest in the historical Calvin in recent decades. See, for example, William J. Bouwsma, *John Calvin: A Sixteenth Century Portrait* (New York: Oxford University Press, 1988); Cottret, *Calvin;* and Alister E. McGrath, *A Life of John Calvin: A Study in the Shaping of Western Culture* (Cambridge, Mass.: Basil Blackwell, 1990).

5. Cottret, *Calvin*, p. 9.

6. Bouwsma, *John Calvin*, p. 9.

7. Bouwsma indicates that Calvin was four or five years old (*John Calvin*, p. 9); Cottret claims that Calvin was six years old (*Calvin*, p. 10).

8. Cottret, *Calvin*, p. 11.

9. Cottret, *Calvin*, p. 11.

port his education.[10] Partly as the result of a falling out with the Noyonaise ecclesiastical authorities, Calvin's father directed him to switch from the study of theology in preparation for the priesthood to the study of law.[11] Calvin's father died several years later in 1531 in a state of excommunication stemming from that same rupture in relations.[12]

Calvin began his studies in Noyon at the Collège des Capet and then moved to Paris to study at the Collège de la Marche and, eventually, at the Collège de Montaigu.[13] When Calvin's father decided that he would shift his studies from theology to law, Calvin followed his father's urging and completed his formal education at Orléans and Bourges.[14] In addition to his theological and legal training, he excelled in the study of Latin and rhetoric under the tutelage of some of the best humanist teachers in France. During his years of study as a young man in Paris, Orléans, and Bourges, Calvin studied with the leading humanist scholars in France at the time.[15] As a result, he gravitated increasingly toward a life of humanistic scholarship. Notably, his first published book was a commentary on the Stoic Seneca's *De Clementia* in which he attempted to address some problems left by Diderius Erasmus (1469-1536) in his critical editions of Seneca.[16] While the success of Calvin's commentary on Seneca did not achieve the hoped for heights of critical acclaim, the work was solid and augured well for future works by the talented, ambitious, and disciplined young scholar. Commenting on Calvin's formation as a student in Paris, William Bouwsma observes: "The reformism of Paris had been nourished by Italian humanism, which, combining literary classicism and philology, pointed, under the slogan '*ad fontes*,' to the study of Greek and Latin Fathers and the Bible in its original languages. Like Italian humanists, Paris reformers looked to the ancient church as a model for contemporary reform."[17] Calvin's humanistic training as well as the subtle and continuing

10. Cottret, *Calvin*, p. 11.

11. Bouwsma, *John Calvin*, p. 10.

12. Cottret, *Calvin*, p. 11.

13. Cottret, *Calvin*, pp. 12-20.

14. Cottret, *Calvin*, pp. 20-24.

15. Calvin seems to have been particularly influenced by humanist scholars Pierre de l'Estoile and Andrea Alciati. See Cottret, *Calvin*, pp. 20-23, for a fuller account of their influence on him.

16. Cottret, *Calvin*, pp. 64-65.

17. Bouwsma, *John Calvin*, p. 12.

influence of Stoicism would serve him well in his subsequent work as a Protestant reformer. He adeptly employed the tools and skills of humanistic scholarship in his effort to secure Protestant reform in Europe.

The circumstances of Calvin's religious transformation from the French Catholicism of his childhood, youth, and early adulthood to a vigorous Protestantism remain somewhat sketchy.[18] What scholars have pieced together about his conversion to Protestantism points to events in France during the period of his advanced academic studies.[19] Apparently, Calvin's break with his Catholic roots did not result from one catastrophic event; more likely, he moved by subtle steps over the course of months, or perhaps years, to the point at which he embraced the Protestant cause. He did not provide the exact date and circumstances of his metamorphosis into deeper Christian commitment as a "lover of Jesus Christ."[20] As was characteristic of the man generally, he rarely spoke about himself and his private experiences. The closest he came to a description of what took place in this all-important period of evangelical transformation can be found in the preface to his *Commentary on the Book of Psalms* written many years after the events described:

> My condition, no doubt is much inferior to his [David's], and it is unnecessary for me to stay to show this. But as he was taken from the sheepfold, and elevated to rank of supreme authority; so God, having taken me from my originally obscure and humble condition, has reckoned me worthy of being invested with the honorable office of a preacher and minister of the gospel. When I was as a very little boy, my father had destined me for the study of theology. But afterwards, when he considered that the legal profession commonly raised those who followed it to wealth, this prospect induced him suddenly to change his purpose. Thus it came to pass, that I was withdrawn from the study of philosophy, and was put to the study of law. To this pursuit I endeavored faithfully to apply myself, in obedience to the will of my father; but God, by the secret guidance of his providence, at length gave a different direction to my course. And first, since I was too obstinately devoted to the superstitions of Popery to be easily extricated from so profound an abyss of mire, God by a sudden conversion subdued and brought my

18. Cottret, *Calvin,* pp. 65-70.
19. Cottret, *Calvin,* pp. 65-70.
20. Cottret, *Calvin,* p. 89.

mind to a teachable frame, which was more hardened in such matters than might have been expected from one at my early period in life. Having thus received some taste and knowledge of true godliness, I was immediately inflamed with so intense a desire to progress therein, that although I did not altogether leave off other studies, I yet pursued them with less ardour.[21]

As a newly committed Protestant faced with life in exile, Calvin sought a quiet place to study and to carry on his humanistic scholarship. He fled in 1533 to the relative safety of Basel, Switzerland.[22] Though he intended to pursue a quiet life of humanistic scholarship during his Swiss exile, such was not to be the case for this brilliant young humanist Protestant.

During an unplanned detour on the way to Bern, Guillame Farel — a somewhat older and more zealous Protestant compatriot — prevailed upon Calvin to go with him to Geneva in order to help with the newly birthed Protestant movement there.[23] To break down Calvin's resistance to the prospect of a likely conflicted public life of religious leadership, Farel fulminated about the certain prospect of divine judgment should Calvin continue to demur! Calvin relented and began what would turn out to be a rather futile first attempt to solidify and advance deep-level religious reform in Geneva.

The situation in Geneva into which Calvin stepped was contentious and confused. He arrived in Geneva in the summer of 1536.[24] He came to Geneva in the midst of political and religious change already in full swing. The Reformation in Geneva preceded Calvin's arrival by as much as three years, but things had neither solidified nor settled down.[25] Calvin and Farel attempted to bring order and stability to the cause of Protestant reform while also pushing the reform of communal life forward to its logical conclusions.

In addition to the many responsibilities and projects he undertook

21. Cottret, *Calvin*, p. 67.
22. Cottret, *Calvin*, pp. 73-76.
23. Cottret, *Calvin*, pp. 118-20.
24. Cottret, *Calvin*, p. 118.
25. The initial Protestant transformation of Geneva began on Good Friday, 1533. It culminated on Sunday, May 21, 1536, when the citizenry officially embraced Protestantism. Calvin came to Geneva in the summer of 1536. For a fuller account, see Cottret, *Calvin*, pp. 114-18.

during his first period in Geneva (1536-38), Calvin participated in a delegation of Protestant scholars who engaged with Roman Catholic theologians in Lausanne.[26] In the midst of these debates, fellow Protestant Pierre Caroli accused Calvin of holding to a unitarian view of the doctrine of God. Caroli's charges stemmed from Calvin's refusal to sign a statement of adherence to traditional creedal statements. Calvin's reluctance to sign on the dotted line arose from his concern to base every theological claim solely on the text of Scripture. Even though the charges of Unitarianism by Caroli were ultimately proven false, this incident marked the beginning of a series of conflicts over the doctrine of the Trinity that would dog Calvin for many years.[27] The Caroli affair may well have spurred him to develop further and to articulate more explicitly his admittedly implicit views on the doctrine of God as Trinity.

Calvin's first stint in Geneva ended rather unceremoniously after only a few short years. Calvin and Farel apparently pushed too hard and too fast; the Genevan citizenry revolted against their too hasty and too heavy-handed measures to solidify and extend Protestant reform. It did not help matters that Calvin was a foreigner and not a citizen of Geneva (a privilege he would not enjoy until the end of his life).[28] Despite early signs of progress toward the radical transformation of the community in light of scriptural teachings and the solidification of the Protestant cause, Calvin and Farel were expelled from Geneva during the week immediately following their defiance of a civil order banning them from preaching on Easter Sunday, 1538. Evidently, Calvin and Farel had asserted themselves in civil judgments concerning religious practice one too many times. The authorities gave them three days to leave town permanently.[29]

Calvin soon found himself in exile from his place of exile. His four-year sojourn in Strasbourg (1538-41) proved to be very important for his life and thought in several respects. As a result of the prodding of the leading Strasbourg Protestant Martin Bucer, Calvin was ordained and

26. Cottret, *Calvin*, pp. 121ff.

27. Karl Barth provided a helpful treatment of the Caroli controversy in his early lectures on Calvin's theology. Karl Barth, *The Theology of Calvin*, trans. Geoffrey W. Bromiley (Grand Rapids: Eerdmans, 1995), pp. 309-45.

28. Calvin did not enter the bourgeoisie in Geneva until 1559; Bouwsma, *John Calvin*, p. 27. This meant, among other things, that Calvin was never able to stand for election to public office.

29. Cottret, *Calvin*, pp. 130-31.

served as pastor of the French Protestant congregation.[30] After some matchmaking and prodding from friends, he married Idelette du Bure, the widow of a former Anabaptist. He also adopted her children as his own.[31] Later in life, Calvin would recall that these Strasbourg years were among the most peaceful and enjoyable years of his entire life.[32] His pastoral experience in the expatriate French Protestant congregation in Strasbourg would prove invaluable in subsequent years of his ministry. If nothing else, his experience as a parish pastor helped to moderate his more impatient impulses for radical reform of belief and life among the people in his charge.

After a period of continued civil and ecclesial unrest and a string of inept pastoral leaders, the municipal leadership of Geneva attempted to recall Calvin from Strasbourg. Evidently, his letter in response to Catholic Bishop Sadoleto in which he very effectively parried the bishop's attempt to bring the Genevans back into the Roman fold made a very favorable impression on the Genevan populace. In addition, some of Calvin's supporters in Geneva eventually managed to gain the upper hand in the civil government. These two developments led to the extension of an invitation for Calvin to return to the place where he did not desire to go in the first place and where he was not completely sure he wanted to return. After some considerable wrestling with the matter, he finally agreed to return to Geneva in September 1541.[33]

Calvin picked up in preaching and in his efforts to reform the city according to the Protestant faith essentially where he had left off, and he continued to struggle for wholesale reform of town and church for the next eighteen years until his death in 1564. For most of the next decade, Calvin engaged in a series of pitched battles with several well-established Genevan

---

30. Bouwsma, *John Calvin,* pp. 20-21, and Cottret, *Calvin,* pp. 134-35.

31. Idelette had a boy and a girl from her previous marriage to an Anabaptist. Calvin and Idelette had one child together; Alexandre Ganoczy, "Calvin's Life," trans. David L. Foxgrover and James Schmitt, in *The Cambridge Companion to John Calvin,* ed. Donald K. McKim (Cambridge: Cambridge University Press, 2004), p. 14. Sadly, the boy died a few days after birth. Years later, when Idelette died, Calvin wrote touchingly to a number of friends about the deep pain that he felt over these losses; Bouwsma, *John Calvin,* p. 23. Bouwsma argues that the couple actually had three children, none of whom survived infancy; Cottret, *Calvin,* p. 23.

32. Cottret, *Calvin,* p. 134.

33. Cottret, *Calvin,* p. 157.

families and with the interlocking municipal entities that made up the Genevan government. In his recent biography of Calvin, Bernard Cottret helpfully points out that Calvin was not the iron-fisted theological dictator of Geneva that he is often portrayed to have been:

> Geneva, in fact, was never a theocracy. Although they interpenetrated each other more than today, the religious and the political powers, the ministry and the magistracy, were never one and the same. Calvin indeed had to fight step-by-step to maintain the autonomy of the church against the ascendancy of the councils. The question of excommunication was at the center of the debate. Was it a religious action, as Calvin maintained, or did it come under the civil jurisdiction, as his adversaries wished? To sum up, Calvin did not take over the state; he was neither a commanding general nor an ayatollah. On the contrary, he only wanted to guarantee a minimum of liberty of action to the church.[34]

While Calvin and the Genevan civil authorities clashed over many matters, the main point of tension concerned the authority to administer excommunication. Calvin insisted that the ecclesial authorities had the sole stewardship of this crucial point of church discipline and that the civil government had no business meddling in exclusively ecclesial matters. He did, however, affirm the right of the Genevan civil authorities to promote and enforce right worship of God, the suppression of idolatry, and the punishment of immorality.[35] He argued that the pastors and the Consistory ought to have the sole right to determine admission to and exclusion from the Lord's Table. Though he met fierce opposition over this matter, Calvin eventually prevailed.

Along these lines, it is important to point out another bit of evidence for the actual nature of Calvin's relationship to the civil authorities in Geneva. He argued strongly for weekly celebration of the Eucharist in Geneva, but ultimately he lost this battle with one of the town councils and had to settle for Eucharistic celebration only four times a year.[36] Only in

---

34. Cottret, *Calvin*, p. 159.

35. Calvin, *Institutes* 4.20.1.

36. Elsie McKee, *John Calvin: Writings on Pastoral Piety*, The Classics of Western Spirituality series (New York: Paulist, 2001), p. 104. Cottret notes that the Eucharist was celebrated in Geneva on "Christmas, Easter, Pentecost, and the first Sunday in September"; Cottret, *Calvin*, p. 166; see also p. 129.

the final few years of his life did Calvin enjoy unopposed influence over Genevan life.[37]

During this second Genevan period, Calvin's scholarly and pedagogical output was phenomenal. He produced commentaries on approximately two-thirds of the Bible.[38] He wrote and rewrote his summary of practical biblical teaching for faithful Christian living, *The Institutes of the Christian Religion,* until he eventually produced the epitome of mature Protestant thought in the sixteenth century.[39] He engaged in voluminous correspondence and lectured regularly. During this period, he also produced confessions of faith and a number of catechetical materials for common use.[40] He preached every Sunday and several times during the week. He wrote untold numbers of polemical tracts and treatises against movements he deemed to be damaging to the life and health of the church. During the latter part of his second Genevan period, he also founded the Academy of Geneva as a concrete institutional expression of his Protestant humanism.

No account of Calvin's life and work, no matter how brief, can avoid mention of the Servetus affair. Even though this was not the major issue in his life and ministry that Calvin's detractors have made it out to be, it deserves some attention here because it says something significant about how he viewed such matters as the doctrine of the Trinity, the practice of baptism, and ecclesial pedagogy. In brief, the Genevan civil authorities accomplished what several other European cities intended to do: they arrested the notorious Spanish physician, Servetus, and found him guilty of promulgating Anabaptist and Unitarian teachings.[41] The sentence passed by the council was death by fire. Even though he had long opposed Servetus from afar, Calvin repeatedly paid pastoral visits to him in his

37. Cotrett, *Calvin,* p. 235. See also William G. Naphy, *Calvin and the Consolidation of the Genevan Reformation,* with new preface (Manchester and New York: Manchester University Press, 1994; Louisville: Westminster John Knox, 2003), pp. 208-32.

38. Wulfert de Greef, *The Writings of John Calvin: An Introductory Guide,* trans. Lyle D. Bierma (Grand Rapids: Baker, 1993; originally published as *Johannes Calvijn: Zijn werk en geschriften* [Kampen: De Groot Goudriaan, 1989]), pp. 93-107.

39. For a history of the editions of the *Institutes,* see de Greef, *The Writings of John Calvin,* pp. 195-202.

40. De Greef, *The Writings of John Calvin,* confession: pp. 142-43; catechisms: pp. 131-33.

41. Cottret, *Calvin,* pp. 213-25; and Naphy, *Calvin and the Consolidation of the Genevan Reformation,* p. 183.

prison cell and exhorted him to recant his heterodox views. In these efforts, he was largely unsuccessful.[42] Calvin also attempted to intervene with the civil authorities on Servetus's behalf by changing the means of his execution to beheading — a more swift and humane means of execution than incineration. Calvin's appeal on Servetus's behalf met with rejection by the civil authorities.[43] Thus, while Calvin did not prevent the burning of Servetus, he also did not single-handedly bring it about. Nonetheless, Calvin did perceive that Servetus's teaching in the church about the doctrine of the Trinity and the sacrament of baptism posed very serious threats to the church's welfare at the levels of both theory and practice. In the Servetus episode, we see the elements of baptism, the Trinity, and ecclesial pedagogy at play, but here these elements lack integration into a dynamic nexus.

After a protracted period of struggle, Calvin eventually prevailed over the last of his detractors in Geneva.[44] For a few brief years at the end of his life, he enjoyed the triumph of his views in Genevan church and society. This is not to say, however, that he was ever satisfied with the reform of belief and practice among the Genevan populace; he was not. Though his final victories in Geneva were far from hollow, they seem not to have brought satisfaction and peace for the determined reformer. In this late period of triumph, his health — which had been a source of discomfort for some years — declined markedly. After a struggle with several protracted illnesses, Calvin died at the age of fifty-four on May 27, 1564.[45]

Calvin's influence beyond Geneva deserves brief note. As an exile from his beloved France for most of his adult life, he maintained a lively interest in the Protestant cause in his homeland. Near the end of his life, he deployed scores of pastors to work clandestinely in France for the cause of reform.[46] This covert operation contributed a great deal to the growth of the Huguenots and may well have played a factor in the civil unrest in France that would later erupt into bitter violence in the decades following Calvin's death.[47]

---

42. Cottret, *Calvin,* pp. 224-25.

43. Cottret, *Calvin,* p. 224.

44. Naphy, *Calvin and the Consolidation of the Genevan Reformation,* pp. 208-35.

45. Cottret, *Calvin,* p. 261.

46. David Steinmetz, *Calvin in Context* (New York: Oxford University Press, 1995), p. 19.

47. Eire, *War Against the Idols,* pp. 271-75.

Calvin's influence extended far beyond the Swiss cantons and his native land. Geneva offered refuge not only to droves of French Protestants, but also to Protestants from many different countries. Protestants from France, Hungary, England, Scotland, and the Netherlands found refuge in Geneva. Many future leaders of Reformed Protestant churches learned the ways of high-commitment, biblically based Protestant Christian faith from Calvin. When these Protestant refugees returned to their various homelands, they brought with them the teachings they had acquired and internalized from him.[48] There was even an attempt at one point to establish a Genevan missionary outpost in the New World; the Brazilian mission was a relatively short-lived endeavor and ultimately came to a tragic end.[49]

Space does not permit the telling of the story of Calvin's influence in early American public and ecclesial life. Suffice it to say that his thought exerted significant influence on the emerging new political and cultural reality that became the United States of America. As witness to the influence of Calvin's thought, the British initially referred to the American Revolution as "the Presbyterian Revolt." The leading theological lights during the period leading up to and including the Revolution included Calvinists like Jonathan Edwards and John Witherspoon. Calvin's theology exerted significant influence on the political evolution of American government and on the early character of American cultural life.

The Baptismal Rite

The baptismal rite Calvin developed for use in Geneva arose from a long history in Western Christianity. It grew out of the Roman liturgical subfamily in the early Western church.[50] This particular liturgical family, as one would expect from the larger history of Western Europe, eventually emerged as the dominant if not the sole liturgical tradition during the medieval period.[51] The Roman baptismal liturgy included:

---

48. Eire, *War Against the Idols*, pp. 279-81.

49. Cottret, *Calvin*, pp. 236-39.

50. For a detailed treatment, see Hughes Oliphant Old, *The Shaping of the Reformed Baptismal Rite in the Sixteenth Century* (Grand Rapids: Eerdmans, 1992), pp. 1-20.

51. Maxwell Johnson, *The Rites of Christian Initiation: Their Evolution and Interpretation* (Collegeville: Liturgical Press [A Pueblo Book], 1999), p. 177.

Pre-Baptismal Rites
  Anointing
  Renunciation

Baptism Proper
  Baptism

Post-Baptismal Rites
  White garment
  Anointing
  Imposition of hands and prayer by bishop
  Anointing of forehead by bishop
  Eucharist.[52]

The post-baptismal prayer and the anointing by the bishop stand out in the Roman liturgy. That these acts could only be performed by a bishop laid the groundwork for the separation of the Roman baptismal rite into a sacrament for infants (pre-baptismal rites and baptism proper) and the sacrament of confirmation for older children or young adolescents (post-baptismal rites).[53]

Though there is evidence for the practice of infant baptism as early as the second and third centuries, by the fifth century the dramatic shift from adults to infants in baptism was in full swing.[54] Infant baptism soon replaced adult conversion as the norm.[55] Though the characteristics of the candidates for baptism changed dramatically, the rite itself did not. For the next thousand years, the Western church baptized infants in a rite that had been constructed on the premise of adult conversion to Christian faith.[56] Most of the modifications to the baptismal liturgy that took place during

52. Johnson, *The Rites of Christian Initiation*, p. 157.

53. See Johnson, *The Rites of Christian Initiation*, pp. 203-13, for a fuller treatment of the fracture of the Roman baptismal rite and the emergence of confirmation as a sacrament.

54. Tertullian (c. 160–c. 225), Hippolytus (c. 170–c. 236), Origen (c. 185–c. 254), and Cyprian of Carthage (d. 258) attest to the practice of paidobaptism. See Johnson, *The Rites of Christian Initiation*, pp. 59, 65, 67, and 77. See also Everett Ferguson, "Baptism," in *Encyclopedia of Early Christianity*, 2nd ed., ed. Everett Ferguson, Garland Reference Library of the Humanities, vol. 1839 (New York: Garland, 1998), p. 162.

55. Johnson, *The Rites of Christian Initiation*, pp. 180-81.

56. Old, *The Shaping of the Reformed Baptismal Rite*, pp. 6-7.

the medieval era condensed elements of the standard rite into shorter and shorter liturgical units of time.[57] Eventually, the entire complex of catechesis and baptism was reduced to a single liturgical event. Rather than fundamental reform of the rite to address the predominant reality of paidobaptism, the church baptized infants using a rite that had been developed for adult converts during the third and fourth centuries. Baptismal catechesis effectively vanished from the scene for several centuries in Western Christianity.[58]

The emergence of the sacrament of confirmation in the early medieval period further shaped the liturgical and pedagogical environment into which Calvin stepped. The standard medieval practice entailed the administration of the first two-thirds of the early church Roman baptismal liturgy in a single liturgical event for newborn babies. The remaining third of the original rite — post-baptismal anointing and admittance to the Eucharist — was administered some years later. The separation of the baptismal rite into two segments and eventually into two distinct and interrelated sacraments arose out of the Western church conviction — originating with Cyprian — that only a bishop could administer the second post-baptismal anointing that conferred the Holy Spirit upon the baptizand.[59] The shortage of bishops combined with the distances between parishes in several dioceses contributed to the chronological separation of the elements of the Roman baptismal rite. The sacrament of confirmation would have been administered only to children old enough to understand and confess the rudiments of Christian faith.[60] Summarizing baptismal practice immediately prior to the sixteenth century in Western Christianity, Maxwell Johnson observes:

> On the eve of the Reformation, then, baptism itself had become: a rite administered almost exclusively to infants as a precautionary step, i.e., a rite for the dying, designed to rescue the candidate from the power of original sin and death; a rite filled with exorcisms designed to snatch

57. Johnson, *The Rites of Christian Initiation,* p. 216; and Old, *The Shaping of the Reformed Baptismal Rite,* p. 11.

58. Johnson, *The Rites of Christian Initiation,* pp. 215-16; and Old, *The Shaping of the Reformed Baptismal Rite,* p. 17.

59. Johnson, *The Rites of Christian Initiation,* pp. 203-13; and Old, *The Shaping of the Reformed Baptismal Rite,* pp. 26-30.

60. Johnson, *The Rites of Christian Initiation,* pp. 212-13.

the infant away from the grasp of Satan; a self-contained rite with no necessary relationship to the public liturgical life of the Church; a rite in which catechesis proper had been replaced by the exorcisms themselves; a rite leading to a process of catechetical formation which was limited to the memorization of a few texts; and a rite increasingly narrowed by scholastic theology to the categories of matter, form, intention, and dominical institution. Such is the rite and its interpretation inherited by both Protestants and Roman Catholics in the sixteenth century.[61]

The rich complex of the baptismal rite, the doctrine of the Trinity, and ecclesial pedagogy characteristic of the catechumenate of the early church had lain in ruins for several centuries prior to the Protestant Reformation.

As the Reformation dawned, leading reformers made small but significant changes to the medieval Latin rite. At first, these early Protestant leaders called for only rather modest changes; these small changes, however, proved to be cracks in the dyke. The first innovation involved simply translating the text of the liturgy from Latin into the vernacular.[62] Because translation always and inevitably entails interpretation, this move led the way toward more sweeping changes in the baptismal rite. Within a short period of time, more and more voices sounded the call for wholesale reform of the rite according to the form of the practice outlined in Scripture. On the basis of the Protestant principle of return to Scripture, the move to reform the rite led to the abolition of the sacrament of confirmation and innumerable liturgical accretions to the baptismal rite itself that had developed over the centuries.[63]

In his recent book on the development of the Reformed baptismal rite, John Riggs traces the influences of the first generation of Protestants like Martin Luther, Huldreich Zwingli, and Martin Bucer on Calvin's theory and practice of baptism.[64] Riggs argues that both Luther and Zwingli exerted strong influence on the development of Calvin's approach to baptism. In addition to the elimination of confirmation and various non-biblical practices, Riggs argues that Calvin appropriated and incorporated

---

61. Johnson, *The Rites of Christian Initiation*, p. 233.

62. Old, *The Shaping of the Reformed Baptismal Rite*, pp. 21-22.

63. Johnson, *The Rites of Christian Initiation*, pp. 286-87.

64. John W. Riggs, *Baptism in the Reformed Tradition: An Historical and Practical Theology*, Columbia Series in Reformed Theology (Louisville: Westminster John Knox, 2002).

both Luther's emphasis on divine promise in baptism and Zwingli's stress on the public oath-taking aspects of the rite.[65]

Calvin was influenced not only by the first generation of Protestant reformers but also by the forceful emergence of Anabaptism.[66] Increasingly, he sought to fend off assaults from this quarter. In particular, he opposed believer's baptism — with its foundation in voluntarism — as the only acceptable norm for the rite.[67] He countered the challenge posed by the Anabaptists with a vigorous defense of the practice of infant baptism in terms of covenantal theology and a robustly Augustinian conviction of the primacy of grace.[68]

Calvin abhorred the practice of emergency baptism. The belief that the unbaptized would be condemned to eternal damnation combined with high infant mortality rates resulted in a pattern in which midwives would baptize newborn babies immediately upon delivery. He argued strongly against this practice because it relied upon a highly questionable view of divine grace and lacked any substantial notion of membership in the covenantal community. He insisted forcefully and consistently that baptism belonged solely to the church as the steward of the grace of the Triune God. Further, he maintained that it should be administered only by those men duly called by God and set apart by the church to serve as pastors.[69] For these reasons, Calvin also worked to abolish the practice of private baptisms. In Geneva, baptisms were to be performed by a properly called and trained pastor in the midst of the gathered worshipping community during regularly scheduled services of worship.[70]

In contrast to ancient church practices, Calvin did not link baptism with particular days or seasons in the church calendar. He maintained that any and all days would be appropriate for the celebration of the sacrament of baptism, "provided that there be Sermon along with it."[71] Baptism could be celebrated either during one of the four Sunday services or dur-

---

65. Riggs, *Baptism in the Reformed Tradition*, pp. 50-51.

66. Old, *The Shaping of the Reformed Baptismal Rite*, pp. 109, 142, and 177-78.

67. Old, *The Shaping of the Reformed Baptismal Rite*, pp. 100 and 108-9.

68. Old, *The Shaping of the Reformed Baptismal Rite*, pp. 142-44.

69. Calvin, *Institutes* 4.15.20.

70. McKee, *John Calvin*, p. 135.

71. Calvin, "Ordinances for the Supervision of Churches in the Country: February 3, 1547," in *Calvin: Theological Treatises*, trans. J. K. S. Reid, Library of Christian Classics, vol. 22 (Philadelphia: Westminster, 1954), p. 78. See also McKee, *Pastoral Piety*, p. 135.

ing one of the weekday services. If on Sunday, the first service at dawn or the early afternoon catechism service was the preferred setting. According to Calvin scholar Elsie McKee, Calvin himself seems not to have baptized during the main service on Sundays; instead, he usually baptized during one of the weekday services.[72]

Calvin and the company of pastors around him made sure that baptisms took place in the space normally designated for worship by the gathered community. Baptismal fonts in and around Geneva were located adjacent to or beneath the elevated pulpit.[73] Calvin did not favor adjacent baptisteries, nor did he deem it appropriate to locate the font at the entrance to the church or off to the side of the chancel. The font had to be in closest proximity to the pulpit in order to signify the close interrelation between baptism and the proclamation of the Word.[74] By making the font vertically adjacent and subordinate to the pulpit Calvin intended to promote a properly sacramental view of baptism. All superstitious beliefs and practices associated with the bath would not be tolerated. This core practice of the church required proper interpretation by intimate linkage with the distinctive narratives and proclamation of the gospel message.[75]

What was the shape of the Genevan baptismal rite as developed by Calvin? Aside from a couple of small changes in subsequent years, the Genevan baptismal rite did not change in any substantial way after the definitive form given to it by Calvin soon after his return to Geneva from Strasbourg in September 1541.[76] He published his baptismal rite in the 1542 *La Forme Des Prieres et Chantz Ecclesiastiques.*

According to this manual, baptisms were to be celebrated at the end of the service of worship. Baptisms were allowed during either Sunday or weekday services. Usually, the preacher for the service performed the rite; however, the parents could request another pastor to preside at the baptism.[77] Often Calvin and his colleagues would baptize several children at a time.[78]

The baptismal liturgy contained several sections. The rite opened with an orienting recitation of Psalm 124:8 that served to emphasize the priority

---

72. McKee, *John Calvin*, p. 135.
73. Calvin, "Draft Ecclesiastical Ordinances," in *Calvin: Theological Treatises*, p. 66.
74. Calvin, "Draft Ecclesiastical Ordinances," p. 66.
75. Calvin, *Institutes* 4.14.4.
76. McKee, *John Calvin*, p. 136.
77. McKee, *John Calvin*, p. 136.
78. McKee, *John Calvin*, p. 136.

of divine initiative and grace, especially as distilled in the sacrament of baptism.[79] This epigrammatic beginning stressed the sole sovereignty of God in salvation over and against both medieval superstitions with regard to the material substances used in the rite and the Anabaptist tendency toward voluntarism. Immediately following the tone-setting proclamation of God's gracious sovereignty in salvation, the presiding minister turned to the parents and asked simply and directly if they were presenting their child for baptism. With an affirmative response from the parents, the rite continued.

Next, the minister launched into a lengthy baptismal exhortation. This theologically dense speech accounted for nearly half of the spoken text of the Genevan baptismal liturgy. The exhortation began with an account of the predicament of original sin into which all human beings are born and the utter impossibility of saving oneself from divine judgment and death.[80] Only complete renunciation of trust in self (and any other human means) will prepare the way for the gift of grace, rebirth, and entrance into the reign of God. The gift of regeneration through Jesus Christ given by the Father and actualized by the Holy Spirit in the life of the baptizand consists of both mortification and vivification.[81] The twofold regeneration described here had already been accomplished objectively once and for all in the death and resurrection of Jesus Christ. Application of and participation in the salvific effects of Christ's passion depend on the work of the Holy Spirit.[82] Not only does God justify the baptizand by grace, but also the Holy Spirit begins to transform the baptizand. The new life produced by the Spirit in the baptizand will be pleasing to the Father and will emulate the pattern of the incarnate Son of God in waging battle against the devil, sin, and the disordered desires of the flesh.[83] Building on the themes of imparted grace, sanctifying transformation, and engraftment into the church understood as the Body of Christ, the minister also proclaimed the covenantal promises of the Triune God to be the God not only of adult believers but also of their children.[84] This section of the baptismal rite culmi-

---

79. Calvin, *La Forme Des Prieres Ecclesiastiques* (hereafter, *La Forme*), in vol. 2, *Johannis Calvini Opera Selecta*, ed. Peter Barth and Wilhelm Niesel (Munich: Christian Kaiser, 1962), p. 31.

80. Calvin, *La Forme*, p. 31.

81. Calvin, *La Forme*, p. 32.

82. Calvin, *La Forme*, pp. 31-32.

83. Calvin, *La Forme*, p. 32.

84. Calvin, *La Forme*, p. 33.

nated with a reading and an interpretation of the account of Jesus blessing the children in Matthew 19:13-15. The use of this particular passage highlighted Christ's welcome of little children into his kingdom.[85]

The opening exhortation explaining the meaning of baptism led directly into a prayer of invocation. This prayer emphasized God's infinite mercy, covenantal promises, the remission of original sin through justification, and sanctification by means of the Holy Spirit appropriate to communion with the risen Christ. The prayer of invocation concluded with the Lord's Prayer.[86]

Next, the minister turned to the parents presenting the child for baptism and asked if they desired to have their child baptized in the name of the Trinity.[87] The question appears to have functioned as a follow-up to the immediately preceding didactic material and the prayer of invocation. This second question to the parents aimed to guarantee that the parents understood and desired authentic Christian baptism and not some sort of Roman Catholic "fire insurance" for their child. The long, carefully worded interpretation of the meaning of baptism clearly differentiated the Genevan rite from the medieval Latin rite.[88] It also drew unmistakably Augustinian boundaries around the rite so as to set it apart from the Anabaptist theory and practice of baptism.[89] Upon receiving an affirmative reply from the parents, the minister proceeded into the next major section of the rite.

In response to the parental affirmation to have the child baptized in the name of the Trinity, the minister next directed the parents to claim and carry out their vocation as the primary Christian educators for their child.[90] They were charged specifically to teach the received trinitarian doctrine of the church as encapsulated by the Apostles' Creed to the child as he or she came of age.[91] Specifically, the parents promised to emphasize

85. Calvin, *La Forme*, p. 33.
86. Calvin, *La Forme*, pp. 34-35.
87. Calvin, *La Forme*, p. 35.
88. Calvin, *La Forme*, pp. 35-37.
89. Old is certainly correct to maintain that the development of the Reformed baptismal rite must be understood in reference to a revival of Augustinian commitments with respect to the primacy of grace. See Old, *The Shaping of the Reformed Baptismal Rite*, p. 286.
90. Calvin, *La Forme*, p. 35.
91. Calvin, *La Forme*, p. 35. McKee notes that "in the late 1540s the Apostles' Creed and the Lord's Prayer came to be recited by the father or the godfather instead of the minister." McKee, *John Calvin*, p. 136.

in their domestic religious instruction that the One God who exists as Three Persons was to be the sole object of their common worship and life.[92] As the summary and pinnacle of the Triune God's activity in human history, they were also to teach the story of the incarnation, death, resurrection, and ascension of Jesus Christ the Son of God to the child presented for baptism.[93] Additionally, the presiding pastor admonished them to instruct their growing child that the Holy Spirit had made them participants in Jesus Christ and members of the Body of Christ, the church.[94] This trinitarian framework would set the stage for further instruction about the whole of the Bible and the Christian life as guided by the Ten Commandments and as summarized by Jesus as love for God and love for neighbor.[95] Upon receiving the curriculum that they were to teach their child across the years from the baptismal font to adulthood in their home, the pastor invited the parents to affirm before the Triune God and the gathered church their intention to so teach and guide their child.[96]

After these pedagogical admonitions to the parents regarding their responsibilities for teaching practical trinitarian and Christological beliefs, the minister read the story of Jesus blessing the children in Matthew 19. The rite calls for interpretation of this passage in terms of the baptism presently unfolding before the parents and the gathered assembly.[97]

With all of the foregoing summed up and brought to bear in the crux of the rite, the minister then turned to the parents yet again and asked if they wanted to have their child baptized.[98] Again, the parents were to respond with a simple affirmation. The minister then asked for the name of the child. When the parents provided an acceptable name, the minister would impose the name on the child at the epicenter of the rite.[99] This point of the rite deserves further comment.

In his research on the Genevan State Archives, William G. Naphy has uncovered municipal records listing names disallowed by Calvin and his

92. Calvin, *La Forme*, p. 35.
93. Calvin, *La Forme*, pp. 35-36.
94. Calvin, *La Forme*, p. 36.
95. Calvin, *La Forme*, p. 36.
96. Calvin, *La Forme*, p. 36.
97. Calvin, *La Forme*, p. 37.
98. Calvin, *La Forme*, p. 37.
99. For a full discussion of the issue of baptismal names, see Naphy, *Calvin and the Consolidation of the Genevan Reformation*, pp. 144-53.

pastoral colleagues for use in the baptismal rite.[100] Evidently, Calvin and the company of pastors sought to extend their reform according to the plain and authoritative sense of Scripture even to the selection of names for infants. Names like Jesus, Pentecost, the names of the Three Wise Men, as well as Claude and Martin (local favorites associated with Genevan saints) were strictly forbidden by Calvin and his pastoral colleagues on the grounds that such names promoted popish idolatry and superstition.[101] Though Calvin does not highlight the controversy over baptismal names in his writings, the Genevan civic records of the time provide evidence of a huge crisis in Geneva over the matter of baptismal practice that lasted eight years![102] A riot in church erupted in the middle of a church service on August 26, 1546, when the presiding minister rejected the supplied name of the baby at the baptismal font and imposed an arbitrarily chosen biblical name instead.[103] The resulting conflict over baptismal names flared up intermittently — with occasional riots in church — for several years.[104] William Naphy notes that this controversy became entwined with growing resentment against the influence of the French exilic community in Geneva and that it was this conflict as much as anything that lay at the heart of the persistent opposition Calvin encountered during the second period of his ministry in Geneva:

> The whole dispute over baptismal names, beginning from 1546, was a consistent element in the opposition to Calvin and the ministers. Many other clashes did occur but, other than attacks on the French, this is the single most recurring source of conflict. It is also apparent that this issue became a central rallying-point for opposition to the French and their growing social, economic, and political influence. Indeed, the start of the controversy over baptismal names coincided with a sharp increase in anti-French outbursts. It should also be clear that relying wholly on Calvin's version of Genevan events has allowed this affair to be over-looked almost totally. Thus the image of the ministers facing constant

100. Naphy, *Calvin and the Consolidation of the Genevan Reformation*, pp. 145-46.
101. Naphy, *Calvin and the Consolidation of the Genevan Reformation*, p. 145.
102. Naphy notes that the protracted controversy over baptismal names coincided with "a sharp increase in anti-French outburst" in Geneva; *Calvin and the Consolidation of the Genevan Reformation*, p. 153.
103. Naphy, *Calvin and the Consolidation of the Genevan Reformation*, p. 146.
104. Naphy, *Calvin and the Consolidation of the Genevan Reformation*, p. 153.

disobedience and immorality is in stark contrast to the provocative nature of the ministers' actions, which is apparent in the other primary sources. The Genevans appear to have been striving, unsuccessfully, to maintain their traditions and customs in the face of growing foreign influence. In any case it is clear that many Genevans viewed the actions of the ministers as an unacceptable infringement of their liberties as Genevan citizens. They showed as strong a desire as the ministers to oppose insolence. Most important of all, this policy set the ministers on a course which meant that they would have to admonish and humiliate members of Geneva's ruling elite in public on a regular basis. In the end this served only to prolong and indeed aggravate the tensions which already existed in Geneva as a result of the influx of so many French refugees. Many Genevans must have come to share Berthelier's view that the ministers were insulting them and that they could endure no more.[105]

Some of the Genevan citizenry who balked at this level of intrusion into private life at the point of the baptismal font were hauled before the town council for disciplinary action. As mentioned, Calvin and his pastoral colleagues eventually prevailed over the strong opposition mounted by several well-established and powerful Genevan families on this highly contentious matter.

Returning to our journey through the Genevan baptismal rite itself, we find that immediately following the imposition of the name on the baptizand, the minister would put "pure and clean" water on the head of the child, saying simply, "In the name of the Father, and of the Son, and of the Holy Spirit."[106] It is important to note that the minister was not instructed to say, "I baptize you in the Name . . ." as in the Latin rite. Nor was the pastor to say, "You are baptized in the Name . . ." as in the Eastern Orthodox liturgical tradition. In this liturgy, Calvin instructed the pastor simply to apply the water in the Triune Name ("In the name of the Father, the Son, and the Holy Spirit") without any reference to the subtle question of agency.

The Genevan baptismal rite concluded in short order after the application of the water in the Triune Name. The concluding short prayer asked God the Father to give grace to make the newly baptized a true member of

---

105. Naphy, *Calvin and the Consolidation of the Genevan Reformation*, p. 153.

106. "Au Nom du Pere, et du Filz, et du sainct Espirit." Naphy, *Calvin and the Consolidation of the Genevan Reformation*, p. 38.

his Son Jesus Christ by bearing appropriate fruit.[107] The baptismal rite concluded with a benediction that drew from the final words of the risen Christ to the church in Matthew 28:20. Invoking the promise of Christ's presence along with the command to teach and baptize in the Triune Name, the pastor brought the service to an emblematic conclusion.

Immediately following the conclusion of the liturgical text per se, Calvin supplied two further instructions for ministers performing baptism. First, he directed them to conduct the entire baptismal liturgy in a voice sufficiently loud to be heard by all. Further, they should use the common language of the people *(language vulgaire)* when administering baptism.[108] Pastors should perform baptism in this way so that the gathered assembly would understand the meaning of the sacrament and, perhaps, so that each baptismal celebration would serve as an occasion for baptismal renewal and strengthening of the baptismal faith and life of all those gathered.

Second, the ministers were to avoid all liturgical accoutrements. Even if some traditional embellishments may have had some solid theological or pastoral warrants, they were now to be avoided in Geneva on the grounds that worship pleasing to God must be carried out strictly according to the pure and simple teaching of Scripture. Pastors should administer the rite in a scripturally based practice without ornamentation or elaboration. According to Calvin, to do otherwise would amount to claiming that human beings knew better than the Triune God what the rite should entail.[109]

Stepping Back from the Baptismal Gestalt

The Meaning of Baptism

The core of Calvin's understanding of the meaning of baptism has a decidedly Augustinian cast to it. He habitually preceded discussions of his understanding of the meaning of baptism with a general treatment of sacra-

---

107. Naphy, *Calvin and the Consolidation of the Genevan Reformation*, p. 38.

108. Naphy, *Calvin and the Consolidation of the Genevan Reformation*, p. 38.

109. "Pour le moins, nous avons telle forme de Baptesme que JESUS Christ a ordonnée, que les Apostres one gardée et suyvie, que l'Eglise primitive a eu en usage: et ne nous peult on reprendre d'autre chose, sinon que nous ne voulons pas ester plus sage, que Dieu mesme." *La Forme*, p. 38.

ments. In this definitional material, he quite explicitly and consistently drew upon Augustine's sacramental theology:

> We have in the sacraments another aid to our faith related to the preaching of the gospel. It is very important that some definite doctrine concerning them be taught, that we may learn from it both the purpose for which they were instituted and their present use.
>
> First, we must consider what a sacrament is. It seems to me that a simple and proper definition would be to say that it is an outward sign by which the Lord seals on our consciences the promises of his good will toward us in order to sustain the weakness of our faith; and we in turn attest our piety toward him in the presence of the Lord and of his angels and before men. Here is another briefer definition: one may call it a testimony of divine grace toward us, confirmed by an outward sign, with mutual attestation of our piety toward him. Whichever of these definitions you may choose, it does not differ in meaning from that of Augustine, who teaches that a sacrament is "a visible sign of a sacred thing," or "a visible form of an invisible grace," but it better and more clearly explains the thing itself. For since there is something obscure in his brevity, in which many of the less educated are deceived, I have decided to give a fuller statement, using more words to dispel all doubt.[110]

Calvin aimed for continuity with Augustine in his sacramental theology, even if he felt the need to spell out in some detail a number of things implicit in Augustine's approach to the subject.

In many ways for Calvin, the crux of the matter concerned the proper way that the sacramental sign and the thing signified in the sacrament must be properly distinguished. He argued for a crucial distinction between the baptismal sign of water and the divine reality to which the sign served as pointer.[111] The baptismal rite had as its meaning and substance none other than the crucified, risen, and ascended Jesus Christ.[112] Nothing but the singular event of the death and resurrection of Jesus Christ can bring about salvation for human beings. Thus, Calvin argued that human souls are cleansed not with "holy water," but solely with the blood of

---

110. Calvin, *Institutes* 4.14.1.

111. Calvin, "Catechism of the Church of Geneva," *Theological Treatises*, p. 132. See also *Institutes* 4.14.15.

112. Calvin, *Institutes* 4.14.16.

Christ.[113] That most central event in all of human history can never be repeated or reenacted. Its effects can only be applied. Thus, the sign and the thing signified must be distinguished, but not completely separated.[114]

In Calvin's view, the great mistake of medieval Latin Christianity involved a too close identification of the sign and the thing signified. That "thingification" of grace — to coin a phrase — resulted in a magical conception of baptism in which the application of the water itself, apart from the norms conveyed in the proclamation of the gospel narrative and without faith, brought about salvation and eternal life with the Triune God. Calvin partially differentiated himself from the Augustinian sacramental tradition at precisely this point. He strongly emphasized the sole efficacy of Christ's death and resurrection for human redemption. This led him to the conclusion that baptism was not absolutely essential for salvation.[115] Some people in admittedly extraordinary circumstances — like the repentant thief on the cross — had not been baptized, but had been saved, nonetheless, solely on the basis of faith in Jesus Christ. Similarly, by the grace and mercy of God, children who died in infancy prior to baptism were assuredly received into heaven on the basis of God's covenantal promises made to and by their parents.[116]

Calvin's conviction on the radical character of saving grace did not, however, lead him to treat baptism as an "empty sign."[117] Unlike Zwingli (and Barth), he argued for a sacramental view of baptism because he believed the Triune God worked in and through the rite.[118] Calvin's convic-

---

113. Calvin, *Institutes* 4.15.2. See also Calvin, "Catechism of the Church of Geneva," *Theological Treatises*, p. 133.

114. Calvin, *Institutes* 4.14.15-16.

115. Calvin, *Institutes* 4.15.20 and 4.16.26.

116. Calvin, *Institutes* 4.15.22.

117. Calvin, *Institutes* 4.15.17. See also Riggs, *Baptism in the Reformed Tradition*, pp. 54-58.

118. Calvin believed that sacraments were not "empty signs" and that the Triune God effected what had been promised when they were properly administered. *Institutes* 4.14.15-17. For Barth's views on baptism, see his *Church Dogmatics*, 4/4 (fragment), trans. G. W. Bromiley, ed. G. W. Bromiley and T. F. Torrance (Edinburgh: T & T Clark, 1969). Barth argued that Calvin did not go far enough in reforming the church according to Scripture at the point of baptism. In opposition to Calvin and in some degree of resonance with Zwingli, Barth argued that baptism constituted no more and no less than the paradigm of *human response* to divine grace. In this claim, Barth sought to "understand Zwingli better than he understood himself or could make himself understood" (p. 130).

tion on this point aimed to counter the Anabaptist radicals by means of an argument about divine integrity. He held that the trustworthiness of the Triune God impels us to believe that God will faithfully execute the promises made in baptism in the administration of the rite and in the future unfolding of the life of the baptizand. Strictly speaking, Calvin did not believe salvation required baptism; nevertheless, he believed that the promises of the Triune God come to realization in the baptismal rite when celebrated according to the simple and plain teaching of Scripture because God will do what God promises to do.[119] Forgiveness of sins, union with Christ, engraftment into the Body of Christ, deliverance from death, and assurance of future resurrection all actually and ordinarily take place in the celebration of the sacrament of baptism because God has promised to do them in the rite.[120]

Calvin's emphasis on the efficacy of divine promises points to another Augustinian dimension of his understanding of baptism. He affirmed and extended what Maxwell Johnson has described as Augustine's "sacramental minimalism."[121] Baptismal validity for Augustine and Calvin involved only the application of water in the Triune Name to a person. With this minimal condition met, baptism administered even by heretical or schismatic groups would count as objectively valid. Calvin echoed Augustine in this matter and brought into bold relief the Augustinian conviction as to the necessity of the proclamation of the Word in the celebration of the sacraments.[122] Calvin insisted, therefore, on a preached sermon immediately prior to baptism. His deep concern about the superstitious distortion of sacraments may explain why the Genevan baptismal liturgy tends toward an excess of words surrounding rather minimal liturgical action. Calvin's Augustinian minimalism combined with his relentless commitment to reform every liturgical practice according to Scripture and the evangelical teaching that arose from it led him to eschew all but the basics in the baptismal liturgy. He called for the abolition of the many elaborate sub-practices that added to the baptismal rite over the centuries. In particular, Calvin stripped the rite of such practices as exorcism, anointing with oil, the use of salt, the *ephaphtha*

---

119. Calvin, *Institutes* 4.14.17.
120. Calvin, *Institutes* 4.14.17.
121. Johnson, *The Rites of Christian Initiation*, p. 151.
122. Calvin, *Institutes* 4.14.3.

ceremony, the giving of candles, and the use of milk and honey at the Eucharistic table.[123] He viewed such practices as holdovers of an earlier idolatrous view of the meaning of baptism. He believed that baptism ought to function like the clear and unmistakable seal on a royal letter containing the message of the saving action of God in the death and resurrection of Jesus Christ.[124]

What about the efficacy of baptism? If the question of validity deals with the objective pole of the baptismal complex, the question of efficacy has to do with the subjective dimension of the rite.[125] Characteristically, Calvin differentiated these two aspects of the baptismal rite while simultaneously holding them together. The question of subjectivity with regard to the meaning of baptism points to a difficult set of issues in his thought; namely, the relation of faith, election, and the secret work of the Holy Spirit. According to Calvin, the Triune God gave the sacraments to the church in order "to establish and increase faith."[126] The objective validity of baptism must meet with faith on the part of the baptizand in order for grace of the sacrament to effect fundamental transformation of life. In Book III of the *Institutes,* he defined faith as "a firm and certain knowledge of God's benevolence toward us, founded upon the truth of the freely given promise in Christ, both revealed to our minds and sealed upon our hearts through the Holy Spirit."[127] The latter part of this Triune definition of faith is crucial for understanding the efficacy of baptism in the life of the baptizand. Inasmuch as it is a trusting knowledge of the benevolent disposition of the Triune God made known through the proclamation of the gospel, faith comes as a gift of the Triune God; saving faith is not an innate human capacity. Even though Calvin asserted that all human beings have an innate — if distorted — awareness of God, authentic or saving faith comes only through the secret work of the Holy Spirit in the depths of a person's mind and heart.[128]

The origin of faith points to a deeper and even more controversial is-

123. See Calvin, *La Forme,* p. 38.

124. Calvin, *Institutes* 4.14.5.

125. For discussions of the distinction between validity and efficacy of baptism, see especially Riggs, *Baptism in the Reformed Tradition,* pp. 60-70. For the Augustinian background to this distinction, see Johnson, *The Rites of Christian Initiation,* pp. 147ff.

126. Calvin, *Institutes* 4.14.9.

127. Calvin, *Institutes* 3.2.7.

128. Calvin, *Institutes* 3.1.4.

sue in Calvin's thought: election. In his view, the Triune God gives saving faith only to a limited number of human beings. Only those chosen by God for salvation are given genuine and enduring faith. God gives those destined for damnation only a dim awareness of genuine faith:

> For though only the predestined to salvation receive the light of faith and truly feel the power of the gospel, yet experience shows that the reprobate are sometimes affected by almost the same feeling as the elect, so that even in their own judgment they do not in any way differ from the elect [cf. Acts 13:48]. . . . Although there is a great likeness and affinity between God's elect and those who are given a transitory faith, yet only in the elect does that confidence flourish which Paul extols, that they loudly proclaim Abba, father [Gal. 4:6; cf. Rom. 8:15]. Therefore, as God regenerates only the elect with incorruptible seed forever [1 Pet. 1:23] so that the seed of life sown in their hearts may never perish, thus he firmly seals the gift of his adoption in them that it may be steady and sure. . . . The reprobate never receive anything but a confused awareness of grace, so that they grasp a shadow rather than the firm body of it. For the Spirit, strictly speaking, seals forgiveness of sins in the elect alone, so that they apply it by special faith to their own use.[129]

At the deepest level of Calvin's interpretation of the meaning of baptismal efficacy, we come to highly troubled waters.[130] The doctrine of predestina-

---

129. Calvin, *Institutes* 3.2.11.

130. Undoubtedly the most controversial of all of Calvin's teachings, the fundamental problem concerns the image of God that Calvin's doctrine of election evokes. Many have balked at the notion that a loving God would choose to create some or many people for damnation. Calvin's defense consisted of a resort to the mystery and unknowability of God's secret design for creation. To his credit, Calvin did not treat this radioactive subject under the doctrine of God (as with much subsequent Calvinist doctrine), but rather within the context of redemption. I. John Hesselink helpfully analyzes the pastoral significance of Calvin's situating of this doctrine in the context of faith. See Hesselink, *Calvin's First Catechism: A Commentary, Featuring Ford Lewis Battles' Translation of the 1538 Catechism* (Louisville: Westminster John Knox, 1997), pp. 93-100. Perhaps Calvin's treatment of this subject would have been met with less objection and hostility through the centuries if he had sounded a more agnostic tone with regard to knowing the size and composition of the reprobate. Even though he asserts that only God truly knows who the reprobate are and that, consequently, we must view all persons as potentially elect (see *Institutes* 4.1.3), one wonders if he occasionally had specific persons in mind when talking about the reprobate. Note Calvin's comment in the current quotation that "experience shows" that it is possible to

tion functioned as a crucial component in his understanding of authentic baptismal faith. All depends upon the freedom and grace of God; human capacities and initiatives count for nothing. Even faith itself comes as a divine gift. All human grounds for self-confidence are utterly smashed and taken away from us. He aimed to give all glory to the Triune God alone; human boasting has no place in his understanding of one's ultimate status before God.

The connection between faith, election, the sacrament of baptism, and the ascended Jesus Christ can be found in Calvin's pneumatology. The Holy Spirit, working secretly and inconspicuously in the heart, creates faith in the elect and thereby brings together the validity of baptism with its efficacy. Only the Holy Spirit can connect a person to Jesus Christ, who reigns in heaven. In other words, the Holy Spirit creates saving faith in Jesus Christ to the glory of the Father. For Calvin, the efficacy of baptism required a Triune grammar.

What does this mean for infants and children? Calvin did not make the absurd claim that newborn infants or very young children were in possession of faith. In his treatment of the question of baptismal efficacy in the case of infants and young children, he aimed to strike a crushing blow at the Anabaptists, who argued for believer's baptism precisely on the issue of the necessity of faith in relation to baptismal efficacy. He pursued a two-pronged assault against the Anabaptists on this matter. The first strategy involved fundamentally challenging the Anabaptist argument about the origin and nature of faith in Jesus Christ. The second strategy involved reframing the Anabaptists' biblical arguments for the qualifications for baptism.

To the challenge of the necessity of faith on the part of the baptizand, Calvin argued that the baptism of children was micro-eschatological. That is, children were baptized in hope and promise. Their faith would come about as they grew into maturity. "To sum up, this objection can be solved without difficulty: infants are baptized into future repentance and faith, and even though these have not yet been formed in them, the seed of both lies hidden within them by the secret working of the Spirit."[131] While elect

---

recognize the reprobate by their false or inconstant faith. As the result of pitched battles, Calvin may have violated his own teaching that only God knows those who are elect and those who are reprobate.

131. Calvin, *Institutes* 4.16.20.

infants do not have faith based on trusting knowledge of the saving acts of the Triune God in history, the Holy Spirit causes the "seeds" of faith and repentance implanted in them and watered in baptism to grow into authentic maturity as their life unfolds.[132]

The second line of attack concerns the covenantal nature of baptism. Calvin resolved the endless debate about whether or not children were baptized in the New Testament not by pointing to particular proof texts in which infants or children were baptized, but rather by locating baptism within the larger biblical framework of covenantal theology. Calvin's biblical solution to the question of infant baptism turned on his argument that just as the (male) children of Hebrew parents had been included in the covenantal community via circumcision prior to their understanding of and commitment to God's covenant with the people of Israel, so the parents belonging to the community of the New Covenant had the right and the obligation to present their children for baptism. Stressing the underlying continuity of substance in the two outward forms of circumcision and baptism, Calvin argued:

> Indeed, it is most evident that the covenant which the Lord once made with Abraham [cf. Gen. 17:14] is no less in force today for Christians than it was of old for the Jewish people, and that this word relates no less to Christians than it then related to the Jews. Unless perhaps we think that Christ by his coming lessened or curtailed the grace of the Father — but this is nothing but execrable blasphemy! Accordingly, the children of the Jews also, because they had been made heirs of his covenant and distinguished from the children of the impious, were called a holy seed [Ezra 9:2; Isa. 6:13]. For this reason the children of Christians are considered holy; and even though born with only one believing parent, by the apostle's testimony they differ from the unclean seed of idolaters [1 Cor. 7:14]. Now seeing that the Lord immediately after making the covenant with Abraham, commanded it to be sealed in infants by an

132. Riggs sees a contradiction here in Calvin's thought; *Baptism in the Reformed Tradition*, p. 70. He argues that baptism would not offer anything to the infant of believing parents that it did not already possess by virtue of election. Riggs may well have identified a point of tension or a rough edge in Calvin's thought here; nevertheless, Calvin's conviction with respect to the inseparability of the sign and the thing signified would appear to deal with Riggs's objection in that, for Calvin, what is promised in baptism is really imparted in the administration of the sacrament.

outward sacrament [Gen. 17:12], what excuse will Christians give for not testifying and sealing it in their children today?[133]

To be sure, members of the church were permitted and obligated to present their children for baptism inasmuch as the promise of inclusion in the Body of Christ in Acts 2:39 was given to believers and their children.[134]

The status of babies of believers who died without having been baptized was an important but exceptional matter in Calvin's understanding of baptism. He had no particular theological difficulty with the death of unbaptized infants. He argued that "infants are not barred from the Kingdom of Heaven just because they happen to depart the present life before they have been immersed in water."[135] His view of the immeasurable love of God would not permit him to accede to the Augustinian-inspired medieval notion that infants must be baptized as soon as possible after birth in order to ensure their salvation.

We have now traced several main features of Calvin's interpretation of the meaning of the baptismal rite. With the analysis of his understanding of baptismal validity and efficacy, we began to move toward the deeper theological underpinnings of his understanding of the meaning of the sacrament. To go further in tracing Calvin's understanding of the meaning of the sacrament of baptism, we must now pursue in greater depth the lines of theological investigation opened up by his discussion of the secret work of the Holy Spirit to bring about faith in and union with Jesus Christ. Calvin's interpretation of the meaning of baptism necessarily and inescapably points to his most fundamental beliefs about the nature and activity of the Triune God.

On Practices and Doctrines

Many today think of Calvin as a systematic theologian, due in large measure to the orderly and interconnected character of his *Institutes*. The carefully planned and interrelated *Institutes* do indeed provide ample justification for him to occupy a permanent seat among the pantheon of Christian

133. Calvin, *Institutes* 4.16.6.
134. Calvin, *Institutes* 4.16.15.
135. Calvin, *Institutes* 4.15.22.

theologians. Yet, I would argue that Calvin should not be categorized primarily as a systematic theologian in the modern sense of the term. While his theological vision bears many marks of a work of systematic theology, he nonetheless assiduously avoids philosophical abstraction and eschews the tight interlocking of ideas that the term *systematic* usually implies. Calvin primarily concerned himself with writing for the purpose of the edification and preservation of the church. He wrote in his preface to the king of France affixed to most editions of his *Institutes,* "My purpose was solely to transmit certain rudiments by which those who are touched with any zeal for religion might be shaped to true godliness."[136] Further, his famous opening statements about the necessarily interrelated knowledge of God and knowledge of all things human made the point even more forcefully: "Nearly all the wisdom we possess, that is to say, true and sound wisdom, consists of two parts: the knowledge of God and of ourselves. But, while joined by many bonds, which one precedes and brings forth the other is not easy to discern."[137] Calvin remained committed to this practical emphasis throughout his writings. He always employed theological reflection in the service of the correction and enhancement of ecclesial practice. He made the point rather clearly in his concluding comments on the doctrine of the Trinity in Book I of the *Institutes:*

> Finally, I trust that the whole sum of this doctrine has been faithfully explained, if my readers will impose a limit upon their curiosity, and not seek out for themselves more eagerly than is proper troublesome and perplexed disputations. For I suspect that those who intemperately delight in speculation will not be at all satisfied. Certainly I have not shrewdly omitted anything that I might think to be against me: but while I am zealous for the edification of the church, I felt that it would be better advised for me not to touch upon many things that would profit me but little, and would burden my readers with useless trouble.[138]

Even when dealing with the doctrine that habitually offers theologians the most opportunities for abstract and esoteric theological speculation, Calvin sought to avoid all impractical abstraction and useless speculation. We can see in this a key feature or characteristic of his thought: he attempted

---

136. Calvin, *Institutes,* "Prefatory Address to King Francis I of France," p. 9.
137. Calvin, *Institutes* 1.1.1.
138. Calvin, *Institutes* 1.13.29.

always to limit his theological reflections to those warranted by scriptural teachings and to that which was deemed necessary for meeting the practical challenges of strengthening and preserving the church in a life of vital faith and public witness.

The Doctrine of the Trinity

For Calvin, the theological grammar of baptism was trinitarian to the core. As with his depiction of the Christian life in general, we might be tempted to argue that he put the sole focus on Jesus Christ. Were we to argue for such a Christocentric reading of Calvin we might well miss the deeper theological framework within which he understood baptism. Too narrow a focus on Christ would obscure Calvin's deep and pervasive commitment to the doctrine of God as Trinity and the ways in which his Christology dovetailed with his understanding of the Trinity. His thought was marked by a remarkable reciprocation between Christology and Trinity.[139] While surely Christ is the proper object of baptism, the ultimate cause of baptismal grace resides in the First Person of the Trinity; furthermore, the ability to appropriate subjectively the grace given in baptism comes from the Holy Spirit.

In considering briefly the unique features of each of the Triune Persons as related to baptism, let us begin with what can be known on the basis of the text of Calvin's baptismal liturgy and then compare and complete that information with material from the *Institutes*. By working from the baptismal liturgy, we will gain a sense of what would have been communicated to ordinary churchgoers about the doctrine of the Trinity — at least implicitly — through the celebration of the rite. We will follow the same procedure when we come to the question of the relation among the divine Persons.

In the Genevan baptismal liturgy, Calvin portrays the First Person of the Trinity as eternal, all-powerful, and infinitely benevolent. The Father demands righteousness and justice of human beings.[140] Even though human beings fail to live according to the divine will because of the pervasive power of sin, the First Person desires to provide a remedy for this terrible

---

139. Calvin, *Institutes* 1.13.7-13; 3.1.1-3; and passim.
140. Calvin, *La Forme*, p. 31.

predicament. The first part of that remedy involves making human beings aware of their utter wretchedness and woefully misguided self-reliance.[141] The First Person, however, goes beyond judgment of human sin to provide the means for redemption and reconciliation. The First Person of the Trinity "desires to become our Father."[142]

The central emphasis of Calvin's baptismal liturgy with regard to the First Person has to do with the initiative of grace. Forgiveness of sins would appear to be the main present preoccupation of the Father.[143] In order to effect forgiving grace in history, the Father sent the Son to accomplish redemption in his death and resurrection. That would remain a remote and distant event if the Father did not also send the Holy Spirit to make it possible for human beings to take hold of Jesus Christ by faith. The Father's promise of forgiveness and adoption as well as the selection of water as the earthly vehicle for conveying that promise indicate reliability, trustworthiness, and faithfulness of the Father. What the Father promises to do, the Father does. These promises of human salvation are not only for adult believers. The Father also promises to be the God of the children of believers. The faithfulness and mercy of the Father extend beyond the immediate cohort of believers to include generations of their descendants, provided that those descendants affirm the covenant upon reaching the age of reckoning.[144]

The Father's gracious actions and promises come to fulfillment in the incarnation of the Son of God, the Second Person of the Trinity.[145] Through the recitation of the Western church baptismal creed (the Apostles' Creed) and in the condensed curricular instructions supplied immediately following the creed, the Genevan baptismal liturgy affirmed the Christology of both Nicea and Chalcedon.[146] The Son of God is of the same essence as the Father and the Spirit, and the Son is fully divine and fully human.

---

141. Calvin, *La Forme*, p. 31.

142. Calvin, *La Forme*, p. 32.

143. Calvin, *La Forme*, p. 31.

144. Calvin, *La Forme*, p. 35.

145. Calvin, *La Forme*, p. 33.

146. "En apres que en une seulle essence divine/nous recognoissons le Pere le Filz & le sainct Esprit. Pareillement que nous recepvons pour certaine verité L'histoire qui est escripte en L'evangile touchant la conception, Nativite, Mort, Resurrection et Ascension de JHuChrist." Calvin, *La Forme*, p. 35.

The death and resurrection of Jesus Christ serves as the focal point of Triune grace in human history.[147] The shed blood of Christ on the cross washes away sin and brings about restoration to the Father's original intent for human life by the work of the Holy Spirit.[148] Therefore, the substance or inner meaning of the sacrament of baptism is Jesus Christ, the Son of God. Baptism testifies to and connects the baptizand mystically to the death and resurrection of Jesus Christ. By means of this sacrament, the baptizand enters into union with Jesus Christ and becomes engrafted into the Body of Christ, the church.[149]

Calvin's Genevan baptismal liturgy communicated only what he considered to be the bare essentials about the Second Person of the Trinity. In the *Institutes* he had a good deal more to say about the Person and work of the Son.[150] The treatment of Christology found there expands upon the essentials inscribed in the order for baptism. For instance, in the *Institutes* he explored in detail the Anselmian rationale behind the incarnation as well as the threefold office of Christ as prophet, king, and priest.[151]

Calvin developed his treatment of the Second Person of the Trinity both in the baptismal liturgy and in the *Institutes* as primarily a soteriological and practical matter. His main concern was to interpret the Person and work of the Son of God in terms of the concrete existential predicament of human beings in relation to God. Characteristically, he avoided the temptation to speculate on the ontological depths of the mystery depicted by the Chalcedonian formulation. Calvin was less concerned with the ontological mechanics of the incarnation than with its practical implications.

The grace of the Father in giving the Son would have no meaning or value for human beings through the ages if it were not for the work of the Holy Spirit, who shares the same essence of divinity with them. Beyond

147. "L'accomplissement et de l'un et de l'autre est en nostre Seigneur JESUS, duquel la mort et passion a telle vertu et efficace qu'en participant à icelle, nous sommes comme ensepvelis à peché: afin que noz concupiscences charnelles soyent mortifies. Pareillement, par la vertu de sa resurrection, nous ressuscitons en nouvelle vie, qui est in Dieu: entant que son Esprit nous conduict et gouverne, pour faire en nous les oeuvres, lesquelles luy sont agreables." Calvin, *La Forme*, p. 32.

148. "Car nous n'avons point d'aultre lavement, que son sang." Calvin, *La Forme*, p. 33.

149. Calvin, *La Forme*, p. 34.

150. Calvin, *Institutes* 1.13.7-13, 26, and esp. 2.9-17.

151. Calvin, *Institutes* 2.12 and 2.15.

the assertion of the Father's willingness to forgive sin, the Father also sends the Spirit to work inside the subjectivity of the baptizand, bringing about the self-renunciation and taking hold of Jesus Christ that is characteristic of regeneration. The Father not only calls for mortification of the fleshly nature and spiritual vivification by adherence to Jesus Christ but also makes both possible by the inner working of the Holy Spirit.[152] Further, the Holy Spirit given by the Father enables and equips the baptizand to fight a lifelong battle against the unholy trinity of the devil, sin, and the lust of the flesh to the point of eventual victory.[153] Indeed, the Holy Spirit superintends the growth process of baptized babies to the point at which they recognize and affirm their commitment to God. The Holy Spirit continues to guide them to faith and doxology through the course of their lives.[154]

Calvin devoted Book III of the *Institutes* to pneumatology. Here again, as with Christology, he maintained a practical emphasis. The title of the third section of the *Institutes* communicates this quite clearly, "The Way in Which We Receive the Grace of Christ: What Benefits Come to Us from It, and What Effects Follow."[155] The *Institutes* contain much detail about the subtle and secret work of the Holy Spirit in creating faith and about the mystery of election, but the primary emphasis on the Spirit as the subjective dimension of grace remains consistent with implicit teachings promulgated in the baptismal liturgy itself.

What about the interrelations among the three divine Persons? How might we characterize their relations and the nature of their unity on the

---

152. "Or, quand it nous a remonstré nostre malheurté: il nous console semblablement, par sa misericorde, nous promettant, de nous regenerer pas son sainct Esprit, en une nouvelle vie laquelle nous soit comme une entrée en son Royaulme. Ceste regeneration consiste en deux parties; c'est que nous renoncions à nousmesmes, ne suyvant point nostre proper raison, nostre plaisir, et proper volunté: mais subiugant et captivant nostre entendement et nostre Coeur, à la sagesse et iustice de Dieu, moriffions tout ce qui est de nous et de nostre chair: puis apres, que nous suyvions la lumiere de Dieu, pour complaire et obtemperer à son bon plaisir, comme il nous le monster par sa parolle, et nous y conduict et dirige par son Esprit." Calvin, *La Forme*, pp. 30-31.

153. "Secondement, qu'il nous assistera par son sainct Esprit, afin que nous puissons batailler contre le Diable, le peché, et les concupiscences de nostre chair, iusques à en avoir victoire, pour vivre en la liberté de son Regne, qui est le Regne de iustice." Calvin, *La Forme*, p. 32.

154. Calvin, *La Forme*, p. 34.

155. Calvin, *Institutes* 3.1.

basis of the Genevan baptismal liturgy? There are two ways to answer this question. First, Calvin simply affirmed the crux of Nicene theology that the three divine Persons share the same divine essence *(homoousios)*. The liturgical text for the baptismal rite explicitly stressed the unity of three distinct Persons in the pedagogical directions given to parents.[156] This same message was conveyed implicitly in the use of the Apostles' Creed and in the traditional baptismal formula at the epicenter of the rite.

Second, as is evident from the above description of the work of each of the divine Persons in the baptismal liturgy, Calvin also depicted the relations among the Persons in terms of the economy of salvation. He provided no metaphysical speculation on this subject in the *Institutes;* only a description of how Father, Son, and Holy Spirit work together in harmony for the purpose of redemption in both macro- and micro-historical narratives:

> We know the most perfect way of seeking God, and the most suitable order, is not for us to attempt with bold curiosity to penetrate to the investigation of his essence, which we ought more to adore than meticulously to search out, but for us to contemplate him in his works whereby he renders himself near and familiar to us, and in some manner communicates himself.[157]

The construction of Calvin's baptismal liturgy makes it very difficult to describe the work of one of the Persons without making reference to the other two Persons. He expanded on this theme in the chapter in the *Institutes* devoted to the doctrine of God as Trinity. He argued that the differentiated unity of the Trinity functioned in part to oppose indeterminate conceptions of the divine: "But God also designates himself by another special mark to distinguish himself more precisely from idols. For he so proclaims himself the sole God as to offer himself to be contemplated in three persons. Unless we grasp these, only the bare and empty name of God flits about in our brains, to the exclusion of the true God."[158] Thus, when we turn to the *Institutes,* we find a complementary picture of the relations among the divine Persons.

The larger trinitarian framework lying behind Calvin's description of

---

156. Calvin, *La Forme,* p. 35.
157. Calvin, *Institutes* 1.5.9.
158. Calvin, *Institutes* 1.13.2.

baptism as pointing to and effecting union with Christ readily appears in this text from the chapter on the doctrine of the Trinity in Book I:

> Lastly, our faith receives from baptism the advantage of its sure testimony to us that we are not only engrafted into the death and life of Christ, but so united to Christ himself that we become sharers in all his blessings. For he dedicated and sanctified baptism in his own body [Matt. 3:13] in order that he might have it in common with us as the firmest bond of the union and fellowship which he has deigned to form with us. Hence, Paul proves that we are children of God from the fact that we put on Christ in baptism [Gal. 3:26-27]. Thus we see that the fulfillment of baptism is in Christ, whom also for this reason we call the proper object of baptism. Consequently, it is not strange that the apostles are reported to have baptized in his name [Acts 8:16; 19:5], although they had also been bidden to baptize in the name of the Father and of the Spirit [Matt. 28:19]. For all the gifts of God proffered in baptism are found in Christ alone. *Yet this cannot take place unless he who baptizes in Christ invokes also the names of the Father and the Spirit. For we are cleansed by his blood because our merciful Father, wishing to receive us into grace in accordance with his incomparable kindness, has set this Mediator among us to gain favor for us in his sight. But we obtain regeneration by Christ's death and resurrection only if we are sanctified by the Spirit and imbued with a new and spiritual nature. For this reason we obtain and, so to speak, clearly discern in the Father the cause, in the Son the matter, and in the Spirit the effect, of our purgation and our regeneration.*[159]

This pattern might be characterized as a "Cause-Object-Subject" economic trinitarianism. This pattern holds not only for baptism, but also for Calvin's entire depiction of the economy of salvation. In this sense, the baptismal rite and the theological content of his other writings have a reciprocal relationship. On the one hand, the baptismal liturgy contains in highly concentrated form all that is necessary and possible to know about the revelation of God in the economy of salvation. On the other hand, Calvin's vast array of biblical and theological works functions as various expository dimensions of the "Cause-Object-Subject" economic trinitarianism found in the baptismal liturgy.

If we look at the five-year period preceding the production of the

---

159. Calvin, *Institutes* 4.15.6; emphasis added.

Genevan baptismal liturgy, we find an interesting history of the development of Calvin's theological understanding of the theological grammar of baptism. If we go back to the original editorial layer of the *Institutes*, we find an emphasis that, though never completely lost, may have been obscured for readers of later editions. In the first edition of the *Institutes*, Calvin made clear the baptismal grounding of his teaching:

CATECHISM
OR INSTITUION OF THE CHRISTIAN RELIGION
Of the Church of Geneva previously published in the vernacular
And now at last rendered also in Latin, by
John Calvin.[160]

In this title, Calvin makes quite clear the close interrelation between baptism and catechesis, or doctrinal instruction. He intended the *Institutes* to serve precisely as a pedagogical instrument in the service of the sacrament of baptism. The *Institutes* were his attempt to offer an instruction manual for catechetical teachers who would provide instruction for those baptized babies who were coming of age and who sought admission to the sacrament of the Lord's Supper. He treats the term *institutes* in its Latin meaning of instruction or teaching as roughly equivalent to baptismally based "catechism." For Calvin, this teaching could never be abstract and speculative; it had to have a practical and hortative character. Such teaching would aim to edify or build up the Christian church through the proclamation of the immeasurable grace of the Father to the human family whereby the Son was given over to death as atonement for our sin and raised as the pattern of new and eternal life by the power of the Holy Spirit.

In 1537, Pierre Caroli accused Calvin of anti-trinitarian heresy. He demanded that Calvin demonstrate his trinitarian orthodoxy by signing a statement of adherence to the Apostles', Nicene, and Athanasian creeds.[161] Calvin refused to do so on the grounds that he would only give his allegiance to the plain teachings of Scripture. He argued that church councils, no matter how eminent, were prone to error and were not on par with Scripture. He also pointed out places in his writings in which he had clearly used orthodox trinitarian theological grammar. Though the Caroli

160. Hesselink, *Calvin's First Catechism*, p. 7.
161. Hesselink, *Calvin's First Catechism*, p. 110.

affair dogged him for many years and may have made him particularly sensitive to the issues at play in the matter of Servetus, Calvin demonstrated repeatedly his impeccable Nicene orthodoxy. The Caroli affair seems to have forced him to make explicit in his writings what had been implicit all along about the doctrine of God. In the latter 1530s and into the early 1540s, Calvin's trinitarian commitments came much more to the fore in his writings.

This can be seen in a brief comparison of his teaching on baptism in the Latin Catechism of 1538 and the Genevan baptismal liturgy of 1542. In the Catechism, Calvin wrote the following on baptism:

> Baptism was given to us by God: first, to serve our faith before him; secondly, to serve our confession before men. Faith looks to the promise by which our merciful Father offers the communication of his Christ, that clothed with him we may share in all his benefits. Baptism especially represents two things: the cleansing which we get in Christ's blood; and the mortification of our flesh which we attain from his death. For the Lord commanded his own to be baptized for forgiveness of sins. And Paul teaches that the church has been sanctified by Christ her bridegroom and cleansed in the bath of water, in the Word of life. Again, he states that we have been baptized into Christ's death, buried together with him in his death, that we may walk in newness of life. These words do not signify that the cause or effective working of cleansing or regeneration inheres in the water, but only that the knowledge of such gifts is received in this sacrament when we are said to receive, obtain, get what we believe to have been given us by the Lord, whether at the time we first acknowledge it, or are more surely persuaded of it as previously acknowledged.
>
> Thus it serves our confession among men. Indeed, it is a mark whereby we openly profess that we wish to be numbered among God's people in order to worship one God in the same religion along with all godly men. Since therefore the covenant of the Lord with us is principally ratified by baptism, we rightly baptize our infants, as sharers in the eternal covenant by which the Lord promises that he will be the God not only of us but also of our descendants.[162]

Calvin gives expression to many of the themes found in the baptismal rite of 1542. Conspicuously absent, however, is a full-orbed and explicit trini-

162. Hesselink, *Calvin's First Catechism*, p. 34.

tarian grammar. In this text, he only mentions the Father and the Son at work in baptism. The Spirit's activity is not mentioned explicitly. This teaching must, though, be seen in relation to his exposition of the third article of the Apostles' Creed earlier in the Catechism. There, Calvin had pointed to the work of the Holy Spirit as that which makes possible all the things associated with baptism: cleansing of sin, mortification and vivification, illumination, and so forth.[163]

When we turn to Calvin's introductory remarks on the exposition of the Apostles' Creed in the same 1538 Catechism, we see quite clearly that he held to the Nicene orthodoxy that would by stages come to permeate his entire theological vision:

> We spoke above of what we obtain in Christ through faith. Now we must hear what our faith ought to look to in Christ and to ponder how it is to be strengthened. This is explained in what is called "the Creed." That is to say, in what way Christ was by the Father for us made wisdom, redemption, life, righteousness, and sanctification. Who the author was or rather who wrote down this epitome of the faith is not of great concern to us, for it contains nothing merely human but has been assembled from very sure testimonies of Scripture. Lest anyone may be perturbed that we confess we believe in Father, Son, and Holy Spirit, we must say a few preliminary things about this matter. When we name Father, Son, and Spirit, we are not fashioning three Gods, but in the simplest unity of God and Scripture *and the very experience of godliness* we are showing ourselves God the Father, his Son, and Spirit. Our understanding cannot conceive of the Father without including the Son at the same time, in whom his living image shines; and the Spirit in whom his might and power are visible. Let us cleave with the total concentration of our mind upon the one God; yet in the meantime let us contemplate the Father with his Son and Spirit.[164]

Calvin's assertion that we know the doctrine of the Trinity not only from Scripture, but also "in the very experience of godliness" immediately stands out in this passage. What could he have meant by it? Inasmuch as the "experience of godliness" has to do with the life based on union with Jesus Christ in his death and resurrection, he surely intended an oblique

---

163. Hesselink, *Calvin's First Catechism*, p. 25.
164. Hesselink, *Calvin's First Catechism*, pp. 21-22; emphasis added.

reference to an existential or practical trinitarianism arising from baptism. It may be the case that Calvin found some inspiration for this line of argument in his reading of Basil of Caesarea's *De Spiritu Sancto* in which Basil argued from the experience of baptismal transformation to the divinity of the Holy Spirit.[165] In any case, Calvin thought at this point that the very character of the experience of the Christian life initiated by baptism bore an unmistakably trinitarian stamp.

In addition to the somewhat surprising assertion that the doctrine of the Trinity may be known from reflection upon the character and quality of life that issues forth from baptism, this passage also points to another distinctive feature of Calvin's practical trinitarianism at this early stage of his thought. We can see the interplay here between the unity and the plurality of the Trinity that will characterize his fully developed trinitarian theological approach to the interpretation of baptism. He worked this alternation between the oneness of God and the three distinct Persons into the 1539 edition of his *Institutes* published in Strasbourg:

> Again, Scripture sets forth a distinction of the Father from the Word, and of the Word from the Spirit. Yet the greatness of the mystery warns us how much reverence and sobriety we ought to use in investigating this. And that passage in Gregory of Nazianzus vastly delights me:
> "I cannot think on the one without quickly being encircled by the splendor of the three, nor can I discern the three without being straightway carried back to the one." Let us not, then, be led to imagine a trinity of persons that keeps our thoughts distracted and does not at once lead them back to that unity. Indeed the words "Father," "Son," and "Spirit" imply a real distinction — let no one think that these titles, whereby God is variously designated from his works, are empty — but a distinction, not a division.[166]

It certainly cannot have escaped Calvin's notice that he came across this vastly delighting statement — which he used several times in his explicit statements on the Triune mystery — from Gregory Nazianzen in the lat-

---

165. See Ellen T. Charry, *By the Renewing of Your Minds: The Pastoral Function of Christian Doctrine* (New York: Oxford University Press, 1997), esp. pp. 116-17. See also Johnson, *The Rites of Christian Initiation*, p. 111.

166. Calvin, *Institutes* 1.13.17. The editorial notation in the McNeill edition indicates that this passage originated in the 1539 Strasbourg edition of the *Institutes*.

ter's sermon, "On Holy Baptism."[167] T. F. Torrance rightly points out that this centrally placed Cappadocian affirmation at the core of Calvin's otherwise largely Augustinian approach to the doctrine of the Trinity makes him a particularly fruitful resource for building bridges between Eastern and Western forms of Christianity.[168]

In the Genevan baptismal liturgy of 1542, the interconnections between the Holy Spirit and baptism as well as a pervasive and thoroughly trinitarian theological grammar for baptism are clearly discernible. The controversy with Caroli combined with his broadening base of experience as pastor and liturgical leader in the French Protestant congregation during his Strasbourg years seems to have motivated Calvin to flesh out and bring to the fore not only his trinitarian pneumatology but also the deep trinitarian theological grammar of baptism. By the time Calvin wrote the "Catechism of the Church of Geneva" in 1545, the section on sacraments in general and on baptism in particular came to have an explicitly trinitarian substructure.[169]

It is interesting to note further along these lines that in the 1543 edition of the *Institutes,* Calvin for the first time shifted from treating the content of the Apostles' Creed in a single chapter to breaking out the content of the creed into a chapter for each of the divine Persons in the Godhead. Later, in

---

167. Calvin, *Institutes* 1.13.17. See also Calvin's *Commentary on the Gospel According to John,* vol. 1, trans. William Pringle (Grand Rapids: Eerdmans, 1949), p. 29. Gregory of Nazianzus, *On Holy Baptism,* Oration xl. 41 (J. Migne, *Patrologia graeca* [Parisiis: Garnier, 1857-91], 36.418; A Select Library of Nicene and Post-Nicene Fathers of the Christian Church, 2nd series [Grand Rapids: Eerdmans, reprint, 1994], 7.375).

168. Torrance writes: "Before we proceed further let me say something about the relation of Calvin to Augustine. It is certainly true that Calvin cites Augustine far more than any other all through his writings, and refers to him time and time again in what he says about the Trinity. However, I find that at every essential point the basic conceptions that Calvin wants to adduce come from Gregory, and from Gregory's theological heir Athanasius the Great. . . . Calvin seems to me to direct his readers to Augustine for two main reasons: because Augustine was the acknowledged *magister theologiae* in the West so that appeal to him had great debating value for Reformed theology, but also because the basic teaching of Gregory Nazianzen was given its most extended Latin interpretation in Augustine's *De Trinitate.* It is hardly surprising, therefore, that Philip Melanchthon quickly discerned the inner connection between Calvin's doctrine of the Trinity and that of Gregory, in spite of the Augustinian overlay, when he put forward the idea that Calvin should also be entitled 'the Theologian.'" T. F. Torrance, *Trinitarian Perspectives: Toward Doctrinal Agreement* (Edinburgh: T&T Clark, 1994), p. 22.

169. Calvin, "Catechism of the Church of Geneva," in *Theological Treatises,* pp. 129-35.

the 1559 final edition of the *Institutes* he further pushed his trinitarian commitments to center stage by utilizing the trinitarian pattern of the Apostles' Creed as the architectonic for the entire work.[170] In this brief evolutionary analysis we can see that Calvin moved from an implicit trinitarianism that undergirded his baptismally based instruction in the faith with an essentially binitarian theological grammar for baptism to an explicit and pervasive trinitarian architectonic for teaching the essentials of the faith with a thoroughly trinitarian interpretation of the meaning of baptism.

Ecclesial Pedagogy

Calvin's trinitarian interpretation of the sacrament of baptism pointed to his theological anthropology.[171] In the preface to the liturgy for baptism, he wove together his practical trinitarian grammar of baptism and his understanding of the human condition to which baptism responds.[172] Baptism functions as a sign and symbol of the Triune economy of salvation for human beings. Father, Son, and Holy Spirit work harmoniously together in history to rescue and to restore fallen humanity.

Calvin built his theological anthropology on the foundation of Augustine's teaching on original sin. Human beings are born into a state of alienation from God characterized by sin, miserable servitude, disease, and spiritual blindness.[173] This condition inevitably results in death. All hu-

---

170. Hesselink, *Calvin's First Catechism,* p. 110.

171. "We cannot have a clear and complete knowledge of God unless it is accompanied by a corresponding knowledge of ourselves. This knowledge of ourselves is twofold: namely, to know what we were like when we were first created and what our condition became after the fall of Adam." Calvin, *Institutes* 1.15.1.

172. Calvin, *La Forme,* pp. 30-31.

173. In the *Institutes,* Calvin carefully defined his understanding of human depravity. "There is no doubt that Adam, when he fell from his state, was by this defect alienated from *God.* Therefore, even though we grant that God's image was not totally annihilated and destroyed in him, yet it was so corrupted that whatever remains is frightful deformity. Consequently, the beginning of our recovery of salvation is in that restoration which we obtain through *Christ,* who also is called the Second Adam for the reason that he restores us to true and complete integrity. . . . Now God's image is the perfect excellence of human nature which shone in Adam before his defection, but was subsequently so vitiated and almost blotted out that nothing remains after the ruin except what is confused, mutilated, and disease-ridden. Therefore in some part it now is manifest in the elect, insofar as they have

man efforts at cure prove futile and serve only to aggravate the predicament. Human beings simply cannot help themselves out of the stinking pit of sin and death. Only the Triune God can provide reconciliation through the forgiveness of sins, healing of the fatal wound, and illumination of the understanding. This rescue operation depends on divine initiative and freedom. The sacrament of baptism epitomizes and enacts the entire historical drama of salvation.

This does not mean, however, that the Triune God works by punctiliar fiat inside the mind and heart of the baptizand. Though baptism functions in many ways as *the* defining moment in a person's life, it functions as something far more than a momentary event wrought in the Triune God. In an exposition and commentary on the doctrinal agreement among the Swiss Reformed churches published in 1554, Calvin wrote of the larger impact of baptism on the life of the baptizand:

> Then, seeing that repentance and advancement in it ought to be our constant study even until death, who sees not that baptism is impiously mutilated if its virtue and fruit, *which embraces the whole course of life,* is not extended beyond the outward administration? *Nay, no greater affront to the sacred symbols can be imagined than to hold that their reality is in force only at the time of the actual exhibition. My meaning is, that though the visible figure immediately passes away, the grace which it testifies still remains, and does not vanish in a moment with the spectacle exhibited to the eye.*[174]

Much more than a singular event in which a few drops of water are applied to the head of an infant, baptism serves as the paradigm for the whole of the Christian life. As the paradigm for the ongoing work of transformation by God in the life of the baptizand, baptism attests to the secret work of the Holy Spirit within the heart of the baptized elect to bring the seeds of faith and repentance to full flower. This secret and subtle work of the Spirit, however, ordinarily occurs through the secondary human means of ecclesial pedagogy:

---

been reborn in the *Spirit,* but it will attain its full splendor in heaven." *Institutes* 1.15.4; emphasis added.

174. John Calvin, "Mutual Consent in Regard to the Sacraments" (1554), in *Calvin's Tracts and Treatises,* vol. 2, trans. H. Beveridge, notes by T. F. Torrance (Grand Rapids: Eerdmans, 1958), p. 237; emphasis added.

We see how God, who could in a moment perfect his own, nevertheless desires them to grow into manhood solely under the education of the church. We see the way set for it: the preaching of the heavenly doctrine has been enjoined upon the pastors. We see that all are brought under the same regulation, that with a gentle and teachable spirit they may allow themselves to be governed by teachers appointed for this function. . . . From this it follows that all those who spurn this spiritual food, divinely extended to them through the hand of the church, deserve to perish in famine and hunger . . . today it is his will to teach us through human means.[175]

In a way analogous to his complex and paradoxical linkage between the sign and the thing signified in sacramental theology, Calvin argued that ecclesial pedagogy ought to be taken both with utmost seriousness and with appropriate caution to avoid slipping into the mistaken belief that practices of ecclesial pedagogy produce Christian faith. For him, the sovereign freedom of the Triune God must be preserved at all times and at all costs![176] While the Triune God is not absolutely bound to use practices of ecclesial pedagogy, this does appear to be God's preferred means — along with preaching — for the evocation, establishment, and evolution of authentic Christian faith.

Aimed at establishing an effective approach to ecclesial pedagogy, Calvin sought to revive and reformulate the ancient church's baptismally oriented pedagogical practices. In the third and final part of his 1537 "Articles concerning the Organization of the Church and of Worship" produced during his first stint in Geneva, Calvin stated very clearly the relationship between his pedagogical efforts and the catechumenate of the ancient church:

175. Calvin, *Institutes* 4.1.5.

176. Craig Dykstra makes a similar point about the relationship between religious practices and God's transforming activities in the lives of those who engage in such practices. He writes, "[Practices] are not, finally, activities we do to make something spiritual happen in our lives. Nor are they duties we undertake to be obedient to God. *Rather, they are patterns of communal action that create openings in our lives where the grace, mercy, and presence of God may be made known to us.* They are places where the power of God is experienced. In the end, these are not ultimately our practices but forms of participation in the practice of God." Craig Dykstra, *Growing in the Life of Faith: Education and Christian Practices* (Louisville: Geneva, 1999), p. 66; emphasis added.

The third article concerns the instruction of children, who without doubt ought to make a confession of their faith to the Church. For this purpose, in ancient days, a definite catechism was used for initiating each one in the fundamentals of the Christian religion: and this might be a formula of witness, which each could use to declare his Christianity. The children were individually taught from this catechism, and had to come to testify to their faith to the Church, to which they were unable at their Baptism to render witness. For we see that Scripture has always joined confession with faith; and it has told us that, if we truly believe with the heart, it is right that we ought also to confess with the mouth to that salvation which we believe. Now if this ordinance has ever been proper and appropriate, it is more than ever necessary now, in view of the neglect of the Word of God which we see in most people, and the contempt of parents in instructing their children in the way of God, from which one sees a remarkable rudeness and great ignorance which is quite intolerable in the Church of God.[177]

Never mind the fact that Calvin's conception of the ancient church catechumenate bore little actual resemblance to the thing itself! Even though the catechumenate focused much more on the process of making Christian disciples through the transformation of beliefs and practices — not to mention the fact that the early church catechumenate was designed for adult converts, not baptized babies — Calvin was convinced that early church pedagogy focused on the transmission of essential doctrinal teaching drawn from and illuminating biblical teaching. The point is not whether he had an accurate picture of what went on in the church's educational ministry in the fourth or fifth century (most probably, he did not); rather, the point is that he thought that baptism required a well-developed system of ecclesial pedagogy in order for the reality to which the sacrament pointed to come to full fruition in the lives of the baptized. For Calvin, the fundamental transformation of human life as epitomized in the baptismal liturgy required a comprehensive para-liturgical pattern of ecclesial pedagogy.

What were the aims of ecclesial pedagogy for Calvin? The *telos* of the church's post-baptismal educational efforts entailed helping children and

---

177. Calvin, "Articles concerning the Organization of the Church and of Worship at Geneva proposed by the Ministers at the Council, January 16, 1537," in *Theological Treatises*, p. 54.

youth "exhibit the power of their Baptism" in faith and ongoing repentance (understood as mortification of the flesh and vivification through union with Christ).[178] Even though in baptism the Triune God promises (and in some sense actually fulfills the promise) to deliver the baptizand from sin, the deliverance given to the elect in baptism is "the guilt of sin, rather than . . . the very substance of sin."[179] The baptized person must struggle throughout the entire course of his or her life with the ongoing effects of sin, even if divine judgment for sin has been decisively removed. The fundamental process of exhibiting the power of baptism in one's life follows the dual rhythm of mortification and vivification. One must continually put to death the lingering tendrils of sin while simultaneously taking ever stronger hold of Jesus Christ. The inner trajectory of this dying and rising pattern of Christian life leads to doxology; that is, exhibiting the power of baptism means ultimately to grow in "earnest zeal for worshiping God."[180]

Behind the scenes of ecclesial pedagogy, as it were, the Triune God functions as the sole Teacher of the baptized elect. In some places, Calvin refers to Jesus Christ as the Teacher of the baptized.[181] In other places, he refers to the Holy Spirit as the baptismal Pedagogue par excellence.[182] Behind and through the work of the church's educational ministry, Calvin urged the baptized to see the work of the Triune Teacher.

Calvin's convictions about the character of the Triune God's formational and transformational activities in the life of the baptizand led

178. Calvin's depiction of the Christian life as mortification and vivification has to do with participating in the death and resurrection of Jesus Christ. This conception is an outgrowth of the conviction that baptism is the paradigm for the Christian life (esp. in relation to Romans 6). See *Institutes* 3.3.3-9 and 4.15.4-6.

179. Calvin, *Institutes* 3.3.11.

180. Calvin, *Institutes* 4.16.9.

181. Calvin, *Institutes* 4.8.7: "The Father by a singular privilege ordained the Son as our teacher, commanding him, and not any man, to be heard." See also *Institutes* 2.15.2, 3.1.4 n. 9, 3.2.4 and 6, and 3.20.48 (as listed by J. T. McNeill in "Subject Index" to *Institutes*, p. 1704).

182. Calvin, *Institutes* 4.14.9: "But the sacraments properly fulfill their office only when the Spirit, that inward teacher, comes to them, by whose power alone hearts are penetrated and affections moved and our souls opened for the sacraments to enter in. If the Spirit be lacking, the sacraments can accomplish nothing more in our minds than the splendor of the sun shining upon blind eyes or a voice sounding in deaf ears." See also *Institutes* 1.9.1, 3.1.4 n. 9, 3.2.34, 4.14.9, and 4.17.36 (as listed by J. T. McNeill in "Subject Index" to *Institutes*, p. 1704).

him to emphasize the importance of intentional pedagogical practices in the congregation and in the home. Because the Triune God prefers to utilize ordinary human means to accomplish pedagogical ends, an instructional partnership between the local church and the home is forged anew with each celebration of the sacrament of baptism. Teachers in the church and parents in the home bear significant pedagogical responsibilities in Calvin's vision. Calvin and the company of pastors held parents accountable for the quality of teaching in the home and for regularly bringing their children for instruction in the church.

Calvin understood divine pedagogy to have a trinitarian grammar. If we return to the Genevan baptismal liturgy to look at the content of the teaching to which parents were asked to commit themselves in their homes, we find an integral linkage between baptism, teaching, and the doctrine of the Trinity. Once parents had affirmed their intent to have their children baptized in the name of the Triune God, the presiding pastor would spell out the expectations with regard to the content of that teaching in some considerable detail as an integral part of the baptismal rite.

Parents were exhorted to commit themselves to teaching their child the Christian faith in word and deed. Immediately following the parental affirmation that they desired their child to be baptized in the name of the Trinity, the presiding pastor admonished the parents to teach the basics of Christian belief and practice at home. When their child reached the appropriate age, the parents were to help her or him memorize the Apostles' Creed and to learn how to interpret its essential meaning. It was not enough for parents to promote rote memorization of the Apostles' Creed by their child; they needed also to teach their baptized youngster the explicitly trinitarian character of the mystery of God and the Christian life. Parents committed themselves to teaching the basics of the Christian gospel and essential practices of the Christian faith (such as prayer and following the Ten Commandments) using a trinitarian grammar.[183]

Calvin called upon pastors and elders to use home visitation as an occasion for pedagogical accountability stemming from the pledges made at baptism. Pastors and elders were "to warn and exhort in every house" with respect to the diligence with which parents were teaching the basics of

183. Calvin, *La Forme*, pp. 35-36.
184. Calvin, *Institutes* 4.12.2.

Christian faith and practice to their children.[184] Not only were parents expected to commit themselves in the Genevan baptismal service to providing primary pedagogical leadership for their children, but also they were to see to it that their children regularly participated in the educational activities of the church.

In Calvin's pedagogical vision, domestic pedagogical practices were necessary but insufficient. The church should also educate baptized children (and adults) in the full meaning of their baptism. To that end, every service of worship carried a strongly pedagogical dimension. Preaching in particular was to be a means of in-depth biblical instruction as well as exhortation to faithful living. Liturgy itself — aesthetically spartan though it might have been — provided an effective vehicle for teaching authentic and scripturally based worship of the Triune God. Calvin believed that a rite administered without proclamation of the Word and without explanatory teaching would lead inevitably back to the magical views of the sacraments that were prevalent in the Middle Ages. He believed that the rite itself should have an instructional valence to it. Liturgy should be suffused with pedagogical instruction. Proper liturgical action depended, at least in part, on adequate instruction in the midst of the rite. The conjunction of religious practice and religious instruction set apart the sacrament of baptism from other initiation practices that may also have involved water. The liturgical act must be interpreted in reference to the teaching and proclamation of the scriptural narrative of God's acts of salvation in the life, death, and resurrection of Jesus Christ, the Word of God incarnate. This accounts for much of the wordiness of Calvin's liturgical texts. It also explains why the celebration of baptism could never precede the sermon in Geneva.

Of the four Sunday services in Geneva, Calvin organized the third or noontime service as a practice of ecclesial pedagogy. This catechetical service focused on instruction in the basics of baptismally based Christian discipleship. Calvin scholar Elsie McKee provides helpful information on this catechetical service:

> The catechism service at noon in each Genevan parish was a regular time of weekly instruction. The substance of the study was Calvin's 1542-1545 catechism, with its fifty-five divisions of questions on faith and the Apostles' Creed, law and the Decalogue, prayer and the Lord's Prayer, and the sacraments. The chief purpose of the catechism services

was to prepare children and others for admission to the Lord's Supper, and so it became the custom on the four Sundays each year prior to the celebration of the supper to have a public examination of the candidates who were considered ready to give an account of their faith. Calvin's catechism was a summary of the doctrine Genevans were supposed to understand, but in the examination the children were asked a series of much simpler questions.[185]

Those much simpler examination questions began with economic trinitarianism as depicted by the Apostles' Creed, moved through the Decalogue, culminated in the account of the death and resurrection of Jesus Christ, continued with prayer, and concluded with the sacraments of baptism and the Lord's Supper.[186] This abbreviated curriculum dovetailed with the core curriculum outlined for parents in the baptismal liturgy, with Calvin's larger catechetical writings, and with his *Institutes*.

Fathers were expected to bring their baptized children to the weekly catechism services in each parish. Failure to present children at the service would be reported to the Consistory. If appropriate admonitions and warnings continued to go unheeded and the children still were not brought to the Sunday pedagogy services on a regular basis, then the matter would be turned over to the civil authorities, who would determine appropriate punishments.[187]

The close connection between practices of ecclesial pedagogy and practices of ecclesial discipline seem quite heavy-handed to most contemporary readers. Two things must be kept in mind, however, in order to properly interpret Calvin's close connection between ecclesial pedagogy and discipline. First, Calvin and the company of pastors administered baptism on a fairly indiscriminate basis in Geneva. As long as they were not excommunicate, Genevan parents could present their children for baptism. Since it did not make sense to require faith of infants, they would be baptized on the basis of covenantal promises made by the Triune God in the hope that the Holy Spirit would give the gift of faith and repentance to the child in the future.

Second, only those who provided adequate evidence of faith would be allowed to partake of the holy meal. The pastors worried that those who

185. McKee, *John Calvin*, p. 101.
186. McKee, *John Calvin*, pp. 101-4.
187. Calvin, "Draft Ecclesiastical Ordinances," in *Theological Treatises*, p. 69.

came to the Lord's table unprepared would fall into the sort of divine judgment described in 1 Corinthians 11:17-34. Faith, a notoriously difficult matter to observe directly, would be verified only indirectly on the basis of public profession of faith, mastery of the rudiments of the Catechism, and evidence of a Christian pattern of life.

Post-baptismal catechesis, then, functioned as a form of church discipline in Calvin's Geneva.[188] In the early church, the predominant pattern of initiation entailed a period of engagement in a well-defined pattern of practices of ecclesial pedagogy culminating in the conjoined celebration of baptism and the Eucharist during the Easter vigil. The period of post-baptismal catechetical instruction would have been relatively brief. This instruction would have focused mainly on the meaning of the sacramental realities experienced in and around the baptism-Eucharist liturgical complex. In marked contrast, Calvin required engagement in a rigorous and extended pattern of post-baptismal catechetical formation on the way to participation in the Eucharist. Since he assumed paidobaptism as the normative practice, a prolonged and well-developed pattern of post-baptismal catechesis made sense.

In Calvin's vision, ecclesial pedagogy did not conclude when a young person successfully passed the catechetical examination and participated in the Eucharist. The baptismal covenant required a lifelong process of learning and growth in faith. In a passage reminiscent of Cyprian, Calvin wrote of the church that "there is no other way to enter into life unless this mother conceive us in her womb, give us birth, nourish us at her breast, and lastly, unless she keep us under her care and guidance until, putting off mortal flesh, we become like the angels [Matt. 22:30]. Our weakness does not allow us to be dismissed from her school until we have been pupils all our lives."[189] There is, then, no such thing as adolescent graduation from the church's educational ministry for Calvin. Post-baptismal catechesis began at the baptismal font and continued in principle until the mourners lowered the baptizand's coffin into the ground.

Calvin believed that such lifelong post-baptismal catechesis should

---

188. Calvin rejected confirmation as a sacrament. He described it in the preface to his Genevan Catechism in rather caustic terms. "In fact, the whole business [of confirmation] consists in nothing but theatrical gesticulations, or rather the wanton sport of monkeys, without even imitative skill." "Catechism of the Church of Geneva," in *Theological Treatises*, p. 91.

189. Calvin, *Institutes* 4.1.4.

have a decidedly trinitarian cast. In his masterful treatment of the comprehensively trinitarian character of Calvin's approach to the many dimensions and complexities of the divine-human relationship, Philip Butin points out that Calvin saw the necessary interconnectedness of baptism, the Trinity, and ecclesial pedagogy:

> Calvin saw an intrinsic connection between trinitarian baptism and the long catholic tradition of comprehensive catechesis of the baptized in Christian worship, doctrine, and practice. Through this connection of baptism and catechesis, trinitarian baptism was understood as a visible reflection of the comprehensiveness of God's grace for each aspect of the Christian life.[190]

For Calvin, the basis and the content of the instruction about the character of baptismal grace were thoroughly trinitarian in character. Butin's observations about this interplay in Calvin's thought resonates well with the efforts undertaken here to demonstrate that Calvin understood the sacrament of baptism, the doctrine of the Trinity, and practices of ecclesial pedagogy to belong necessarily together.

Summary and Assessment

The Genevan reformer offers us several important and usable themes with regard to the nexus of baptism, the Trinity, and ecclesial pedagogy. First, Calvin's reform of the baptismal rite itself offers several important insights that may be appropriated today. In order to avoid the notion that the baptismal rite was somehow magical, he reaffirmed Augustine's teaching that a sacrament has to have both the Word of God and material substance. The reemphasis on the teaching of the Word meant that the baptismal liturgy itself carried a teaching valence. For Calvin, the liturgical celebration of baptism functioned as a form of ecclesial pedagogy. We can see again this emphasis on the pedagogical dimensions of worship in the catechetical service offered every Sunday in Geneva.

Second, the various dimensions of Calvin's interpretation of the

---

190. Philip W. Butin, *Revelation, Redemption, and Response: Calvin's Trinitarian Understanding of the Divine-Human Relationship* (New York: Oxford University Press, 1995), p. 107.

meaning of baptism may also serve as a constructive resource for today. In contradistinction to Gregory of Nyssa and most of the early church fathers, Calvin avoided the problem of over-identification of the sacramental sign and the thing signified. His view of sacramentality was rather complex. He held something of a middle position between the extreme of over-identification of the thing and the thing signified and a complete rupture of the two at the other extreme (as in the case of Zwingli and Barth). The water does not save anyone in and of itself; only the atoning death and life-conferring resurrection of Jesus Christ can wash away sin and reconcile one to the Triune God. Yet, inasmuch as baptism serves as a testimony to the Triune promise of grace and because the Triune God can be counted on to faithfully carry out promises that are made, baptism can be said to bring about that to which it testifies.

Calvin interpreted baptism as mystical participation in the death and resurrection of Jesus Christ. It symbolizes and enacts union with Christ. Calvin's Christocentrism, however, is thoroughly and unapologetically trinitarian. He taught that the twin baptismal themes of mortification and vivification are not only paradigmatic for the entirety of the Christian life, but also that their grammar is trinitarian. The Father wills for the baptized elect to enter into faithful union with Jesus Christ and this is made possible by the secret and persistent work of the Holy Spirit in the subjectivity of the baptizand throughout his or her life.

Third, Calvin's trinitarian grammar of baptism turns out to be paradigmatic not only for the shape of the Christian life, but also for the interpretation of all ecclesial practices. For example, Bible reading, preaching, and prayer can only be interpreted by Calvin in reference to the Triune grammar of grace operative within the entire economy of salvation and as distilled and condensed in the Genevan baptismal rite. The assessment of Calvin's contribution on this subject resonates well with Butin's claim to the effect that

> as a "means of grace" and a sacrament, baptism — with its explicitly Trinitarian basis, pattern, and dynamic — makes the triune grace of God visible and tangible as the basis, pattern, and dynamic of the divine-human relationship. At the same time, baptism renders the comprehensiveness of God's Trinitarian grace visible in the Christian life.... The implication of baptism for the divine-human relationship is thus that the visible outworking of God's Trinitarian grace in the life of be-

lievers implies the comprehensive integration of Christian belief, worship, and practice.[191]

If, as Butin claims, it is true that Calvin researchers have historically tended to underestimate the pervasive trinitarianism in his thought, such is doubly the case with respect to both the paradigmatic role of baptism and the interplay of baptism, Trinity, and pedagogy for Calvin.

Contemporary thinkers concerned with practical trinitarianism might well benefit from taking seriously the increasing importance Calvin gave to the trinitarian pattern of the Western baptismal creed as the essential pattern for organizing the content of ecclesial pedagogy. We saw in our analysis of the baptismal liturgy that the first item of the "core curriculum" provided to parents concerned teaching the basics of Nicene trinitarianism. Calvin introduced this as the first thing parents should teach their growing child because it provided the indispensable theological framework for the teaching of essential Christian beliefs and practices. In the Latin Catechism of 1538, he emphasized that the doctrine of the Trinity should be taught not only on the basis of scriptural interpretation, but also from reflection upon the unfolding experiences of baptismal grace. In the *Institutes,* we observed that Calvin repeatedly expanded his treatment of the doctrine of the Trinity until the final edition of 1559. In that edition, it both headed up the treatment of the knowledge of God derived from revelation and it served as the architectonic for the entire project. Calvin, then, provided insight as to the importance of the doctrine of the Trinity for organizing the entire enterprise of post-baptismal Christian education.

We can also learn something of crucial importance with regard to the teaching-learning process in post-baptismal practices of ecclesial pedagogy. In the baptismal liturgy, we see the importance that Calvin attached to the parental vocation to serve as the primary Christian educators for the baptized. The baptismal liturgy spelled out in rather lengthy detail the expectations for parents. The Genevan baptismal rite emphasized that parenting was to be a form of ecclesial pedagogy. Teaching baptized children the essential beliefs and practices of the Christian faith was a major component of the vocation of parents. Both religious and civil authorities would hold parents accountable for their efforts in domestic catechesis during regular visits by pastors and elders.

191. Butin, *Revelation, Redemption, and Response,* pp. 112-13.

Calvin viewed parenting in relation to the practice of ecclesial pedagogy. Parents had the duty to teach the curriculum prescribed in the baptismal liturgy. They were also expected to provide for the regular participation of their children in the pedagogical activities of the church. Parents had the duty to bring their children every Sunday to the noontime catechetical service.

Finally, Calvin saw the need to reformulate the ancient church's catechumenate in such a way as to address the needs of his contemporary context. It is clear that he retained the intimate connection between the sacrament of baptism and ecclesial pedagogy. Because most of those being baptized in his day were infants, Calvin perceived the need to reformulate the relationship between baptism and catechesis. He made catechesis a largely post-baptismal endeavor. With Hughes Oliphant Old, we might even cautiously go so far as to categorize Calvin's educational vision as a form of mystagogical catechesis. Calvin assumed that learners had already been baptized and that they needed to participate in a structured pattern of teaching over a lifetime in order to live into the meaning of baptismal grace. The sacrament in and of itself was insufficient to produce committed Christian people; intentional post-baptismal instruction in home and church would lead to a life of Christian discipleship. In this sense, it seems fair to characterize Calvin's conception of ecclesial pedagogy as a paraliturgical practice, the aim of which was to bridge the gap between liturgy and life.

Some aspects of Calvin's way of configuring the relationship between baptism, the Trinity, and ecclesial pedagogy may need, however, to be altered or jettisoned for use in the context of contemporary American mainline churches. Three areas in particular require critical scrutiny and reformulation: the relation between election and baptism, ecclesial pedagogy as an instrument of church discipline, and strategies for pursuing parental accountability.

Calvin integrated his understanding of baptism and the doctrine of election by means of the secret work of the Holy Spirit. Baptismal validity only required the application of some form of water and the invocation of the Triune formula. Baptismal efficacy was another matter. Calvin argued that the Holy Spirit only brings the implanted seed of faith to full flower in the elect. Faith does not come to maturity in the reprobate, even though a measure of faith may be given to them temporarily only to have it ripped away from them later as a testimony to divine judgment. Even though Calvin had clearly stated that it is not for human beings to determine who were among the elect and the reprobate, he appears to have slipped over this line and made judgments about the fate of particular people based on his pastoral experience. He would have been on sounder biblical and theological ground if he had simply affirmed that faith is a gift of the Triune God for which the faithful can only render humble thanks, rather than developing in too much detail the possible implications of this teaching. If judgment really belongs to God, then the baptized ought to assume that all people are elect. No one ought to look upon another as reprobate.

Even though he moderated some of the earlier reforming zeal that resulted in his ouster from Geneva in 1538, Calvin continued to be concerned about church discipline and purification, which may have led him into theological transgression. With regard to baptism, it would have been adequate to affirm that faith comes by way of the inner working of the Holy Spirit in partnership with human means. If some do not respond appropriately as youth, one cannot fairly conclude they are possibly among the reprobate. It only means that one should assume that the Spirit has not yet brought them to the point of affirming faith in Jesus Christ. By putting so much weight on the catechetical process with its culmination in admittance to the sacrament of Holy Communion, Calvin may well have too closely identified the work of the Holy Spirit with the human agency of ecclesial pedagogy.

The two other related problems with Calvin's legacy are connected with matters under investigation in this study. Post-baptismal catechesis functioned for Calvin as a form of church discipline. Though baptism was to be administered relatively indiscriminately (to the children of church members in good standing), the Eucharist was reserved only for those who provided public witness to their faith in Jesus Christ. This meant that access to the grace symbolized and made real in the celebration of the Lord's Supper was made conditional upon the internalization and recitation of a determinate amount of basic biblical and theological knowledge. In short, one had to pass a theological test before passing from the grace offered in baptism to the grace offered in the Lord's Supper. This is problematic for at least two reasons.

First, to make minimum theological knowledge a requirement for admission to the Eucharist introduces a difficulty that turns out to be a rather slippery slope. What about individuals who are unable to master even the minimum of theological knowledge? What damage might be done to those with significant learning disabilities in the process of attempting to hold them accountable for learning catechetical basics? Does this mean that people with mental disabilities should remain functionally excommunicate even though baptized? What happens when someone loses mental acuity through some form of dementia or a severe brain injury? Of course, exceptions to cover these extreme pastoral situations might well be made while still upholding Calvin's schema, but that would seem to be increasingly untenable on pastoral as well as theological grounds. Though Calvin should be applauded for his efforts to instill meaningful church discipline, the conception of ecclesial pedagogy as one of the main mechanisms of such discipline needs to be radically changed.

The second problem with making mastery of basic theological knowledge the condition of entrance to the Eucharist concerns the nature of grace itself. There appears to be a disconnect in Calvin's thought on the subject of grace as related to baptism and to the Eucharist. In the case of baptism, he affirmed the importance of the primacy of grace. First, grace is given in and through the sacrament; then, one spends the rest of one's life growing into an apprehension of the meaning of baptismal grace. Why is this not also the pattern with regard to the Eucharist? Calvin himself confessed to possessing little comprehension of this great mystery of grace.[192] Isn't it the case with all who partake of the Eucharistic meal that the experience far exceeds rational comprehension? How can anyone articulate accurately what little comprehension one might have of the experience of encounter in the Eucharist? It would seem to be more consistent on theological as well as epistemological grounds to treat the Eucharist in a fashion similar to baptism. I would argue against Calvin that churches should administer both sacraments to young children, inclusive of infants. The key principle at work here would be that the experience of Triune grace embodied and conveyed in the sacrament precedes and funds a life of discipleship characterized by growing ever more deeply into an apprehension of it. In one sense, this would recover at a deeper level the early church catechumenate with its culmination in the differentiated unity of the baptism-Eucharist event. Metaphorically, this would mean that after having been born anew one would not have to wait a decade or more for the spiritual sustenance that is apparently so crucial to nourishing faith that Calvin argued a losing battle for its weekly administration.

192. Calvin, *Institutes* 4.17.7.

Finally, Calvin's concern with ecclesial pedagogy as one of the central mechanisms of church discipline resulted in practices that undercut the vocation of parents as the primary religious educators of their children. While he should be lauded for the way in which the baptismal liturgy communicated so clearly and forcefully that parents were expected to teach the basics of trinitarian Christian belief and practice to their children, the means of enforcing those promises leave a lot to be desired. In Calvin's context of close cooperation between civil and ecclesial authorities in reforming patterns of living to make them more resonant with the teachings of Scripture, accountability for ecclesial pedagogy in the home through regular pastoral visitation and discipline by the Consistory and, if need be, by the town council made sense. In a different set of historical, ecclesial, and political circumstances this pattern of discipline comes across as nothing less than authoritarian. Even in Calvin's Geneva one wonders about the degree to which religious instruction in the home was motivated more by the avoidance of punishment and public humiliation than by genuine love for God and love for the children in question. The distinctive proclamation of Triune grace manifest in Jesus Christ would appear to be undercut by methods of discipline which, albeit unintentionally, emphasized judgment and meritorious conduct.

One final difficulty in Calvin's thought requires comment before we conclude our treatment of the Genevan reformer. Though we can see the nexus of baptism, the Trinity, and ecclesial pedagogy in Calvin's thought, it has a serious limitation. This problem comes to light when we begin, not with baptism, but with the doctrine of the Trinity. When we read his *Institutes* from beginning to end as he laid them out, we encounter his teaching on the doctrine of the Trinity early on in the first book. Though he references the baptismal liturgy at a key point in that discussion, the linkage between the Trinity and baptism comes across as rather thin; furthermore, it is difficult if not impossible to get to ecclesial pedagogy from his treatment of the doctrine of the Trinity. Without an explicit grounding in or reference to baptism, Calvin's teaching on the Trinity tends to move in an abstract direction — this despite his stated intentions. Even though he protests repeatedly against speculative doctrine disconnected from the concrete life of the church, his failure to make the close relationship between the doctrine of the Trinity and the sacrament of baptism (with little explicit attention to ecclesial pedagogy at that particular juncture) results in an almost gravitational pull toward the abstract and the disembodied.

Likewise, the underdevelopment of the linkage between the doctrine of the Trinity and the sacrament of baptism resulted in only an implicit connection with practices of ecclesial pedagogy.

Conversely, when we begin with the baptismal rite in Calvin's thought and work out its interpretation, the connections between the rite and the doctrine of the Trinity on the one hand and patterns of ecclesial pedagogy on the other become quite explicit and compelling. In this regard, Calvin's work toward a reinvention of the ancient church's catechumenate remains impressive.

It would seem to be the case that the more Calvin moved away from the explicit framing of the *Institutes* as a form of baptismally grounded catechesis, the more he undercut his claims about the edificatory and pedagogical function of doctrine. Ironically, beginning with the 1543 edition of the *Institutes* and continuing into the final edition of 1559 he jettisoned Luther's architectonic in favor of the explicitly trinitarian architectonic supplied by *the* baptismal creed of the Western Christian tradition (the Apostles' Creed). Calvin unintentionally lost the concrete, practical, and pedagogical coordinates for his doctrinal teachings about the mystery of God revealed in Scripture.

Calvin was a practical trinitarian theologian of the first order whose doctrinal insights avoided wild flights of metaphysical speculation. In his trinitarian thought, he made some important linkages with the rite of baptism, attended to theological anthropology, and paid serious attention to ecclesial practices of formation. Calvin concerned himself with forming generations of the baptized into the doxological life. We can still learn much from his efforts, particularly if we trace the trajectories of his thought radiating out from the baptismal rite.

CHAPTER 5

Baptizing and Teaching in the Triune Name

The great faiths provide meaning and purpose for their adherents. The question is: can they make space for those who are not its adherents, who sing a different song, hear a different music, tell a different story? On that question, the fate of the twenty-first century may turn.

Jonathan Sacks, *The Dignity of Difference*

In the previous two chapters, we saw how intrinsic and necessary relations between the sacrament of baptism, the doctrine of the Trinity, and ecclesial pedagogy come into clear focus in the works of Gregory of Nyssa and John Calvin by privileging baptism. It remains for us in this concluding chapter to consider the implications of holding baptism, the doctrine of the Trinity, and ecclesial pedagogy together for contemporary efforts to foster vital Christian faith in congregations.

While I have sought to recover significant formulations of the crucial nexus of baptism-Trinity-pedagogy from two pivotal periods of the past in the previous two chapters, I want here to outline the elements of a *contemporary* trinitarian practical theology of Christian formation based on the baptism-Trinity-pedagogy nexus. To do this, I will draw upon, but not be captive to, the perspectives provided by Gregory of Nyssa and John Calvin.

Considering in condensed form what we can glean from Gregory of Nyssa and John Calvin will provide a running start for the constructive task. We will focus on some key points of convergence around the issues relevant to the constructive task and then move into a sketch of some of the issues in contemporary context that will necessarily differentiate our approach to relating baptism, the Trinity, and ecclesial pedagogy from those represented by our conversation partners from the fourth and the sixteenth centuries. All of this will be in service to a concluding section that will provide the outlines of a contemporary approach to educational ministry based on the nexus of baptism-Trinity-pedagogy.

What We Can Learn from Gregory of Nyssa and John Calvin about the Baptism-Trinity-Pedagogy Nexus

In the work of both Gregory of Nyssa and John Calvin, we found evidence of a deep and necessary linkage between baptism, the Trinity, and ecclesial pedagogy that came to light when we used baptism as an interpretive lens. The previous two chapters helped to make the case that contemporary efforts to extract trinitarian insights from either Gregory or Calvin apart from consideration of the deep intertwining of this doctrine with baptism and with ecclesial pedagogy run the risk of distorting the complexity and richness of the theological treasures to be found in their work. As we push ahead toward a delineation of key features of a contemporary trinitarian practical theology of Christian formation, several convergent themes in the work of these two pastor-teachers come into view. It will prove useful to name the points of overlap between the two as a way to get our bearings in the constructive task.

One of the chief difficulties with mining the work of Gregory or Calvin for nuggets of insight on the subject of the doctrine of God as Trinity concerns the nature and function of doctrine itself. Both Gregory and Calvin understood Christian doctrine as inherently rooted in the life and practices of the church. Looking through the lens of the baptismal rite, we saw something of the close relation of trinitarian doctrinal development and ecclesial pedagogy. Gregory and Calvin both developed an understanding of the Triune God that arises wholly or in part from reflection upon the practice of baptism. Sacramental practice in this case funds and orients the development of doctrine and issues forth into an understanding of the Christian life that is inherently pedagogical in character. More specifically, the doctrine of the Trinity both reflected the life of the church at the point of baptism and carried normative intent with respect to shaping the life of the church. We attended to the explicitly practical character of their doctrines of the Trinity in relation to the edification of the church and its individual members through lifelong baptismally oriented pedagogy. For both of these thinkers the doctrine of the Trinity was ultimately a practical matter born of a complex understanding of the relationship between practice and theological reflection.

The practical character of the doctrine of the Trinity comes through in the way in which both Gregory and Calvin understood the relation of practice and doctrine and also in the way they interpreted baptism as entrance into participation in divine reality. Gregory argued that baptism has to do with participation in the Trinity itself. Calvin emphasized that baptism points to and makes actual union with Jesus Christ (carefully couched in trinitarian terms). Gregory's emphasis on the Trinity carried a distinctively Christological valence; Calvin made clear that his emphasis on union with Christ could only be understood in a thoroughly trinitarian framework. In both Gregory and Calvin we see in the life that issues from baptism a dynamic interplay between trinitarian and Christological emphases.

This convergence of interplay between Christology and trinitarian doctrine found in Gregory of Nyssa and Calvin serves to underscore Moltmann's recent claims in *The Crucified God* and in *The Trinity and the Kingdom* as to the reciprocal relationship between the cross and the Trinity.[1] Moltmann writes in *The Crucified God* that

> what happens on the cross manifests the relationships of Jesus the Son, to the Father, and vice versa. The cross and its liberating effect makes possible the movement of the Spirit from the Father to us. The cross stands at the heart of the trinitarian being of God; it divides and conjoins the persons in their relationships to each other and portrays them in a specific way. . . . Anyone who really talks of the Trinity talks of the cross of Jesus, and does not speculate in heavenly riddles.[2]

Later in that same work, Moltmann argues further for the close practical interconnection between Christology and trinitarian doctrine when he ar-

---

1. See also Miroslav Volf, *Exclusion and Embrace: A Theological Exploration of Identity, Otherness, and Reconciliation* (Nashville: Abingdon, 1996), p. 127.

2. Jürgen Moltmann, *The Crucified God: The Cross of Christ as the Foundation and Criticism of Christian Theology* (New York: Harper & Row, 1974), pp. 206-7.

gues that "the material principle of the doctrine of the Trinity is the cross of Christ. The formal principle of knowledge of the cross is the doctrine of the Trinity."[3] He develops this same theme by coming at it from the other side (that is, from the point of view of the doctrine of the Trinity) in his later work, *The Trinity and the Kingdom:*

> God is love. That means God is self-giving. It means he exists for us: on the cross. To put it in trinitarian terms — the Father lets his Son sacrifice himself through the Spirit. The Father is crucifying love, the Son is crucified love, and the Holy Spirit is the unvanquishable power of the cross. The cross is at the centre of the Trinity.[4]

Gregory and Calvin would likely affirm Moltmann's fundamental insights concerning the reciprocity of the cross and the doctrine of the Trinity in the Christian life. They would likely point out, however, a glaring deficiency in Moltmann's vision. Unlike Gregory and Calvin, Moltmann fails to provide concrete ecclesial grounding for his treatment of the mutuality of Trinity and cross. Insofar as Moltmann does not connect his claim about the mutual disclosure of the cross of Christ and the Trinity to the concretely existing church and to embodied people by way of baptism, his argument tends toward abstraction and runs the risk of failing to connect with the actual life of local congregations. Further, to the extent that he does not explicitly attend to the pedagogical dimensions of his practical trinitarian claims, Moltmann's perspective runs the risk of functioning as an idealistic vision that will perpetually falter at the point of moving beyond the academy and into the pews and classrooms of local churches. Gregory and Calvin help us to see that the mutual implication of Trinity and cross will become a generative commitment for the lived Christianity in congregations only when and to the extent that such claims are grounded in the sacrament of baptism and take seriously the practice of ecclesial pedagogy.

Another point of convergence for Gregory and Calvin concerns the relationship between what we can and cannot know about the Triune mystery. Neither of them granted that human beings have access to knowledge of the inner being of the Triune God, even if the baptized do have the priv-

---

3. Moltmann, *The Crucified God,* pp. 240-41.
4. Jürgen Moltmann, *The Trinity and the Kingdom: The Doctrine of God* (San Francisco: Harper & Row, 1981), p. 83.

ilege of access to more reliable knowledge than do the unbaptized. In this respect, both thinkers champion an apophatic theme in their approach to the mystery of God, though much more explicitly developed in Gregory than in Calvin. Following from the affirmation that there are discernible limits to our knowledge of the Trinity, both asserted that reliable knowledge of the Trinity is only available through that which has been revealed in and through Scripture. From the biblical witness we can only know about God's activities "for us"; we cannot know what constitutes the mystery of the Trinity in and of itself apart from the activities of creation and redemption. Furthermore, Gregory and Calvin remind us that the disclosures found in Scripture aim at practical effects: salvation, healing, and growth in doxological holiness.

Building on their sense of the limits of human knowledge of the Trinity, both Gregory and Calvin conveyed a rich understanding of the function of religious language in relation to religious life. They teach us that scriptural language points reliably, though not exhaustively, to the Triune mystery. Because of this, they counsel avoidance of reification and the making of false idols out of the concepts and language conveyed by Scripture. The Triune God can be worshipped but never fully comprehended. By implication, this understanding of the nature and function of religious language in reference to the mystery of God would seem to call for a way of life marked by a generous Christian humanism characterized by a deeply committed relativism. Gregory and Calvin would urge us to hold onto biblically based and ecclesially developed theological convictions, but with a good measure of intellectual humility.

A further point of convergence in the contributions of Gregory and Calvin about the baptism-Trinity-pedagogy nexus uncovered by approaching their thought through the lens of baptism pertains to the pedagogical dimensions of a baptismally based doctrine of the Trinity. Gregory and Calvin demonstrated how the complex interplay of the baptismal rite and the doctrine of the Trinity can give rise to an unmistakably pedagogical emphasis. When we privilege baptism in their work, we see not only its close connections with the doctrine of the Trinity (and, thereby, one key aspect of its practical character), but also the inherently pedagogical character of their understandings of the Christian life. They shared the conviction that the pedagogical dimensions of the life of Triune faith initiated and oriented by baptism are pervasive and central, not incidental and ancillary. In other words, Gregory and Calvin help us to see that the juxtaposition of baptism and the Trinity necessarily calls forth a robust emphasis on ecclesial pedagogy.

Being baptized in the Triune Name entails a lifetime of learning and growth. Both Gregory and Calvin affirm that living the Christian life in relation to the divine reality into which one enters in baptism requires reflecting ever more deeply on the meaning of the core elements of baptism itself. Baptism provides a kind of paradigm for the Christian life that makes possible growth in both understanding and virtue. The baptized spend the entirety of their lives in the school of faith that is the church. For Calvin, graduation comes only at the point of death; for Gregory, death marks only a transition into yet higher levels of learning. The life issuing forth from having been baptized into the Triune Name is for them inherently and necessarily pedagogical in character inasmuch as it entails continually seeking understanding and an ever more profound personal encounter with the Triune mystery.

Gregory and Calvin tell us that this inherently pedagogical Christian life aims at a specific purpose. They agree that the *telos* of baptism and the Christian life that issues forth from it has to do with worshipping the Triune God. Baptism and teaching in the Triune Name come to fulfillment in doxological praise. The baptized learn and grow across the course of their lives into the dynamic and joyful practice of doxology. Ultimately, growing in the life initiated and oriented by baptism aims at personal engagement with the Trinity in ever deeper thanksgiving and enjoyment. To paraphrase the answer to the first question of the Westminster Shorter Catechism: the purpose of the baptismal life is to glorify and enjoy the Triune God forever.[5] This love for the Trinity, in turn, issues forth in an overflowing of love for neighbors near and far.

There is at least one major point of convergence between Gregory and Calvin with which we must part company from them. Both Gregory and Calvin were pre-modern figures who lived in varying degrees within the long shadow of Constantinianism or Christendom. Gregory and Calvin shared more with each other about their conceptions of cooperation between ecclesial and civil authorities than either of them does with those of us who live in twenty-first-century America marked by a clear separation

---

5. The Westminster Shorter Catechism, in *The Constitution of the Presbyterian Church (U.S.A.): Part I: Book of Confessions* (New York and Atlanta: Office of the General Assembly, 1983), 7.001.

between church and state. Living on this side of the Enlightenment means, among other things, that we have to configure and live out the baptism-Trinity-pedagogy nexus in some ways that differ markedly from both Gregory and Calvin. Before we turn to our constructive work more directly, we will have to spend a bit more time limning some of the key differences between the world we inhabit on this side of modernity and the worlds that Gregory and Calvin knew.

Reflections on the Contemporary Context

By privileging the baptismal rite, we have seen something of the way in which Gregory of Nyssa and John Calvin held together the nexus of baptism, the Trinity, and pedagogy. It simply will not do to bring their insights forward into the present as if their worlds were like the one we inhabit. We cannot move directly from identification of key insights from thinkers in the pre-modern past to application of those insights in a late modern or a postmodern context.[6] Instead, we must both draw from them and think with them as we seek to negotiate the baptism-Trinity-pedagogy nexus today. This means that we may well sometimes employ the baptism-Trinity-pedagogy nexus in different ways and for different ends than would have been the case with either of them.

Gregory and Calvin knew nothing of modern science, medicine, and technology. They took for granted that the earth was the center of the universe. Patriarchy reigned unabashedly in every aspect of society. Speech was not free and human rights had not become a key feature of moral discourse. No one had yet heard Kant's cry "Aude sapere" or his description of Enlightenment as "man's emergence from his self-incurred immaturity."[7] They lived long before the Enlightenment and the revolutions in America

---

6. For this reason, I intend to differentiate my position from such perspectives as those offered by the Radical Orthodoxy movement, MacIntyre's anti-modernity project, and Debra Dean Murphy's recent work in Christian education and liturgy. To be sure, each of these points of view makes important contributions to contemporary discussions of various kinds. I part company with them all, however, at the point of wholesale dismissal of Enlightenment modernity.

7. Immanuel Kant, "An Answer to the Question: 'What Is Enlightenment?'" in *Kant: Political Writings*, Cambridge Texts in the History of Political Thought, 2nd enlarged ed., ed. Hans Reiss (Cambridge: Cambridge University Press, 1991), p. 54.

and France. They could not envision the rise of such fields as nuclear medicine, chemical engineering, and subatomic physics. Unknown to them, too, were such human-oriented fields of study as psychology, sociology, history, and economics. The invention of the modern notions of selfhood, the discovery of antibiotics, and the historical-critical approach to the study of Scripture all came into existence on this side of modernity.

More specifically, neither Gregory nor Calvin ever considered such uniquely American arrangements as the separation of church and state, the separation of powers of government, the Bill of Rights, touch-screen voting, or churches as volunteer societies. They would not likely have embraced or valued the increasing religious and cultural pluralism that so marks contemporary American society.

Gregory and Calvin could never have imagined the many disturbing downsides to modernity. They did not have to contend with the hegemony of disembodied reason, the hubris of anti-historicism, and the widespread revolt against established authority and tradition. They knew nothing of the Jewish Holocaust, mass media manipulation of consumer appetites, or wars for oil. They did not have to worry about the specters of biological terrorism, airplanes as bombs, or the ever looming specter of nuclear annihilation. Likewise, they did not have to struggle with dominant forms of thought marked by the displacement of God and the narcissistic cunning that seeks to mask the inherently religious character of the self-preservation agenda of modern thought as secularism.[8]

There are three main reasons to take these key differences between our context and the pre-modern contexts of Gregory and Calvin into account when moving forward constructively in relation to the baptism-Trinity-pedagogy nexus. First, it is important to stress today that we cannot go back behind the Enlightenment, even if we wanted to do so. Culturally and intellectually, we have passed over a cultural Rubicon. While we can learn from and even appropriate insights from past thinkers, we must also grapple with our own set of issues. This needs to be said clearly and boldly as a counterpoint to those contemporary voices who would advocate for dealing with the problems of modernity through nostalgic appropriation of pre-modern eras and thought forms. To equal what others may have ac-

---

8. David S. Pacini, *The Cunning of Modern Religious Thought* (Philadelphia: Fortress, 1989). Each of the essays in this book addresses and elucidates aspects of the Augustinian-influenced self-preservation impulse at the heart of modern thought.

complished in the past in their social and historical situations requires that we do similar things in very different ways. The position I take calls for thinking with Gregory and Calvin about issues of common concern without attempting simply to repristinate their conclusions. A contemporary trinitarian practical theology of Christian formation that takes its cues from the baptism-Trinity-pedagogy nexus may well take a shape different in certain key respects from that operative in the thought of either of our two main conversation partners.

Second, I want to stake out a position that both affirms and criticizes elements of modernity. I cannot affirm the position that modernity needs no correction. Nor can I affirm the view that justice and liberation require relegating every feature of modernity to the trash heap. Moral philosopher Cornel West's criticism of Radical Orthodoxy spokesman John Milbank's overblown critiques of modernity captures something of the point of view espoused here:

> [Milbank] fails to appreciate the moral progress, political break-throughs, and spiritual freedoms forged by the heroic efforts of modern citizens of religious and secular traditions. It is just as dangerous to overlook the gains of modernity procured by prophetic religious and progressive secular citizens as it is to overlook the blindness of Constantinian Christians and imperial secularists. And these gains cannot be preserved and deepened by reverting to ecclesiastical refuges or sectarian orthodoxies. Instead they require candor about our religious integrity and democratic identity that leads us to critique and resist Constantinian Christianity and imperial America.[9]

One suspects that many of the severest critics of modernity would not actually want to live in a world stripped of the positive goods that have come from it. Who would really want to live in a social context devoid of critical reason, free speech, separation of church and state, individual autonomy, scientific method, racial and ethnic pluralism, and commitment to universal human rights?[10] There are important and valuable gains that we have received precisely from modernity.

---

9. Cornel West, *Democracy Matters: Winning the Fight Against Imperialism* (New York: Penguin, 2004), pp. 162-63.

10. The position taken here differs markedly from that articulated by Debra Dean Murphy in her recent work on worship and Christian education. She argues for recovery of

This is not to say, however, that everything about modernity is fine and dandy. We certainly cannot turn a blind eye to the totalitarian blood-shed and the genocides of the previous century as if they had nothing whatsoever to do with the presuppositions and agendas of modernity. Likewise, the damage done by Western colonialism dressed up in modern garb as well as the profound disfigurations of sexism and racism but-tressed by disembodied, male-oriented reason cannot be responsibly ig-nored. Further, the clever covering over of the inherently religious charac-ter of modernity in the guise of secularism seems no longer tenable or desirable.[11] Thus, in sketching out the contours of a contemporary trini-tarian practical theology of Christian formation based on the baptism-Trinity-pedagogy nexus, we will seek to avoid the Scylla of the rejection of modernity and the Charybdis of uncritical embrace of it.

Philosopher Stephen Toulmin captured well the delicate balancing act espoused in the current study with regard to the contemporary context when he wrote that "as things now stand, we can neither cling to Modernity in its historic form, nor reject it totally — least of all despise it. The task is rather, to reform, and even reclaim, our inherited modernity, by *humanizing* it."[12] For Toulmin, this means recovering the humanist side of modernity and bringing it into dynamic interaction with its physico-mathematical side.[13] Toulmin argues that humanizing modernity implies recovering prac-tical philosophy with particular emphases on rhetoric, particularity, local situatedness, and timeliness.[14] Such themes, I would argue, comport well

---

trinitarian sensibilities, Christian particularity, and the close connection between worship and ecclesial pedagogy by rejecting modernity. In contradistinction to her view, the position taken here seeks to affirm such things as the doctrine of the Trinity, the particularities of Christian identity, and ecclesial pedagogy in close connection with the liturgical core of con-gregational life and to put these matters into dynamic interaction with modernity. Murphy seems inspired by Milbank and others of similar ilk to blame modernity for all of the ills of contemporary churches. I find this line of argument deeply ironic and problematic. Her anti-modern vituperation can be seen in her attacks on the educational visions of Roman Catholic educators Gabriel Moran, Thomas Groome, and Mary Boys. See Debra Dean Murphy, *Teaching That Transforms: Worship as the Heart of Christian Education* (Grand Rapids: Brazos, 2004), pp. 29-94 passim.

11. Pacini, *The Cunning of Modern Religious Thought*, pp. 58-59.

12. Stephen Toulmin, *Cosmopolis: The Hidden Agenda of Modernity* (New York: The Free Press, 1990), p. 180.

13. Toulmin, *Cosmopolis*, p. 180.

14. Toulmin, *Cosmopolis*, pp. 186-92.

with an emphasis on the local, bodily practice of baptism and the processes of ecclesial pedagogy resulting in a way of life shaped by engagement with Triune reality understood as both transcendent and practical.

Third, I want to restrict my constructive treatment to an important but limited range of issues. A full-blown treatment of a trinitarian practical theology of Christian formation for the contemporary situation would entail a much more comprehensive and trenchant exploration of the complex features of the current context. Here, I will focus only on the crucial issue of faith formation in relation to the development of both Christian identity and openness.[15] In this, I find a high degree of resonance with Robert W. Pazmiño when in his work on the Trinity and ecclesial pedagogy he writes:

> The affirmation of identity preserves Christian distinctives, including the recognition that God has created all persons with intrinsic dignity and worth. The affirmation of openness signals the need to respect and care for all others in educational encounters and, more generally, in life. . . . The common good of humanity necessitates occasions to *mix* with non-Christians as well as occasions to *huddle* with persons of like faith in wrestling with past, current, and future challenges around the globe.[16]

By "identity and openness," I mean the challenge of forming individuals and communities in such a way that honors the irreducible particularities of Christian identity while fostering a generous and democratic openness to non-Christian "others." Jeffrey Stout's statement, "Democracy will suffer greatly, I fear, if orthodox Christians are unable to find a way to maintain their convictions while also taking up their responsibilities as citizens," aptly states the underlying concern of the approach taken here.[17]

---

15. This term is similar to Vanhoozer's *loyalty-openness,* which he describes as the ability to simultaneously hold particular Christian convictions and engage in conversation with those who do not share Christian convictions. See Kevin J. Vanhoozer, "Does the Trinity Belong in Theology of Religions? On Angling in the Rubicon and the 'Identity' of God," in *The Trinity in a Pluralistic Age: Theological Essays on Culture and Religion,* ed. Kevin J. Vanhoozer (Grand Rapids: Eerdmans, 1997), p. 64. I prefer the term *identity* over Vanhoozer's term *loyalty* because the former implies for me both one's character and one's posture in reference to that character.

16. Robert W. Pazmiño, *God Our Teacher: Theological Basics in Christian Education* (Grand Rapids: Baker Academic, 2001), pp. 167-68.

17. Jeffrey Stout, *Democracy and Tradition* (Princeton: Princeton University Press, 2004), p. 116.

James Fowler's developmental scheme sheds further light on the approach I wish to develop. In *Stages of Faith: The Psychology of Human Development and the Quest for Meaning*, Fowler depicts "conjunctive faith" in terms that resonate deeply and well with the perspective I am attempting to develop. Fowler describes this mature form of faith in this way:

> [Conjunctive faith] accepts as axiomatic that truth is more multidimensional and organically interdependent than most theories or accounts of truth can grasp. Religiously, it knows that the symbols, stories, doctrines, and liturgies offered by its own or other traditions are inevitably partial, limited to a particular people's experience of God and incomplete. [Conjunctive faith] also sees, however, that the relativity of religious traditions that matters is not their relativity to each other, but their relativity — their *relativity* — to the reality to which they mediate relation. Conjunctive faith, therefore, is ready for significant encounters with other traditions than its own, expecting that truth has disclosed and will disclose itself in those traditions in ways that may complement and correct its own. . . . This position implies no lack of commitment to one's own truth tradition. Nor does it mean a wishy-washy neutrality or mere fascination with the exotic features of alien cultures. Rather, Conjunctive faith's radical openness to the truth of the other stems precisely from its confidence in the reality mediated by its own tradition and in the awareness that that reality overspills its mediation. The person of [Conjunctive faith] makes her or his own experience of truth the principle by which other claims to truth are tested. But he or she assumes that each genuine perspective will augment and correct aspects of the other, in a mutual movement toward the real and the true.[18]

Fowler has aptly articulated an orientation to faith marked by commitment and relativism. As a result of searching faithfulness lived in supportive community, this orientation tends to arise at midlife. I believe that communities that embrace the dynamics of the baptism-Trinity-pedagogy nexus may be able to effectively foster the conditions that produce people who live with both deep Christian commitment and creative openness to others.

How might such faith be developed in Christian churches today? In

---

18. James W. Fowler, *Stages of Faith: The Psychology of Human Development and the Quest for Meaning* (San Francisco: Harper & Row, 1981), pp. 186-87.

order to answer this question, we must go forward into the constructive task proper.

Strategic Principles for Baptizing and Teaching in the Triune Name

The world today positively drips with religion and religious instruction. Contrary to those who argue that religion is a thing of the past, the world appears in several respects to be more religious today than ever before. Nearly all of the major conflicts in the world have an unmistakably religious dimension to them. Hinduism, Islam, Judaism, and Christianity all face serious challenges from fundamentalists who are willing to engage in or support from afar acts of violence against those who are religiously or culturally "other." For this reason, Jonathan Sacks, the chief rabbi for the United Kingdom, in his book *The Dignity of Difference: How to Avoid the Clash of Civilizations* writes prophetically: "The great faiths provide meaning and purpose for their adherents. The question is: can they make space for those who are not its adherents, who sing a different song, hear a different music, tell a different story? On that question, the fate of the twenty-first century may turn."[19]

Sacks finds a Christian counterpart on this theme in the work of Croatian systematic theologian Miroslav Volf, who writes: "It may not be too much to claim that the future of our world will depend on how we deal with identity and difference. The issue is urgent. The ghettos and battlefields throughout the world — in the living rooms, in inner cities, or on the mountain ranges — testify indisputably to its importance."[20]

A similar call for the development of religiously committed pluralism comes from Diana Eck in her recent study of religious diversity in contemporary American life. Eck's call resonates with the concern of both Sacks and Volf:

> We must embrace the religious diversity that comes with commitment to religious freedom, and as we move into the new millennium we must

19. Jonathan Sacks, *The Dignity of Difference: How to Avoid the Clash of Civilizations* (London and New York: Continuum, 2003), p. 43.

20. Volf, *Exclusion and Embrace*, p. 20.

find ways to make the differences that have divided people the world over the very source of our strength here in the U.S. It will require moving beyond a laissez-faire inattention to religion to a vigorous attempt to understand the religions of our neighbors. And it will require the engagement of our religious traditions in the common tasks of civil society. Today, right here in the U.S., we have an opportunity to create a vibrant and hopeful pluralism, in a world of increasing fragmentation where there are few models for a truly pluralistic, multireligious society.[21]

The challenge pointed to by Sacks, Volf, and Eck requires thoughtful response from mainline Protestant churches. Can they make space for those who are not its adherents, who sing a different song, hear a different music, and tell a different story? Does the sacrament of baptism have anything to do with this? Might we find any resources in that most distinctively Christian teaching about God — the doctrine of the Trinity — for any clues about how to live into a faithful understanding of how to teach for identity and openness? What kind of ecclesial pedagogy would foster deeply committed Christians who, precisely because of their Christian commitments, would make space for others who sing a different song and tell a different story?

As that part of religions concerned with reproducing the faith in future generations, religious leaders charged with pedagogical responsibilities can do tremendous good and also incalculable harm in the world today. Those charged with such responsibilities in the various religious communities can teach exclusion, separation, and even violence. They can also teach respect, toleration, and cooperation with their neighbors near and far. What constitutes the difference between lethal and life-giving religious pedagogy, especially in its Christian forms? The key factor has to do with the way in which human differences are understood and addressed. The capacity for openness and care for those who are different marks the shape of the divide between religious pedagogies that diminish or destroy life and those that support and uphold life.

Let me try here to connect the dots a little more clearly on the crucial interplay between baptism, Trinity, and Christian education and this set of issues. When we talk about the sacrament of baptism and the doctrine of

21. Diana L. Eck, *A New Religious America: How a "Christian Country" Has Become the World's Most Religiously Diverse Nation* (New York: HarperSanFrancisco, 2001), p. 25.

God as Trinity, we are talking about two of the most exclusive and Christian-specific elements of our religion. When it comes to teaching about God, no other religion in the world espouses belief in one God in three co-equal Persons in the way in which we do as Christians.[22] Christians are neither polytheists nor undifferentiated monotheists; Christians are specifically trinitarian monotheists who believe that the One God exists as three distinct, yet perfectly related Persons. On the distinctive Christian teaching of the doctrine of God Karl Barth wrote: "The doctrine of the Trinity is what basically distinguishes the Christian doctrine of God as Christian, and therefore what already distinguishes the Christian concept of revelation as Christian, in contrast to all other possible doctrines of God or concepts of revelation."[23] The doctrine of the Trinity is distinctively Christian in character. For all its richness and beauty, the doctrine of the Trinity does not tend to lend itself to easy bridge-building with neighbors of other faiths or of no religious faith at all.

Baptism, likewise, has to do with Christian particularity. A person gets baptized into the Body of Christ in order to receive a particular religious identity. In baptism, old ways of life — including religious ones — must be left behind and renounced in order that the new way of faith and discipleship in relation to Jesus Christ might be established. Baptism involves cutting ties with the forces of evil, injustice, and godlessness and being bound with cords of faith, hope, and love to the Triune God and to neighbor. As Barth observed, "every baptism validly performed in our churches at least confronts us with the problem of the doctrine of the Trinity."[24] Baptism does, in fact, confront the churches with the issue of Christian identity in relation to the Triune God. In so doing, it also poses simultaneously the question of relating to those who do not share the particularities of Christian belief and practice.

There are those in the Christian churches today who seem quite comfortable with emphasizing the particularities and distinctive features of Christian belief and practice over and against everyone else. In the face of various forms of corruption in both society and church, some are calling us to hunker down and to reassert Christian identity by emphasizing the

22. It is possible that some forms of Hinduism contain interesting parallels to the traditional doctrine of God as Trinity.

23. Karl Barth, *Church Dogmatics*, 1/1, trans. G. W. Bromiley, ed. G. W. Bromiley and T. F. Torrance (Edinburgh: T&T Clark, 1975), p. 301.

24. Barth, *Church Dogmatics*, 1/1, p. 379.

separation of the church from the world. I fear that such Christian identity assertion over and against society and culture may all too easily lead to nasty forms of religious chauvinism. Such Christian identity assertion by withdrawal into supposed enclaves of Christian identity and holiness seems to me a dangerous option that easily devolves into nothing less than sophisticated forms of religious tribalism.[25]

Of course, there are also those on the other end of the spectrum in the churches today who want to erase any distinctive marks of Christian identity in the name of establishing good relations with our non-Christian neighbors. On this end of the spectrum, some believe that the way to deal with religious differences entails downplaying them. This point of view would sacrifice Christian identity for the sake of openness. I equally reject this lowest common denominator approach to dealing with religious diversity and the problems it poses for Christian witness in the realm of public engagement. I do not have much enthusiasm for moral monotheism that is embarrassed by the distinctive claims of Christian faith.

Thus, I believe there are two wrong answers and one right answer to the problem of Christian faith formation for public engagement in the increasingly pluralistic world in which we live. I just mentioned the two wrong answers: identity assertion to the point of excluding otherness and openness to non-Christian "others" to the point of losing any meaningful sense of particular religious identity. I believe a better answer involves attempting to hold together identity and openness. Trinitarian theologian Kevin Vanhoozer describes this stance as "open to differences while at the same time minding distinctives."[26] The nexus of the doctrine of the Trinity and the sacrament of baptism may provide the necessary orientation for an approach to Christian education that helps us hold together both identity and openness.

In this study of the baptism-Trinity-pedagogy nexus via the lens of the baptismal rite in the thought of Gregory of Nyssa and John Calvin, we have discovered some very helpful resources to aid in the development of individuals and communities that simultaneously affirm particular religious identity and capacious openness to those who live with different beliefs and practices. To begin, Gregory and Calvin both emphatically proclaimed that we can never know all there is to know about the mystery of

25. Volf, *Exclusion and Embrace*, p. 54.
26. Vanhoozer, *The Trinity in a Pluralistic Age*, p. 68.

the Triune God. Human beings do not have the capacity to comprehend the inner essence of the Trinity. Full and complete knowledge of the Triune God always eludes human comprehension. The mystery of God always exceeds the grandest and most elaborate of human conceptions. Gregory of Nyssa in particular provides a most compelling articulation of the limits of what can be known about the mystery of God. While the particular attributes and functions of each particular Person of the Trinity and something of the character of their interrelationships may be known through revelation, the shared essence of the Trinity remains a mystery for human beings:

> The uncreated Nature alone, which we acknowledge in the Father, and in the Son, and in the Holy Spirit, surpasses all significance of names. For this cause the Word, when He spoke of "the name" in delivering the Faith [that is, in baptism], did not add what it is, for how could a name be found for that which is above every name? — but gave authority that whatever name our intelligence by pious effort be enabled to discover to indicate the transcendent Nature, that name should be applied alike to Father, Son, and Holy Ghost, whether it be "the Good" or "the Incorruptible," whatever name each may think proper to be employed to indicate the undefiled Nature of the Godhead. And by this deliverance the Word seems to me to lay down for us this law, that we are to be persuaded that the Divine Essence is ineffable and incomprehensible: for it is plain that the title of Father does not present to us the Essence, but only indicates the relation to the Son. . . . [T]he knowledge [of the divine Essence] is beyond our capacity, as we have in the profession of faith [in baptism] the doctrine delivered to us that suffices for our salvation.[27]

What has been disclosed is *that* the tri-relational God is one, not *the way in which* that is the case. Knowledge of the inner essence of the Trinity has not been and will not ever be revealed to humanity or to any other creature. Thus, wisdom in the contemporary context, too, consists of being able "to recognize the limits of our knowledge, to be learned about our unknowing, to acknowledge the undisclosedness of God."[28]

---

27. Gregory of Nyssa, *Against Eunomius*, Book I, A Select Library of Nicene and Post-Nicene Fathers of the Christian Church, 2nd series (Grand Rapids: Eerdmans, reprint, 1994), 5.103.

28. Pacini, *The Cunning of Modern Religious Thought*, p. 59.

Even though the way in which the three are one remains perpetually beyond human comprehension for Gregory and Calvin, reliable knowledge about the work of the Triune God in and for creation has been disclosed. The knowledge that is necessary for salvation, healing, and restoration of the human condition has been revealed by God and can be known through Scripture. Both of our conversation partners articulated a rhetorical theory of divine accommodation defined by therapeutic or practical trinitarianism. As the ultimate teacher and healer, the Triune God takes the initiative to come to finite and fallen humanity in comprehensible, though not exhaustive, terms. That which is disclosed to the human family is that which will lead to rescue and restoration. Triune revelation does not aim at solving intellectual puzzles; rather, it is intended to have very concrete and practical effects.

Gregory in particular warned that scriptural language and concepts should not be reified. We should never confuse the likeness of gold for the gold itself.[29] The content of revelation should, however, be taken with utmost seriousness as God-given and trustworthy pointers toward therapeutic connection with the Triune reality. Christian teaching and preaching need, therefore, to emphasize that we do not know all there is to know about the mystery and work of the Triune God. This can proceed perhaps most effectively by way of exegesis of and reflection upon the texts and actions of the baptismal rite in all its fullness.

In Gregory and Calvin we find, then, a fascinating interplay between what can and what cannot be known about the mystery of the Triune God. We see, further, that that which lies beyond our comprehension conditions and qualifies that which we are able to comprehend. Again, Jonathan Sacks proves helpful in bringing out the significance of the interplay between apophasis and cataphasis in the trinitarian thought of both Gregory and Calvin: "The radical transcendence of God in the Hebrew Bible means that the Infinite lies beyond our finite understanding. God communicates in human language, but there are dimensions of the divine that must forever elude us."[30] This means that Christian communities and individuals are entitled to hold well and deeply their distinctively Christian convictions

---

29. Gregory of Nyssa, *Commentary on the Song of Songs,* trans. Casimir McCambley, The Archbishop of Iakovos Library of Ecclesiastical and Historical Sources, ed. N. M. Vaporis, vol. 12 (Brookline, Mass.: Hellenic College Press, 1987), p. 82.

30. Sacks, *The Dignity of Difference,* p. 55.

about the mystery of the Trinity and the economy of salvation, but to do so with intellectual humility and with generosity of spirit.

Such an emphasis as Gregory of Nyssa and Calvin provide on the limits and the practical character of knowledge of the Triune God lays the groundwork for the kind of intellectual humility and openness to others that creative citizenship in a pluralistic democracy requires. In this, the perspective of Jonathan Sacks offers something quite helpful:

> The divine word comes from heaven but it is interpreted on earth. The divine light is infinite but to be visible to us it must be refracted through human understanding. Truth in heaven transcends space and time, but human perception is bounded by space and time. When two propositions conflict, it is not necessarily because one is true and the other false. It may be, and often is, that each represents a different perspective on reality, an alternative way of structuring order, no more and no less commensurable than a Shakespeare sonnet, a Michelangelo painting, or a Schubert sonata. . . . God transcends the particularities of culture and the limits of human understanding. He is my God but also the God of all mankind, even of those whose customs and way of life are unlike mine. That is not to say that God endorses every act done in His name. On the contrary: a God of your side as well as mine must be a God of justice who stands above us both, teaching us to make space for one another, to hear each other's claims, and to resolve them equitably. Only such a God would be truly transcendent — greater not only than the natural universe but also than the spiritual universe capable of being comprehended in any human language, for any single point of view. Only such a God could teach [mankind] to make peace other than by conquest and conversion, and as something nobler than practical necessity.[31]

Sacks, like Gregory of Nyssa, rightly emphasizes the transcendence of God and the human inability to finally and fully grasp the mystery. Sacks, however, does what Gregory and Calvin do not; he helps us to see the profound ethical implications of stressing divine transcendence for public deliberations regarding the common good in a society such as ours. Since none of us can ever claim fully and finally to comprehend the divine mystery, we must make space for those whose conceptions of God and ultimate matters differ from our own. In more technical terms, contemporary trinitarian apophatic

---

31. Sacks, *The Dignity of Difference*, pp. 64-65.

spirituality funded by the baptismal rite may lead to a religious affirmation of epistemic humility in the face of pervasive pluralism and to a deep investment in the practice of democratic conversation in the public arena.

Jeffrey Stout of Princeton University in his 2004 book *Democracy and Tradition* helps to flesh this out even further. Stout carefully criticizes both the Rawlsian liberalism that would inhibit particular religious identity in public ethical discourse and a Christian sectarianism advocated by thinkers like Alasdair MacIntyre and Stanley Hauerwas.[32] Instead, Stout calls upon religious individuals and communities to bring the particularities of their religious identity into public deliberations about the common good as a necessary element of the practice of democratic conversation. Stout writes, "I am trying to articulate a form of pluralism, one that citizens with strong religious commitments can accept and that welcomes their full participation in public life without fudging on its own premises."[33] Christians should own the particularities of their identity and should be willing to provide rational explanations for the positions they hold on various ethical matters. They should also remain open to hearing others' points of view and the reasons behind them. Giving up on the practice of such democratic conversation by religious communities sets up the conditions for a return to the Wars of Religion that ravaged Europe immediately prior to and gave rise to the Enlightenment. Stout calls people with deep religious conviction to engage in the practice of democratic conversation marked by both identity and openness.

Sacks also draws out the implications of his emphasis on the radical transcendence of God in relation to democratic conversation. He urges the religious formation of individuals and communities who can engage in the lively practice of democratic conversation:

> The answer, I have already suggested, is *conversation*, not mere debate but the disciplined act of communicating (making my views intelligible to someone who does not share them) and listening (entering into the inner world of someone whose views are opposed to my own). Each is a genuine form of respect, of paying attention to the other, of conferring value on his or her opinions, even though they are not mine. In a debate one side wins, the other loses, but both are the same as they were before.

---

32. Stout, *Democracy and Tradition*, pp. 118-61.
33. Stout, *Democracy and Tradition*, pp. 296-97.

In a conversation neither side loses and both are changed, because they now know what reality looks like from a different perspective. That is not to say that either gives up its previous convictions. That is not what conversation is about. It does mean, however, that I may now realize that I must make space for another deeply held belief, and if my own case has been compelling, the other side may understand that it too must make space for mine. That is how public morality is constructed in a plural society — not by a single dominant voice, nor by the relegation of moral issues to the private domain of home and local congregation, but by a sustained act of understanding and seeking to be understood across the boundaries of difference.[34]

An ecclesial pedagogy based on a baptismally funded practical trinitarianism must face the challenge of forming people deeply into the particularities of Christian identity and making the dynamics of such particularity a powerful resource for democratic conversation along the lines described by both Stout and Sacks.

It is not only, though, what we do not know about the mystery of the Triune God that provides us with clues about how to teach for identity and openness; it is also what we do know that helps us to meet this challenge. On the basis of Barth's theology of Christ as *the* disclosure of Truth, Stout further calls upon Christians to be open to finding the truth both inside and outside of the church:

> Thus when Christians are considering the question of where truths — in the plural — are to be found, they must be prepared to look both inside the church and outside of it. Wherever they look, they must be suspicious and critical, as well as open to the possibility of needing to change their minds. Wherever they find important truths being spoken by other human beings, they must take themselves to have been addressed by Christ himself, by *the* Truth, *the* Light, *the* Word. Barth refers to true words spoken (or true lives lived) outside the church as secular "parables of the kingdom" (IV/3, 114). As in the case of the New Testament parables, Jesus Christ is their ultimate source as well as the criterion a Christian must use to appraise them.[35]

34. Sacks, *The Dignity of Difference*, p. 83. See also Eck, *A New Religious America*, pp. 369-70.

35. Stout, *Democracy and Tradition*, p. 110.

Stout here affirms a very ancient Christian theological conviction; namely, that all truth, all goodness, all beauty, and all justice have their ultimate source in the Triune God. While Christian communities and individuals cannot know everything there is to know about the mystery of God, what the Triune God has disclosed in Jesus Christ is of such a profound and universal nature that the Christian community can and must learn to think outside the parameters of the church in order to participate in the ongoing work of God in the world — including contemporary American society.

A contemporary approach to baptizing and teaching in the Triune Name should aim to provide young people and adults with the conceptual tools they need for the broad discernment of the Triune God's activities pointed to by Barth and Stout. Christian education for discernment of the subtle and pervasive work of the Triune God in both church and society can equip Christians to join up with those people and groups engaged in endeavors of truth, goodness, beauty, and justice wherever they may be found. Christians do not need other people to hold the same beliefs and to be part of their religious tribe in order to work alongside them in a constructive fashion.

Ecclesial pedagogy conducted in close proximity to the doctrine of the Trinity and the baptismal rite should not only provide tools for discernment, it should also foster "both-and" thinking. Ecclesial pedagogy today should intentionally promote a complex kind of thinking characterized by holding seemingly contradictory things together. Paradox and tension mark central conceptions of the divine in Christianity. God is one and three at the same time. Jesus Christ is one Person with two natures. Ecclesial pedagogy ought therefore to avoid attempts to resolve these basic tensions as if they were merely logic puzzles. The divine antinomies or paradoxes at the center of Christian belief do not lend themselves to easy rational comprehension, nor should they. When teaching about the doctrine of the Trinity, Calvin would employ a statement from one of Gregory Nazianzen's sermons on baptism. Calvin quoted Gregory of Nyssa's close friend on the paradoxical character of trinitarian doctrine and used it as a basis for his own explication of the doctrine. Calvin wrote:

> That passage in Gregory of Nazianzus vastly delights me: "I cannot think on the one without quickly being encircled by the splendor of the three, nor can I discern the three without being straightway carried back to the one." Let us not, then, be led to imagine a trinity of persons that

keeps our thoughts distracted and does not at once lead them back to that unity. Indeed the words "Father," "Son," and "Spirit" imply a real distinction — let no one think that these titles, whereby God is variously designated from his works, are empty — but a distinction, not a division.[36]

These paradoxes function pedagogically as tensions that stretch and challenge minds. They keep the baptized conceptually open. They help to avoid locking in on any human conception and turning it into an idol of the mind. The point is not to find perfect analogies that explain the Triune mystery; rather, the point is to live with these paradoxes until they become habits of mind which, in turn, will make it possible to hold both one's convictions and remain open to other deeply held points of view. Exploiting the notion of being baptized into the One Name That Is Three may yield people who can more easily find ways to affirm unity in the midst of robust diversity of views.

Ecclesial pedagogy developed in relation to baptism and the doctrine of the Trinity should help learners to avoid calcification of conceptualizations of God, world, and self. Educators and church leaders should avoid the temptation to provide easy answers and to offer simple solutions to basic paradoxes precisely because living with such tensions eventually produces people who have a habit of mind that makes it possible for them to engage in the complex demands of life in a pluralistic democracy with both identity and openness. Living the questions posed by the unusual claim about the unity and plurality of God may well shape in a distinctive and decisive manner the complex habits of mind needed for dynamic fellowship in the church and creative citizenship in a radically pluralistic social and political context.

This same habit of mind fostered by an approach to Christian education that takes its cues from a baptismally grounded doctrine of the Trinity can also provide tools for trenchant critique of the social order in both church and society. In his work on the doctrine of the Trinity, Jürgen Moltmann explicates the deep interconnections between a Cappadocian-inspired social doctrine of the Trinity and radical critique of church and

36. John Calvin, *Institutes of the Christian Religion,* ed. J. T. McNeill, trans. Ford Lewis Battles, 2 vols., Library of Religious Classics, vols. 20 and 21 (Philadelphia: Westminster, 1960), 1.13.17. Note the editorial mark in the McNeill edition indicating that this passage originated in the 1539 Strasbourg edition of the Institutes.

society.[37] Moltmann points out that the emphasis on the monarchical unity of God has often been aligned historically with patterns of hierarchy, patriarchy, and domination in both church and society.[38] In contrast, a thoroughly trinitarian doctrine of God carries radical implications for the transformation of social life in church and society. Moltmann writes:

> We have said that it is not the monarchy of a ruler that corresponds to the triune God; it is the community of men and women, without privileges and without subjugation. The three divine Persons have everything in common, except for their personal characteristics. So the Trinity corresponds to a community in which people are defined through their relations with one another and in their significance for one another, not in opposition to one another, in terms of power and possession.[39]

Teaching in relation to the doctrine of God as Trinity has the potential to equip people with the tools for radical prophetic critique of all forms of social injustice, oppression, and the abuse of power. Further on in his exploration of the ecclesial and political implications of the doctrine of the Trinity, Moltmann argues for a profound and inescapable connection between an understanding of God as Trinity and human freedom in the midst of difference:

> It is only in love that human freedom arrives at its truth. I am free and feel myself to be truly free when I am respected and recognized by others and when I for my part respect and recognize them. I become truly free when I open my life for other people and share with them, and when other people open their lives for me and share them with me. Then the other person is no longer the limitation of my freedom: he is an expansion of it. In mutual participation in life, individual people become free beyond the limits of their individuality, and discover the common room for living which their freedom offers. That is the social side of freedom. We call it love and solidarity. In it we experience the uniting of isolated individuals. In it we experience the uniting of things that have been forcibly divided.[40]

37. Moltmann, *The Trinity and the Kingdom*, p. 195.
38. Moltmann, *The Trinity and the Kingdom*, p. 195.
39. Moltmann, *The Trinity and the Kingdom*, p. 198.
40. Moltmann, *The Trinity and the Kingdom*, p. 216.

The love and freedom characteristic of the divine community of Persons in the Trinity corresponds to a radical alternative for life together in the churches and in a pluralistic democracy like that which we find in contemporary America. The vision of a socially egalitarian Trinity should plant the seeds of discontent with all forms of hierarchy, patriarchy, and exploitation both in the church and in society. It is the job of baptismally based trinitarian ecclesial pedagogy to plant such seeds of discontent and to water them with diligence and regularity.

The development of such capacities will doubtless require a lifetime of learning. As with Gregory and Calvin, contemporary efforts in the direction of a trinitarian practical theology of Christian formation will seek to recover ecclesial pedagogy as one of the highest priorities for churches. Far more than a process for civilizing or moralizing the young, ecclesial pedagogy stands at the very heart of the Christian life. Christian individuals and communities need constantly to strive for deeper apprehension of the reality into which they were initiated by baptism. It cannot be stressed enough that the Christian life is inherently and necessarily pedagogical in character.

Finally, a contemporary trinitarian practical theology of Christian formation will have to stress the centrality of love. The writer of the first of the Johannine epistles rightly affirms that whatever else the mystery of God may be, it certainly has to do with the greatest love imaginable. The three Persons of the Trinity share an inexhaustible love for one another and for the creation. To be baptized into the name of the Triune God and to live the Christian life is to be about the business of concrete acts of love understood as solidarity, hospitality, and dialogue. True love has to do with developing and maintaining a particular identity, but refusing to be imprisoned by it.

The writer of 1 John confronts the baptized with a stark and difficult truth. They cannot say that they love the Triune God if they do not simultaneously engage in acts of love toward their neighbors. Those initiated into a transforming relationship with the Triune God are called to love those who are different and "other" — even those who sing different songs and who tell different stories than the company of the baptized. The acid test of all talk about God is ethical behavior toward those who do not hold the same beliefs and who do not engage in the same practices as Christians. If the baptized only love and work alongside those who see the world the way they do, they may actually only be involved in forms of collective narcissism or religious tribalism. To baptize and to teach for identity and openness in the Triune Name is to teach both how to be loved and how to love. There is nothing more subversive or creative in public life than that.

True love means reaching out in kindness and openness to those who are truly "other." True love reaches out in solidarity and friendship. True love considered socially means working for peace, for justice, for the protection of human dignity, and for social righteousness. Human beings have such love inscribed on their bodies in the waters of baptism.

In the final chapter, we will return to St. Peter's Presbyterian Church to see what difference any of this makes for education and formation for Christian discipleship.

CHAPTER 6

Baptizing and Teaching in the Triune Name at St. Peter's Presbyterian Church

Perhaps . . . the churches can get busy on life-long mystagogy and the
life-long return to the font as Christians seek to live out in the Spirit
the implications of their new birth!

Maxwell Johnson, *The Rites of Christian Initiation*

At the beginning of this study, we considered the baptismal liturgy as enacted in a particular congregation of the PC(USA). In returning to the St.
Peter's congregation here at the end of the study, we are in a position to
imagine a number of important changes that could strengthen the life,
witness, and discipleship formation of the congregation. The various insights and discoveries about the baptism-Trinity-pedagogy nexus will
guide the strategic initiatives described below.

Worship

What would it mean to privilege baptism in the liturgical dimensions of
the life of St. Peter's Church? For starters, vessels of water might be placed
at each entrance to the congregation's central worship space. To be sure,
most Protestants would initially resist this as a return to medieval superstitions about blessed water. It need not carry this meaning, however. Pastors
could explain very clearly that ordinary water has been placed in those ves-

sels and that they are there to remind everyone who enters that it is only by passing through the waters of baptism that anyone enters into the Body of Christ.

We might also look at the order of the liturgy and try to find ways to privilege baptism. For example, at the Genesis Presbyterian Church in Austin, Texas, the worship leader stands behind the centrally placed baptismal font and scoops out cascades of water as the invitation to the call to confession is uttered. Each prayer of confession in that congregation becomes an occasion of baptismal renewal. The gathered congregation confesses sin in the context of remembering and giving thanks for the gift of repentance, forgiveness, and renewal bestowed by the Triune God in baptism.

The above example raises the question of physical location of the baptismal font in the worship space of the congregation. Calvin argued for placing baptismal fonts in juxtaposition to the pulpit in order to stress the close connection between forming practice and orienting narrative. Mostly this seems to have worked out as baptismal fonts placed below or off to the side of pulpits. Such a physical arrangement may have inadvertently contributed to the peripheralization of baptism in Reformed churches. Alternatively, the baptismal font could be placed in a prominent position at the same level as the pulpit in order to signify the parity of the ministries of Word and font. Another possibility would involve placing the baptismal font at the center of the central aisle of pews. This placement, particularly if the font were rather formidable in size, would signify something of the central importance of baptism in the life and work of the congregation. If it were large enough, people would have to move around it on their way to or from the chancel area. As a centrally placed obstruction, it would underscore the privileged place of baptism for the community.

In the end, the mystery of God as Trinity leads less to rational comprehension than to doxological praise. Perhaps the doxology proper ought to be relocated to a different place in the liturgy besides the presentation of the morning tithes and offerings. Perhaps the congregation could sing this immediately following the proclamation of the Word as the very first part of the human response of gratitude and commitment to Triune grace.

Every invitation to the celebration of the Eucharist could begin with a remembrance of baptism. Water from the font could be dramatically used. Words of interpretation could explicitly and elegantly link the font and the table by highlighting that baptism functions as the premise for the Eucharist. With a centrally placed baptismal font, partaking of the Eucharistic elements — whether by intinction or by orderly distribution — would entail negotiating the space around the baptismal font.

The benediction and blessing at the close of the service of worship could employ language from the baptismal rite to send the worshippers out into their service in the world. The standard trinitarian benediction used by many congregations could expand slightly to include the baptismal ground for the grace by which the faithful go forth to continue their worship in all the settings of their daily lives.

Next, we need to look at the dynamics involved in the celebration of the baptismal liturgy itself. Calvin's Genevan baptismal liturgy provides several clues toward constructive change. First, the baptismal liturgy itself may need to become even more intentionally pedagogical. To be sure, interpretive elements are clearly in evidence in the current PC(USA) liturgical text. Yet, enhancing this aspect of the celebration may help the participants to see ever more clearly the crucial importance of baptism as the epitomization of the gospel and as the paradigm for the entirety of the Christian life lived in relation to the mystery of God as Trinity. Specifically, the text of the initial interpretation of the rite may need expansion with the implications of baptism for the character of the Christian life made more explicit. Some instruction about the Triune and pedagogical character of the Christian life could come into bold relief in this statement.

A brief word needs to be said about the importance of anointing with oil immediately after the application of water in the Triune Name. The current PC(USA) baptismal liturgy offers anointing with oil as an optional extra. In light of the close connection between the doctrine of the Trinity and the cross, it would seem that proper anointing with oil in the sign of the cross is mandatory following baptism. Maxwell Johnson has stated it well in calling for a reintegration of confirmation into its original place within the baptismal rite proper:

> Confirmation should be placed back where it belongs — as the inseparable concluding seal of the baptismal rite itself whenever baptism takes place. As a consequence, all the debates about knowledge, preparation, and age for confirmation should be terminated. Perhaps then the churches can get busy on life-long *mystagogy* and the life-long return to

the font as Christians seek to live out in the Spirit the implications of their new birth![1]

Both the Triune Name and the sign of the cross should be inscribed on the flesh of baptizands in order to make clear their identity and the reciprocal interplay between following Jesus Christ and living into a baptismally oriented trinitarian pattern of life.

Another change that should be placed on the agenda for reform of the current PC(USA) baptismal rite concerns the interrelation of baptism and the Eucharist. Baptizing adults exclusively, Gregory of Nyssa was able to articulate something of the close connection between font and table in the Christian life. Ecclesial pedagogy prepared baptizands for participation in an initiatory process that culminated in sacred washing and repasting. It also oriented their lifelong journey of appropriating the meaning of this initiation in relation to the Triune mystery. The font led to the table; the table recalled the font. In very different circumstances, Calvin attempted to recover the initiatory patterns of the early church. To do so, Calvin had to change it. For him ecclesial pedagogy came between font and table. To be sure, he sponsored a form of lifelong mystagogical catechesis subsequent to admittance to the Lord's Supper, but he seems to have underemphasized the interconnections between baptism and the Eucharist.

The Reformed tradition, of which the PC(USA) counts itself a proud member, has largely followed Calvin's lead on these matters. With revision of policies related to the necessary conditions for admittance to the Eucharist in recent decades, the time has now come to rethink the equation of baptism, the Eucharist, and pedagogy. If it is true that sheer Triune grace works in the Eucharist as well as in baptism, then perhaps baptized infants ought also to receive the Eucharistic elements on the very day of their baptism. They can then spend the rest of their lives engaged in patterns of ecclesial pedagogy that will help them live into a deeper understanding of the Triune grace that has been bestowed upon them. First let them experience Triune grace sacramentally, then let them live into deeper understandings of it. Let ecclesial pedagogy reclaim its full-fledged status as mystagogical catechesis leading the baptized (and the communicants) into

1. Maxwell Johnson, *The Rites of Christian Initiation: Their Evolution and Interpretation* (Collegeville, Minn.: Liturgical [A Pueblo Book], 1999), p. 373.

ever more fulsome apprehensions of the Triune reality that has grasped them in these sacraments.[2]

Too often, when baptism is celebrated at St. Peter's it appears to be meaningful and engaging only for the principal players in the drama: the officiating pastor, the parents of the baptizand, the attendant family and friends, and an elder. The celebration of baptism often fails to function as an awe-inspiring rite.[3] Nor does it seem to function very effectively as an occasion for those who have been baptized to remember and celebrate the profound orienting event of their lives. Perhaps worship leaders for the congregation could address this problem by providing substantially more time for the celebration of baptism in the service of worship. Instead of treating it as an added extra to the service, baptism could be regarded as the orienting thematic for the entire service on days when it is administered. Each celebration of baptism and every celebration of the Eucharist provide prime opportunities for the baptismal renewal of all the baptized gathered for worship.

Education and Formation for Discipleship

In his book *Will our Children Have Faith?* John Westerhoff made a strong case a number of years ago for abolishing the "schooling-instructional paradigm" in congregations.[4] He argued that the whole life of the congregation functioned to form faith and that specially designated educational programs — with all the trappings of schools — actually distort and diminish the task of ecclesial pedagogy. While Westerhoff was certainly right to emphasize the many ways in which the whole life of the congregation forms people in faith, he was mistaken to think that this formation could take place apart from time, space, and intentionality given to the task. The church school and the range of other intentional settings where intentional Christian teaching takes place have a crucial role in the process of educating and forming disciples. Moreover, the rumors of the demise of the church school are premature and vastly overrated. Yet it is surely the case that par-

---

2. Johnson, *The Rites of Christian Initiation,* p. 225.

3. I am borrowing from Edward Yarnold's title, *The Awe-Inspiring Rites of Initiation: The Origins of the R.C.I.A.,* 2nd ed. (Collegeville, Minn.: Liturgical, 1994).

4. John Westerhoff, *Will Our Children Have Faith?* (Minneapolis: Winston Seabury, 1976), p. 9.

ticipation in church school for one hour a couple times a month cannot and does not adequately equip people to live creatively and dynamically into the meaning of the Triune mystery at the heart of their baptism. It would be equally an error to rely solely on the church school to carry all the freight of Christian formation as it would to jettison entirely the church school (and other venues for intentional pedagogy) in favor of wide partici- pation in the socializing activities of the congregation. Congregations need not make such an either/or choice. Instead, they can affirm that effective ed- ucation and formation for baptismally based discipleship requires partici- pation in both intentional settings for teaching and learning and the wider range of activities that constitute the life of the congregation. Let me un- pack a bit what this might entail for the St. Peter's congregation.

Intentional Pedagogy

In an expanded and reformulated vision for education and formation for discipleship that arises from reflection on the baptism-Trinity-pedagogy nexus, settings for intentional pedagogy continue to play an important role. Reframed as para-liturgical activities that take seriously both Word and sacraments, the church school and other more traditionally oriented educational settings will need to be rethought in some important ways. In what follows here, I will merely lift up some key issues and themes. A more thoroughgoing revision of the church's intentional pedagogical activities will have to wait for another day. The following principles and strategies may help point the way to a more comprehensive re-imagining of this whole aspect of the church's life. To begin the process of such revision in relation to the concerns of this study, I will briefly touch on four dimen- sions of this church's educational ministry: aims, curriculum, methods of teaching, and the role of the teacher.

1. **Aims** Aims have to do with the overarching purpose of the educational enterprise. They tie together all the components and pieces and provide an orienting direction for the entire effort. Aims are sufficiently broad and lofty that their realization can only be gauged in terms of decades, eras, and even whole lifetimes.

The insights gained from this study provide clarification about the aims of the educational ministry for the St. Peter's congregation. All activities related to the intentional pedagogy of this congregation should be organized to serve a single overriding aim: *the formation of committed Christian disciples who continually seek to live out the meaning of baptism through joyful praise of the Trinity and creative engagement in pluralistic democracy.* The baptismal anchor for this way of life will hold together the mystical and the political dimensions of discipleship.[5] The baptized will grow toward the realization of this aim through the twin processes of daily dying to sin and the forces of death and daily rising to new life in Christ by the power of the Holy Spirit.

2. Curriculum The results of this study point to the need to oppose Karl Barth's later views of baptism. The combination of influence from his son's New Testament work on baptism and his own dismay at the high percentage of baptized babies who grew up to serve as Nazi storm troopers led Barth to conclude that Calvin had had a failure of nerve at the point of affirming the sacramental character of baptism. Barth argued that Calvin did not go far enough in reforming everything according to Scripture — including baptism.[6] He concluded that baptism was not a sacrament in which the Triune God was at work; rather, it functions properly as the first and paradigmatic *human response* to Triune grace.[7] Barth saw clearly the implication of this understanding of baptism: infant baptism should be abolished. Only those old enough to understand the meaning of Christian commitment and the life of discipleship ought to be baptized.

In my judgment, Barth erred in rejecting the sacramental character of baptism as the remedy for the dangerous specter of cultural Christianity. The problem lies not with conceiving of baptism in sacramental terms. Infant baptism likewise does not deserve the blame. The failure represented by untold thousands of baptized babies growing up to serve the Nazi death machine likely had more to do with abysmal failures in ecclesial pedagogy than with thinking of baptism in sacramental terms. The lack of robust, prophetic, and dialogical ecclesial pedagogy in which the idols of church

---

5. For a fuller discussion of the juxtaposition of the mystical and political aspects of discipleship, see Johannes B. Metz's *Followers of Christ: Perspectives on the Religious Life and the Church* (New York: Paulist, 1978), pp. 39-44.

6. Karl Barth, *Church Dogmatics*, 4/4 (fragment), The Doctrine of Reconciliation, trans. G. W. Bromiley, ed. G. W. Bromiley and T. F. Torrance (Edinburgh: T&T Clark, 1969), p. ix.

7. Barth, *Church Dogmatics*, 4/4, pp. 134ff.

and culture were unmasked in light of the Triune mystery provides a more adequate accounting for the ecclesial dimensions of the German crisis in the first half of the twentieth century. A similar indictment of the effectiveness of ecclesial pedagogy might well apply to white South African Protestants during the era of apartheid and to the United States of America in the era of Jim Crow segregation or in the current era of American empire.

Programs of intentional ecclesial pedagogy in congregations like St. Peter's ought to be framed as growing out of and in service to the sacrament of baptism in all its fullness. Stephen Fowl in the conclusion to his work *Engaging Scripture* calls for a renewed commitment to baptismally based ecclesial pedagogy as critical to his project of promoting "Christian practical reasoning" related to the interpretation of Scripture:

> The most obvious practices of formation for my particular purposes are those related to baptism and catechesis. Whether catechesis follows or precedes baptism, the crucial point is to note its connection to baptism. That is, if baptism initiates one into the covenant people of God and thereby joins an individual to that people formed by the death and resurrection of Jesus and journeying under the Spirit's guidance toward the kingdom of God, then catechesis helps those individuals to complete the journey successfully. This is done by introducing and beginning to provide the conceptual, moral, and spiritual resources Christians will need to complete their journey. As I already noted, this must involve the development of scriptural knowledge. It is clear that Christians can no longer presume (if they ever really could) that regular church attendance and general cultural awareness would provide Christians with a basic grasp of biblical content. Moreover, catechesis must also provide an initial context within which scripture can be interpreted in the light of the ends towards which Christians live their lives. At present, very few churches attend to catechesis with anything like the diligence it requires.[8]

Conceived as a para-liturgical endeavor, ecclesial pedagogy in mainline Protestant congregations would situate the study of Scripture in a framework that would unlock the transformative potential of a baptismally

---

8. Stephen E. Fowl, *Engaging Scripture: A Model for Theological Interpretation*, Challenges in Contemporary Theology series (Malden, Mass. and Oxford: Blackwell, 1998), pp. 200-201.

funded practical trinitarianism. If this were to be successful, it would effectively eliminate the possibility of seeing worship and education as separate spheres of activity in the life of the church.

In terms of the doctrine of the Trinity, our study of Calvin would seem to indicate that intentional ecclesial pedagogy in congregations ought to foster the development of a concrete trinitarian grammar for understanding what takes place in ordinary Christian practices like prayer, Bible reading, and service to others. Exegeting experiences at the core of the Christian life may help the baptized to develop a richer sense of how their particular lives and the churches fit into the Triune economy of salvation. According to liturgical theologian Gordon Lathrop:

> The whole process, teaching and bath, is recapitulated in the central act of washing in the triune name. That name has been the core content of the teaching. To stand in the bath juxtaposed to that name, then is to be washed with the water filled with the surprising grace of that name, is to be inserted in to the Christian faith. . . . They speak over the bath the name of Jesus Christ and of the Holy Spirit, and thus they stand before the one God, who is known only by the power of the Spirit in the presence of Christ. Insertion in the active pairing of the name of God with the water becomes insertion into the truth and life of God. The teaching of the community will be continually exploring this name, this combination of no name with the name of Jesus Christ, and leading to the pairing of this name with the bath.[9]

The doctrine of the Trinity should be taught as a practical matter arising from reflection upon the language and gestures of worship and in service to creative engagement in the public realm. The liturgical formation experienced by worshippers requires pedagogically oriented times and places outside of worship for reflection, discussion, and exploration if it is to fully shape Christian communal life and spiritual experience.

Ecclesial pedagogy ought also to teach the dynamics of the Christian life in relation to the core constituting practices of the churches. Here the term *core constituting practices* means the Word and sacraments. For example, ecclesial pedagogy could teach about the Triune mystery by focusing on the relationship between baptism, the Eucharist, and the ministry of

---

9. Gordon W. Lathrop, *Holy Things: A Liturgical Theology* (Minneapolis: Fortress, 1993; paperback ed., 1998), pp. 67-68.

the Word. Each practice carries its own unique features and manifestations. Yet the inner meaning or essence of all three is the same: Triune grace. Calvin taught this when he proclaimed that it should "be regarded as a settled principle that the sacraments have the same office as the Word of God: to offer and set forth Christ to us, and in him the treasures of heavenly grace."[10] Baptism, the Eucharist, and the Word in the liturgy, then, can function pedagogically as an analogy for the Trinity. In these core elements of worship, one finds both clear differentiation and shared essence. One could also focus on the relation between baptism, the Eucharist, and pedagogy as a basis for reflection about the Christian teaching of the doctrine of God as Trinity.

Taking some cues from liturgical theologian Don Saliers, we might also think in terms of another triad. Saliers suggests that "Word, Sacrament, and suffering human beings" find their ultimate meaning in Jesus Christ through the illuminating work of the Holy Spirit.[11] This pedagogical analogy carries the advantage of bringing together core liturgical acts with the all too often agonizing depths of human experience. This scheme also has the advantage of identifying Jesus Christ in the depths of each element. Further, the deep meaning of the Word, sacraments, and human suffering turns out to be intelligible only by means of trinitarian grammar.

The love analogy first put forward by Augustine and later developed even further by medieval trinitarian theologian and mystic Richard of St. Victor provides a particularly rich way for baptismally based teaching about the mystery of the Triune God.[12] In depicting baptism as an act of divine love for human beings, the opportunity arises to reflect on the meaning of love itself. Richard's argument that genuine love requires a minimum of three (as opposed to Augustine's two) Persons could prove especially helpful in connecting the doctrine of the Trinity with the most basic experiences of human life.[13]

---

10. John Calvin, *Institutes of the Christian Religion,* ed. J. T. McNeill, trans. Ford Lewis Battles, 2 vols., Library of Religious Classics, vols. 20 and 21 (Philadelphia: Westminster, 1960), 4.14.17.

11. Don E. Saliers, *Worship as Theology: Foretaste of Glory Divine* (Nashville: Abingdon, 1994), p. 230.

12. Augustine, *The Trinity,* in *The Works of Saint Augustine: A Translation for the 21st Century,* Part I — Books, vol. 5: *The Trinity,* trans. Edmund Hill, ed. John E. Rotelle (Brooklyn: New City, 1991), p. 255.

13. Richard of St. Victor, "Book Three of the Trinity," in *Richard of St. Victor: The Twelve*

Finally, ecclesial pedagogy developed in relation to the baptism-Trinity-pedagogy nexus would involve exploration of the various constellations of practices that make up the Christian life. The practices identified by Dykstra and Bass would provide a helpful place to begin. The following practices taken together constitute a compelling vision of the Christian life: honoring the body, hospitality, household economics, saying "yes" and saying "no," keeping Sabbath, testimony, discernment, shaping communities, forgiveness, healing, dying well, and singing our lives.[14] To make use of this constellation of practices according to the vision outlined in this study, two modifications would be necessary. First, the various practices outlined above would have to have more explicit grounding in the core constituting practices of the churches: the Word and sacraments — with even more emphasis on baptism than Dykstra and Bass have already provided.[15] Second, the practice of apophatically charged democratic conversation would have to find a central place in their constellation of practices in order to provide for a robust engagement with many of the pressing issues of contemporary American society.

An emphasis on practices in ecclesial pedagogy would benefit greatly from Kathryn Tanner's insight about the nature of Christian practices. She argues that Christian practices do not function as neat and tidy things; instead, they are ambiguous, inconsistent, and open-ended.[16] This messiness factor makes ecclesial pedagogy and theological education necessary. It also renders them useful for engagement in the complex and untidy processes of creative democratic engagement with the wider public. The ambiguity, inconsistency, and open-endedness of Christian practices help to promote not only identity formation but also inescapable openness to non-Christian "others." If they were too neat and tidy, they could form a hermetic seal around the baptized that might sunder any meaningful ties

---

Patriarchs, The Mystical Ark, Book Three of the Trinity, trans. Grover A. Zinn, The Classics of Western Spirituality series, ed. Richard J. Payne (New York and Mahwah, N.J.: Paulist, 1979), pp. 384-92.

14. Dorothy C. Bass, ed., *Practicing Our Faith: A Way of Life for a Searching People* (San Francisco: Jossey-Bass, 1997).

15. Craig R. Dykstra and Dorothy C. Bass, "A Theological Understanding of Christian Practices," in *Practicing Theology: Beliefs and Practices in Christian Life,* ed. Miroslav Volf and Dorothy C. Bass (Grand Rapids: Eerdmans, 2002), pp. 30-31.

16. Kathryn Tanner, "Theological Reflection and Christian Practices," in Volf and Bass, eds., *Practicing Theology,* pp. 229-34.

with the rough and tumble of the wider pluralistic context of contemporary democratic America. Handled properly, the messiness of practices can function less as a problem to be solved than as a resource to be exploited for the vision of baptismally based discipleship envisioned here.

If baptism remains simply one topic among many covered in the course of the church school curriculum, then the rich potential of the rite for service as a paradigm for the entirety of the Christian life will only languish under a bushel. Only by shifting baptism from the peripheral to the center of both worship and ecclesial pedagogy will such changes as those contemplated here become possible.

3. Methods of Teaching   While teachers at St. Peter's Presbyterian could employ a wide variety of teaching methods, certain techniques would have a high degree of compatibility with the overarching aim and with the curriculum. In particular, methods of teaching that use an action-reflection loop would likely prove most effective. This approach to discipleship would grow out of reflection upon and exploration of the baptismal rite. As a para-liturgical activity linking liturgy and life, the educational ministry of the congregation would need to provide rich opportunities for reflection upon the experience of baptism and baptismal renewal in light of the challenges posed for living out the full meaning of baptism in the social and political context. The particular action-reflection methods used would, of course, have to be scaled according to the learners' ages and stages.

In order to foster constructive habits of interpretation and dialogue necessary for the sort of committed openness called for by the baptism-Trinity-pedagogy nexus, those who teach for discipleship should make generous use of the arts. Visual arts, music, and literature tend to encourage the development of particular points of view that also remain open to other interpretations.

In addition to a liberal use of the arts, ecclesial pedagogy along the lines developed here ought to place a premium on discussion as a method of teaching. Scaled developmentally, the frequent and appropriate use of various kinds of discussion techniques over the course of many years can cultivate the kinds of skills necessary for faithful and creative engagement in a pluralistic democracy. The development of this set of skills is too important to be left solely to the realm of public education. The church needs to teach the complex art of democratic conversation to the baptized. With its long-standing commitments to love, justice, respect for the dignity of each person, and the dynamics of testimony, the Christian community should make frequent and judicious use of this method of teaching.

Baptism points to the limits of all human understanding about the things of God. Theological reflection upon the baptismal rite points to both what can be known and what cannot be known about the mystery of the Trinity. On the one hand, baptism discloses something of the practical revelation of the Trinity on behalf of human beings caught up in the processes of death and sin. On the other hand, the baptismally inspired doctrine of the Trinity leads to apophatic limits. Emphasizing such limits — as well as the paradoxical character of God as simultaneously one and three — has pedagogical value that can result in intellectual humility and graciousness of spirit in the face of differences.

Those charged with educational leadership in congregations need to use pedagogical strategies that address the apophatic limits of baptismally based reflection on the mystery of the Trinity. Such strategies entail the use of such indirect methods of teaching about the mystery of God as parables, practices, artistic expression, and open-ended dialogue. Such methods of instruction are inherently open-textured and gesture toward the transcendent. Greater attention will need to be paid in this way of approaching discipleship education and formation to Jesus' parables, to the arts, and to the pedagogical method of indirection developed by Christian existentialist philosopher Søren Kierkegaard.

Emphasizing baptismally inspired Triune transcendence as a basis for the formation of people who have well-developed capacities for conversation with those who differ calls, too, for the introduction of robust practices of dialogue into ecclesial pedagogy. Stressing the apophatic limits of knowledge of the Triune mystery at the heart of the baptismal rite requires promoting an understanding of the dynamics of dialogical conversation and the exploration and critique of arguments within an overarching framework provided by a common or shared sense of the defining gift of baptism.

4. Role of the Teacher   Calvin's vision for discipleship education and formation has relevance for us today as we think through the implications of the baptism-Trinity-pedagogy nexus for the local church. Calvin envisioned a shared responsibility between home and church for the education and formation of the baptized into mature disciples of Christ. Local churches need to sponsor a similar sort of partnership in order to meet the challenges of helping the baptized to develop a clear sense of Christian identity and to engage creatively in pluralistic democracy.

Today, most parents and other primary caregivers of children and youth in mainline Protestant congregations have effectively abdicated their vocation as primary religious educators of children. Too many parents seem content to let the education and fellowship programs of the church form the faith of their baptized children. The recovery of a strong sense of parental vocation to teach the Triune faith to the baptized at home and in partnership with the church may well prove to be pivotal in the effort to form people with both a strong sense of Christian identity and a radical openness to others. Ecclesial pedagogy must include teaching and modeling that takes place in the home. Change along these lines begins with the baptismal rite.

In Calvin's Genevan baptismal rite, he not only asked parents if they would teach the Christian faith to their children, he also spelled out in considerable detail the curriculum they were expected to use. Contemporary baptismal rites should likewise specify the outlines of the pattern of ecclesial pedagogy that parents should teach in the home. Change of the covenantal questions in the rite itself must be complemented by well-developed courses of baptismal preparation for parents who wish to have their children baptized.

An educational campaign might be waged to help families connect all of their uses of water with the baptismal rite. This is standard practice in the cultures of Eastern Orthodox churches. Helping people to remember baptism whenever they use water at home and in public seems like a simple, yet effective way to cultivate a pervasive awareness of the centrality of baptism as the paradigm for the Christian life.

Deeper still, congregational leaders can promulgate an understanding of the ritual dimensions of everyday life across the lifecycle. For the purposes of illustration, let us turn to an excursus on the work of developmental theorist Erik Erikson on the subject of ritualization and the lifecycle. In his work *Toys and Reasons*, Erikson articulated a schema for understanding human growth across the lifecycle in reference to daily rituals of everyday life.[17] Even though Erikson emphasized the ritual aspects of

---

17. Erik Erikson, *Toys and Reasons: Stages in the Ritualization of Experience* (New York: W. W. Norton, 1977).

everyday life in distinction from highly formalized communal religious rituals, his work in this area might well prove useful for thinking about how to revise the text of the baptismal liturgy in such a way as to highlight the significance of this sacrament for the life situation of each participant in the congregation. If it is true that baptism functions as the paradigm for the entirety of the Christian life, then it ought to have some relevance across the stages of the lifecycle.

Erikson's assertion that "daily custom creates ritual needs which then find periodic fulfillment in grand rituals"[18] may well be one of the keys to strengthening the baptismal rite as the paradigm for the Christian life. Though Erikson focused primarily on the ritualizations that make up daily life, we might well ask about possible ways by which both the baptismal rite epitomizes such daily rituals — thereby giving them their highest meaning — and the possible ways that the grand ritual of baptism might impact in some decisive way the myriad of rituals that make up daily life. Strengthening the conceptual and symbolic ties between the developmental realities of congregants and the baptismal rite itself may equip church members with the vision and insight needed to make good on the promises made in the baptismal liturgy to teach the Christian faith to the new baptizand. Their teaching baptizands the essentials of the Christian life likely depends upon their abilities to exemplify and articulate the range of connections between the way they live their lives and the meaning of the baptismal rite.

The education and formation taking place in the home must find its counterpart within the congregation. This has two aspects. First, the baptismal rite calls upon the congregation itself to function as teacher for the baptized. Second, each congregation identifies a number of people — volunteer and paid — who have particular gifts for teaching.

The entire assembly of St. Peter's Presbyterian makes promises to teach the baptized in each and every celebration of baptism. In order to make good on these promises, the congregation needs to pay attention to the formational value of each aspect of its life. It may make some significant difference in the congregation if its members always have one eye fixed on the task of discipleship formation. The often soul-killing business of maintaining the congregation as a nonprofit institution may find new life and vitality if reframed in relation to the pervasive task of education

18. Erikson, *Toys and Reasons*, p. 79.

and formation for discipleship and the living out of that discipleship through creative engagement with the social and political issues of the day. I will have more to say on the congregation as teacher of the baptized in the following section.

Those who by gifts and training have particular educational responsibilities for helping the baptized to live into mature discipleship have an important part to play in the ecology of formation called forth by the baptism-Trinity-pedagogy nexus. Because of their special role in the congregation, the pastor or pastors of the local church can do a great deal to make baptism more central in the life of the church. For instance, they can initiate many of the changes described above in the discussion of the role that liturgy can play in this new emphasis. They can lift up the centrality and importance of baptism in all its fullness in their preaching. Through preparatory instruction and changes in the liturgy, they can also play a major role in helping parents to discover and own their vocation as primary religious educators for their baptized children. Through their involvement in and primary leadership for the intentional pedagogy of the congregation, pastors signal the central importance of lifelong engagement in mystagogical catechesis. By initiating partnerships and modeling constructive cooperation in the community, pastors can help members see the connections between font and public square. In short, pastors play a key role in helping congregations move toward the realization of the baptismally based embrace of identity and openness we have been exploring.

Non-ordained staff members and lay volunteers also have a key part to play in fostering an engaged discipleship marked by a thoroughgoing trinitarian grammar. They can help to connect the dots between liturgy and life through their leadership of the church's educational ministry. By seeing their own discipleship and ministry of teaching as an outgrowth of baptism, they can inspire learners in the church to get excited about finding out what it means to live out the gift of baptism. By working on deepening their own apprehension of the doctrine of the Trinity, they can help others to learn and grow in their exploration of this joyful mystery. They can model for young disciples the kind of baptismally based life that is marked by both well-defined Christian identity and generous openness to neighbors of all kinds and creeds.

Education and Formation for Discipleship Through Participation in the Whole Life of the Church

The emerging vision of a trinitarian practical theology of Christian forma-tion marked by both the privileging of baptism in all its fullness and the dynamic interplay of baptism, the Trinity, and ecclesial pedagogy does have something important to contribute to various struggles of the St. Pe-ter's congregation. One key implication concerns the issue of finding a ba-sis for unity in the midst of diversity. Gregory and Calvin urge that we un-derstand baptism as the paradigm for the entirety of the Christian life. Its dynamics and character should mark the way in which Christians live out their lives of discipleship together in the context of the church. Gregory of Nyssa called our attention to the importance of the baptismal formula at the epicenter of the rite. Through baptism, the baptized enter into a reality characterized by unity and diversity. Miroslav Volf reflects:

> The resurrected Christ, in whom Jews and Greeks are united through baptism, is not a spiritual refuge from pluralizing corporeality, a pure spiritual space into which only the undifferentiated sameness of a uni-versal human essence is admitted. Rather, baptism into Christ creates a people as the differentiated body of Christ. Bodily inscribed differences are brought together, not removed. The body of Christ lives as a com-plex interplay of differentiated bodies — Jewish and gentile, female and male, slave and free — of those who have partaken of Christ's self-sacrifice. The Pauline move is not from the particularity of the body to the universality of the spirit, but from separated bodies, to the commu-nity of interrelated bodies — the one *body in the Spirit* with many *dis-crete members.*[19]

The One Name That Is Three conditions the quality of life and community into which people enter by passing through the sacred waters. In other words, baptism signifies that the Christian life calls forth a certain reci-procity of unity and diversity — in church, yes, but also in society. It pro-vides the symbolic markers for a unity not based in uniformity but in real and definite differences. Though Volf does not make an explicit link with baptism in his description of "embrace" of the other, the implicit baptis-

---

19. Miroslav Volf, *Exclusion and Embrace: A Theological Exploration of Identity, Other-ness, and Reconciliation* (Nashville: Abingdon, 1996), p. 48.

mal connection runs just below the surface when he writes: "As a meta-phor, embrace implies that the self and the other belong together in their mutual alterity. For the self shaped by the cross of Christ and the life of the triune God, however, embrace includes not just the other who is a friend but also the other who is the enemy."[20] Church members need not find unity in ideological positions on questions of ordination or patriotism, but in their common birth in the waters of baptism. Entering into the mystery of One Name That Is Three means that the basis of unity lies in being grasped by Triune grace. Understood in this way, baptism can provide the grounds for deeply faithful and creative citizenship by extrapolating experiences of unity and diversity inside the community of faith outward into the public realm.

20. Volf, *Exclusion and Embrace*, p. 146.

An Overture to a Trinitarian Practical Theology
of Christian Formation

In this study, I have sought to make the case that the baptismal rite, the doctrine of the Trinity, and practices of ecclesial pedagogy belong inseparably together. After considering the features and issues associated with the embodied practice of baptism as found in a particular congregation, we took some depth soundings in the fields of theology and Christian education in order to gain some deeper insight about the complex interplay of baptism, the Trinity, and pedagogy. From there, we looked at two pastor-theologians of the past — Gregory of Nyssa and John Calvin — as exemplars and resources for thinking about the inner dynamics of this crucial nexus. We then moved into a consideration of how some of the key insights from Gregory and Calvin might help us articulate and be guided by the baptism-Trinity-pedagogy nexus in our contemporary context. Lastly, we returned to the St. Peter's Presbyterian Church to see how the principles mapped out in chapter 5 might inform specific strategic initiatives for worship, education, and congregational life in service to the forming of deeply grounded and publicly engaged disciples of Christ.

In closing, I want to outline what I think could be a way forward toward the development of a more full-blown trinitarian practical theology of Christian formation. While baptism in all of its fullness would serve as the cornerstone of such a conversation, a more comprehensive effort would have to be broadened to include considerations of the Eucharist and the Word — as well as the dynamic interplay between the Word and sacraments. In other words, the primary formative practices of Christian churches would constitute the bedrock for such a comprehensive trinitarian practical theology of Christian formation. This larger project would be suffused with a rich trinitarian grammar throughout and would give prominence to the challenges and complexities posed not only by the pedagogical vector created by the juxtaposition of the baptismal rite and the doctrine of the Trinity, but also by the complexities of pastoral care and the multitudinous forms of Christian witness.

A project of this magnitude would likely require teams of people working collaboratively on different aspects of the challenge. Professors, graduate students, pastors, laypeople, and empirical researchers from a variety of social science fields would all need places around the research table. Such varied perspectives would give the conversation a series of interrelated feedback loops that would generate real dynamism, creativity, and multiplicity of perspectives as attempts are made to effectively address formational concerns in contemporary contexts. Such sustained conversations might well be generative of the kinds of insights that would help both church and academy to adapt more quickly and more effectively to the challenges posed by rapidly changing social and cultural contexts in the contemporary situation.

These conversations might focus throughout on the widest possible implications of the engagement of individuals and communities in the baptismal theme of transformation from death to life. In so doing, they might address not only the dynamics of individual formation and transformation but also the complex dynamics of significant change in local and global contexts. In these days of denominational retrenchment and phased collapse, I believe that much of the initiative for such a collaborative enterprise would have to come from theological schools.

It is my hope that such an enterprise would result in a number of creative initiatives that would foster the identity and openness needed for the times in which we live and appropriate to the mystery of being baptized into the One Name of Father, Son, and Holy Spirit.

Bibliography

Anderson, E. Byron, and Bruce T. Morrill, eds. *Liturgy and the Moral Self: Humanity at Full Stretch Before God: Essays in Honor of Don E. Saliers.* Collegeville, Minn.: Liturgical, 1998.

Anderson, Ray. *The Shape of Practical Theology: Empowering Ministry with Theological Praxis.* Downers Grove, Ill.: InterVarsity, 2001.

Augustine. *The Trinity.* In *The Works of Saint Augustine: A Translation for the 21st Century.* Part I — Books. Vol. 5: *The Trinity.* Translated by Edmund Hill, O.P. Brooklyn: New City, 1991.

Ayres, Lewis. "On Not Three People: The Fundamental Themes of Gregory of Nyssa's Trinitarian Theology as Seen in *To Ablabius: On Not Three Gods.*" In *Re-Thinking Gregory of Nyssa,* edited by Sarah Coakley. Malden, Mass.: Blackwell, 2003.

Balás, David L. "Gregory of Nyssa." In *Encyclopedia of Early Christianity.* 2nd ed. Edited by Everett Ferguson. Vol. 1839 in Garland Reference Library of the Humanities. New York: Garland, 1999.

Balthasar, Hans Urs von. *Presence and Thought: An Essay on the Religious Philosophy of Gregory of Nyssa.* Translated by Mark Sebanc. San Francisco: Ignatius (A Communio Book), 1995.

Barnes, Michel René. *The Power of God: Δύναμις in Gregory of Nyssa's Trinitarian Theology.* Washington, D.C.: Catholic University Press of America, 2001.

Barth, Karl. *Church Dogmatics,* 1/1, *The Doctrine of the Word of God.* 2nd ed. Translated by G. W. Bromiley. Edited by G. W. Bromiley and T. F. Torrance. Edinburgh: T & T Clark, 1975.

———. *Church Dogmatics,* 4/4 (fragment), *The Doctrine of Reconciliation.* Edited by G. W. Bromiley and T. F. Torrance. Edinburgh: T & T Clark, 1969.

———. *The Epistle to the Romans.* Translated from the 6th ed. by Edwyn C. Hoskyns. New York: Oxford University Press, 1933; Oxford paperback ed., 1968.

————. *The Theology of John Calvin.* Translated by Geoffrey W. Bromiley. Grand Rapids: Eerdmans, 1995.

Bass, Dorothy, ed. *Practicing Our Faith: A Way of Life for a Searching People.* San Francisco: Jossey-Bass, 1997.

————. *Receiving the Day: Christian Practices for Opening the Gift of Time.* San Francisco: Jossey-Bass, 2000.

Battles, Ford Lewis. *Analysis of the Institutes of the Christian Religion of John Calvin.* Grand Rapids: Baker, 1980.

————. *Interpreting John Calvin.* Edited by Robert Benedetto. Grand Rapids: Baker, 1996.

Benson, Peter L., and Carolyn H. Elkin. *Effective Christian Education: A National Study of Protestant Congregations — A Summary Report on Faith, Loyalty, and Congregational Life.* Minneapolis: Search Institute, 1990.

The Book of Common Worship. Prepared by the Theology and Worship Ministry Unit for the Presbyterian Church (U.S.A.) and the Cumberland Presbyterian Church. Louisville: Westminster John Knox, 1993.

Bouwsma, William J. *John Calvin: A Sixteenth-Century Portrait.* New York: Oxford University Press, 1988.

Brown, Peter. *The Body and Society: Men, Women, and Sexual Renunciation in Early Christianity.* Vol. 13, new series, Lectures on the History of Religions. New York: Columbia University Press, 1988.

————. *Power and Persuasion in Late Antiquity: Towards a Christian Empire.* The Curtis Lectures, University of Wisconsin, Madison, 1988. Madison: University of Wisconsin Press, 1992.

————. *Society and the Holy in Late Antiquity.* Berkeley: University of California Press, 1982.

Browning, Don S. *A Fundamental Practical Theology: Descriptive and Strategic Proposals.* Minneapolis: Fortress, 1991.

Browning, Robert L., and Roy A. Reed. *The Sacraments in Religious Education and Liturgy: An Ecumenical Model.* Birmingham, Ala.: Religious Education Press, 1985.

Butin, Philip W. *Revelation, Redemption, and Response: Calvin's Trinitarian Understanding of the Divine-Human Relationship.* New York: Oxford University Press, 1995.

Caldwell, Elizabeth Francis. *Rethinking the Sacraments for Children.* Cleveland: Pilgrim, 1996.

Calvin, John. *Calvin: Theological Treatises.* Translated by J. K. S. Reid. Vol. 22, Library of Christian Classics. Philadelphia: Westminster, 1954.

————. *Commentary on the Gospel According to John.* Vol. 1. Translated by William Pringle. Grand Rapids: Eerdmans, 1949.

————. *Institutes of the Christian Religion.* Edited by J. T. McNeill. Translated by Ford Lewis Battles. 2 vols. Library of Christian Classics, vols. 20 and 21. Philadelphia: Westminster, 1960.

————. "John Calvin: Catechism of 1538." Translated by Ford Lewis Battles. In I. John

Bibliography

Hesselink, *Calvin's First Catechism: A Commentary, Featuring Ford Lewis Battles'
Translation of the 1538 Catechism.* Louisville: Westminster John Knox, 1997.

———. *La Forme des Prieres Ecclesiastiques.* In *Johannis Calvini Opera Selecta.* Vol. 2.
Edited by Peter Barth and Wilhelm Niesel. Munich: Christian Kaiser, 1962.

———. "Mutual Consent in Regard to the Sacraments" (1554). In *Calvin's Tracts and
Treatises.* Vol. 2. Translated by H. Beveridge. Notes by T. F. Torrance. Grand
Rapids: Eerdmans, 1958.

Charry, Ellen T. *By the Renewing of Your Minds: The Pastoral Function of Doctrine.* New
York: Oxford University Press, 1997.

Coakley, Sarah, ed. *Re-thinking Gregory of Nyssa.* Malden, Mass.: Blackwell, 2003.

The Constitution of the Presbyterian Church (U.S.A.), Part II: Book of Order. Louisville:
Office of the General Assembly, 2001-2.

Cottret, Bernard. *Calvin: A Biography.* Translated by M. Wallace McDonald. Grand
Rapids: Eerdmans, 2000. Originally published in French as *Calvin Biographie,*
1995.

Daniélou, Jean. *From Glory to Glory: Texts From Gregory of Nyssa's Mystical Writings.*
Translated and edited by Herbert Musurillo. New York: Scribner's Sons, 1961; reprint, Crestwood, N.Y.: St. Vladimir's Seminary Press, 2001.

———. *Platonisme et Théologie Mystique: Doctrine Spirituelle de Saint Grégoire de
Nysse.* Théologie: Études Publiées Sous la Direction de la Faculté de Théologie S.J.
de Lyon-Fourvière. No. 2. Nouvelle edition. Revue et augmenté. Aubier: Éditions
Montaigne, 1944.

Dewey, John. *Democracy and Education: An Introduction to Philosophy of Education.*
New York: The Free Press, 1916; paperback ed., 1966.

———. *How We Think.* Great Books in Philosophy series. Amherst, N.Y.: Prometheus,
1991.

Dowey, Edward A., Jr. *The Knowledge of God in Calvin's Theology.* Expanded ed. Grand
Rapids: Eerdmans, 1994. Originally published New York: Columbia University
Press, 1952.

Dujarier, Michel. *A History of the Catechumenate: The First Six Centuries.* Translated by
Edward J. Haasl. New York: Sadlier, 1979.

Dykstra, Craig R. *Growing in the Life of Faith: Education and Christian Practices.* Louisville: Geneva, 1999.

Dykstra, Craig R., and Dorothy C. Bass. "A Theological Understanding of Christian
Practices." In *Practicing Theology: Beliefs and Practices in Christian Life.* Edited by
Miroslav Volf and Dorothy Bass. Grand Rapids: Eerdmans, 2002.

Eck, Diana L. *A New Religious America: How a "Christian Country" Has Become the
World's Most Religiously Diverse Nation.* New York: HarperSanFrancisco, 2001.

"Edict of Milan." In *The Concise Oxford Dictionary of the Christian Church.* Edited by
E. A. Livingstone. Oxford: Oxford University Press, 1977.

Eire, Carlos M. N. *War Against the Idols: The Reformation of Worship from Erasmus to
Calvin.* Cambridge: Cambridge University Press, 1986; paperback reprint, 1997.

Elm, Susanna. *Virgins of God: The Making of Asceticism in Late Antiquity.* Oxford Classical Monographs. New York: Oxford University Press, 1996.

Erikson, Erik. *Toys and Reasons: Stages in the Ritualization of Experience.* New York: W. W. Norton, 1977.

Farley, Edward. *Theologia: The Fragmentation and Unity of Theological Education.* Philadelphia: Fortress, 1983.

Ferguson, Everett. "Baptism." In *Encyclopedia of Early Christianity.* 2nd ed. Edited by Everett Ferguson. Vol. 1839, Garland Reference Library of the Humanities. New York: Garland, 1998.

Feuerbach, Ludwig. *The Essence of Christianity.* Translated by George Eliot. Amherst, N.Y.: Prometheus, 1989.

Fichte, Johann Gottlieb. *The Science of Knowledge.* Edited and translated by Peter Heath and John Lachs. Cambridge: Cambridge University Press, 1982; n.p.: Meredith Corporation, 1970.

————. *The Way Toward the Blessed Life or The Doctrine of Religion.* Translated by William Smith. London: John Chapman, 1849.

Finn, Thomas M. *Early Christian Baptism and the Catechumenate: West and East Syria.* Vol. 5, *Message of the Fathers of the Church,* edited by Thomas Halton. Collegeville, Minn.: Liturgical (A Michael Glazier Book), 1992.

Foster, Charles R. *Educating Congregations: The Future of Christian Education.* Nashville: Abingdon, 1994.

Fowl, Stephen E. *Engaging Scripture: A Model for Theological Interpretation.* Challenges in Contemporary Theology series. Edited by Gareth Jones and Lewis Ayres. Malden, Mass., and Oxford: Blackwell, 1998.

Fowler, James W. *Becoming Adult, Becoming Christian: Adult Development and Christian Faith.* San Francisco: HarperSanFrancisco, 1984.

————. *Faith Development and Pastoral Care.* Theology and Pastoral Care series. Edited by Don S. Browning. Philadelphia: Fortress, 1987.

————. *Faithful Change: The Personal and Public Challenges of Postmodern Life.* Nashville: Abingdon, 1996.

————. *Stages of Faith: The Psychology of Human Development and the Quest for Meaning.* San Francisco: Harper & Row, 1981.

————. *To See the Kingdom: The Theological Vision of H. Richard Niebuhr.* Nashville: Abingdon, 1974.

————. *Weaving the New Creation: Stages of Faith and the Public Church.* San Francisco: HarperSanFrancisco, 1991.

Fowler, James W., and Sam Keen. *Life Maps: Conversations on the Journey of Faith.* Edited by Jerome Berryman. Waco, Tex.: Word, 1978.

Friere, Paulo. *Pedagogy of the Oppressed.* Translated by Myra Bergman Ramos. New York: Continuum, 1970; reprint, 2000.

Ganoczy, Alexandre. "Calvin's Life." Translated by David L. Foxgrover and James Schmitt. In *The Cambridge Companion to John Calvin.* Edited by Donald K. McKim. Cambridge: Cambridge University Press, 2004.

Gardner, Howard. *Intelligence Reframed: Multiple Intelligences for the 21st Century.* New York: Basic, 1999.

de Greef, Wulfert. *The Writings of John Calvin: An Introductory Guide.* Translated by Lyle D. Bierma. Grand Rapids: Baker, 1993.

Gregory of Nyssa. *The Catechetical Oration of St. Gregory of Nyssa.* Translated by J. H. Srawley. London: Society for Promoting Christian Knowledge, 1917.

————. *Commentary on the Song of Songs.* Translated by Casimir McCambley. Vol. 12, The Archbishop of Iakovos Library of Ecclesiastical and Historical Sources. Edited by N. M. Vaporis. Brookline, Mass.: Hellenic College Press, 1987.

————. *Gregorii Nysseni Epistulae.* Vol. 8, Part 2. Edited by Gregorius Pasquali. In *Gregorii Nysseni Opera.* Edited by Werner Jaeger. Leiden: E. J. Brill, 1959.

————. *Gregory of Nyssa: Life of Moses.* Translated by Abraham J. Malherbe and Everett Ferguson. The Classics of Western Spirituality: A Library of the Great Spiritual Masters series. Edited by Richard J. Payne. New York: Paulist, 1978.

————. *The Life of Saint Macrina.* Translated by Kevin Corrigan. Toronto: Peregrina, 1997.

————. *Oratio Catechetica.* Opera Dogmatica Minora. Part 4. Edited by Ekkehardus Mühlenberg. In *Gregorii Nysseni Opera.* Vol. 3, Part 4. Edited by Wernerus Jaeger, Hermannus Langerbeck, and Henricus Dörrie. Leiden: E. J. Brill, 1996.

————. *Select Writings and Letters of Gregory, Bishop of Nyssa.* Translated by William Moore and Henry Austin Wilson. Vol. 5, A Select Library of Nicene and Post-Nicene Fathers of the Christian Church (NPNF). 2nd series. Grand Rapids: Eerdmans, reprint, 1994.

Groome, Thomas H. *Christian Religious Education: Sharing Our Story and Vision.* San Francisco: Harper & Row, 1980.

Gunton, Colin E. *The One, the Three, and the Many: God, Creation and the Culture of Modernity: The 1992 Bampton Lectures.* Cambridge: Cambridge University Press, 1993.

Harris, Maria. *Fashion Me a People: Curriculum in the Church.* Louisville: Westminster John Knox, 1989.

————. *Teaching and Religious Imagination: An Essay in the Theology of Teaching.* San Francisco: Harper & Row, 1987.

Hesselink, I. John. *Calvin's First Catechism: A Commentary, Featuring Ford Lewis Battles' Translation of the 1538 Catechism.* Louisville: Westminster John Knox, 1997.

Hiltner, Seward. "The Meaning and Importance of Pastoral Theology." In *The Blackwell Reader in Pastoral and Practical Theology.* Edited by James Woodward and Stephen Pattison. Oxford: Blackwell, 2000.

Hodgson, Peter C. *God's Wisdom: Toward a Theology of Education.* Louisville: Westminster John Knox, 1999.

Jaeger, Werner. *Early Christianity and Greek Paideia.* Cambridge, Mass.: The Belknap Press of Harvard University Press, 1961.

Jerome. *Lives of Illustrious Men.* Vol. 3, A Select Library of Nicene and Post-Nicene Fathers. 2nd series. Grand Rapids: Eerdmans, reprint, 1989.

Johnson, Maxwell. *The Rites of Christian Initiation: Their Evolution and Interpretation.* Collegeville, Minn.: Liturgical (A Pueblo Book), 1999.

Jones, Serene. *Calvin and the Rhetoric of Piety.* Columbia Series in Reformed Theology. Louisville: Westminster John Knox, 1995.

Kant, Immanuel. "An Answer to the Question, 'What Is Enlightenment?'" In *Kant: Political Writings.* Cambridge Texts in the History of Political Thought. 2nd enlarged ed. Translated by H. B. Nisbet. Edited by Hans Reiss. Cambridge: Cambridge University Press, 1991.

———. *Anthropology from a Pragmatic Point of View.* Translated by Victor Lyle Dowdell. Revised and edited by Hans H. Rudnick. Carbondale and Edwardsville: Southern Illinois University Press, 1978.

———. *Critique of Practical Reason.* Translated by Lewis White Beck. 3rd ed. Library of Liberal Arts. New York: Macmillan, 1993.

———. *Critique of Pure Reason.* Translated by Norman Kemp Smith. New York: St. Martin's, 1965.

———. *Religion within the Limits of Reason Alone.* Translated by Theodore M. Greene and Hoyt H. Hudson. New York: Harper & Row, 1960.

Kavanagh, Aidan. *The Shape of Baptism: The Rite of Christian Initiation.* Studies in the Reformed Rites of the Catholic Church, Vol. 1. New York: Pueblo, 1978.

Kelley, J. N. D. *Early Christian Creeds.* 3rd ed. New York: Longman, 1972.

Kelsey, David H. *Between Athens and Berlin: The Theological Education Debate.* Grand Rapids: Eerdmans, 1993.

———. *To Understand God Truly: What's Theological about a Theological School.* Louisville: Westminster John Knox, 1992.

LaCugna, Catherine Mowry. *God for Us: The Trinity and Christian Life.* New York: HarperCollins, 1991; New York: HarperCollins Paperbacks, 1993.

Laird, Martin. *Gregory of Nyssa and the Grasp of Faith: Union, Knowledge, and Divine Presence.* Oxford Early Christian Studies series. Oxford: Oxford University Press, 2004.

Lathrop, Gordon W. *Holy Ground: A Liturgical Cosmology.* Minneapolis: Fortress, 2003.

———. *Holy People: A Liturgical Ecclesiology.* Minneapolis: Fortress, 1999.

———. *Holy Things: A Liturgical Theology.* Minneapolis: Fortress, 1993; paperback ed., 1998.

Loder, James E. *The Logic of the Spirit: Human Development in Theological Perspective.* San Francisco: Jossey-Bass, 1998.

Loder, James E., and W. Jim Niedhardt. *The Knight's Move: The Relational Logic of the Spirit in Theology and Science.* Colorado Springs: Helmers and Howard, 1992.

Lyotard, Jean-François. *The Postmodern Condition: A Report on Knowledge.* Vol. 10, Theory and History of Literature. Translated by Geoff Bennington and Brian Massumi. Minneapolis: University of Minnesota Press, 1984.

MacIntyre, Alasdair. *After Virtue: A Study in Moral Theory.* 2nd ed. Notre Dame, Ind.: University of Notre Dame Press, 1984.

Marx, Karl. "Theses on Feuerbach." In *The Marx-Engels Reader.* 2nd ed. Edited by Robert C. Tucker. New York: W. W. Norton, 1978 and 1972.

McDougall, Joy Ann. "The Pilgrimage of Love: The Trinitarian Theology of Jürgen Moltmann." Ph.D. diss., University of Chicago, 1998.

McGrath, Alister E. *A Life of John Calvin: A Study in the Shaping of Western Culture.* Cambridge, Mass.: Basil Blackwell, 1990.

McKee, Elsie Anne. *John Calvin: Writings on Pastoral Piety.* The Classics of Western Spirituality series. New York: Paulist, 2001.

Meredith, Anthony. *The Cappadocians.* Crestwood, N.Y.: St. Vladimir's Seminary Press, 1995.

———. *Gregory of Nyssa.* The Early Church Fathers series. Edited by Carol Harrison. London and New York: Routledge, 1999.

Metz, Johannes B. *Followers of Christ: The Religious Life and the Church.* Translated by Thomas Linton. New York: Paulist, 1978.

Mikoski, Gordon S. "H. Richard Niebuhr and Fowler's Evolution as a Theologian." In *Developing a Public Faith: New Directions in Practical Theology: Essays in Honor of James W. Fowler.* Edited by Richard R. Osmer and Friedrich L. Schweitzer. St. Louis: Chalice, 2003.

Moltmann, Jürgen. *The Coming God: Christian Eschatology.* Translated by Margaret Kohl. Minneapolis: Fortress, 1996.

———. *The Church in the Power of the Holy Spirit: A Contribution to Messianic Ecclesiology.* Translated by Margaret Kohl. New York: Harper & Row, 1975.

———. *The Crucified God: The Cross of Christ as the Foundation and Criticism of Christian Theology.* Translated by R. A. Wilson and John Bowden. New York: Harper & Row, 1974.

———. *Experiences in Theology: Ways and Forms of Christian Theology.* Translated by Margaret Kohl. Minneapolis: Fortress, 2000.

———. *God in Creation: A New Theology of Creation and the Spirit of God.* The Gifford Lectures 1984-1985. Translated by Margaret Kohl. San Francisco: Harper & Row, 1985. Reprint, Minneapolis: Fortress, 1993.

———. *The Source of Life: The Holy Spirit and the Theology of Life.* Translated by Margaret Kohl. Minneapolis: Fortress, 1997.

———. *The Spirit of Life: A Universal Affirmation.* Translated by Margaret Kohl. Minneapolis: Fortress, 1992.

———. *The Theology of Hope: On the Ground and the Implications of a Christian Eschatology.* Translated by James W. Leitch. New York: Harper & Row, 1967.

———. *The Trinity and the Kingdom: The Doctrine of God.* Translated by Margaret Kohl. San Francisco: Harper & Row, 1981.

———. *The Way of Jesus Christ: Christology in Messianic Dimensions.* Translated by Margaret Kohl. Minneapolis: Fortress, 1993.

Moore, Mary Elizabeth Mullino. *Teaching as a Sacramental Act.* Cleveland: Pilgrim, 2004.

Murphy, Debra Dean. *Teaching That Transforms: Worship as the Heart of Christian Education.* Grand Rapids: Brazos, 2004.

Naphy, William G. *Calvin and the Consolidation of Geneva.* Louisville: Westminster John Knox, 2003. Originally published New York: Oxford University Press, 1994.

Nelson, C. Ellis. *Where Faith Begins.* Richmond: John Knox, 1967.

Niebuhr, H. Richard. *Faith on Earth: An Inquiry into the Structure of Human Faith.* Edited by Richard R. Niebuhr. New Haven: Yale University Press, 1989.

———. *Radical Monotheism and Western Culture: With Supplemental Essays.* Library of Theological Ethics. New York: Harper & Row, 1970; Louisville: Westminster John Knox, 1993.

Old, Hughes Oliphant. *The Shaping of the Reformed Baptismal Rite in the Sixteenth Century.* Grand Rapids: Eerdmans, 1992.

"Ὁμόφωνος." In *A Patristic Greek Lexicon.* Edited by G. H. W. Lampe. Oxford: Clarendon, 1961.

Osmer, Richard R. *The Teaching Ministry of Congregations.* Louisville: Westminster John Knox, 2005.

Osmer, Richard R., and Friedrich L. Schweitzer, eds. *Developing a Public Faith: New Directions in Practical Theology: Essays in Honor of James W. Fowler.* St. Louis: Chalice, 2003.

Pacini, David S. *The Cunning of Modern Religious Thought.* Philadelphia: Fortress, 1987.

Palmer, Parker J. *The Courage to Teach: Exploring the Inner Landscape of a Teacher's Life.* San Francisco: Jossey-Bass, 1998.

Pannenberg, Wolfhart. *Theology and the Philosophy of Science.* Translated by Francis McDonagh. Philadelphia: Westminster, 1976.

Parker, T. H. L. *Calvin: An Introduction to His Thought.* Louisville: Westminster John Knox, 1995.

Paulsell, Stephanie. *Honoring the Body: Meditations on a Christian Practice.* San Francisco: Jossey-Bass, 2002.

Pazmiño, Robert W. *God Our Teacher: Theological Basics in Christian Education.* Grand Rapids: Baker Academic, 2001.

Pelikan, Jaroslav. *Christianity and Classical Culture: The Metamorphosis of Natural Theology in the Christian Encounter with Hellenism.* The Gifford Lectures at Aberdeen, 1992-93. New Haven: Yale University Press, 1993.

Pineda, Ana María. "Hospitality." In *Practicing Our Faith: A Way of Life for a Searching People.* Edited Dorothy C. Bass. San Francisco: Jossey-Bass, 1997.

Philo. *De Vita Mosis.* In *Philo: An English Translation in Ten Volumes.* Vol. 6. Translated by F. H. Colson. The Loeb Classical Library. Cambridge, Mass.: Harvard University Press, 1935.

Pohl, Christine D. *Making Room: Recovering Hospitality as a Christian Tradition.* Grand Rapids: Eerdmans, 1999.

Rahner, Karl. *The Trinity.* Translated by J. Donceel. Introduction, index, and glossary by Catherine Mowry LaCugna. New York: Crossroad, 1997.

Richard of St. Victor. "Book Three of the Trinity." In *Richard of St. Victor: The Twelve*

Patriarchs, The Mystical Ark, Book Three of the Trinity. Translated by Grover A. Zinn. The Classics of Western Spirituality series. Edited by Richard J. Payne. New York and Mahwah, N.J.: Paulist, 1979.

Riggs, John W. *Baptism in the Reformed Tradition: An Historical and Practical Theology.* Columbia Series in Reformed Theology. Louisville: Westminster John Knox, 2002.

Sacks, Jonathan. *The Dignity of Difference: How to Avoid the Clash of Civilizations.* Rev. ed. London and New York: Continuum, 2003.

Saliers, Don E. *Worship as Theology: Foretaste of Glory Divine.* Nashville: Abingdon, 1994.

Schleiermacher, F. D. E. *Brief Outline of Theology as a Field of Study.* Translation of the 1811 and 1830 editions by Terrence Tice. Vol. 1, *Schleiermacher Studies and Translations.* Lewiston, N.Y.: Edwin Mellen, 1990.

————. *The Christian Faith.* Edited by H. R. Mackintosh and J. S. Stewart. Edinburgh: T & T Clark, 1989; reprint.

Schmemann, Alexander. *Of Water and the Spirit: A Liturgical Study of Baptism.* Crestwood, N.Y.: St. Vladimir's Seminary Press, 1974.

Schrag, Calvin O. *The Resources of Rationality: A Response to the Postmodern Challenge.* Bloomington: Indiana University Press, 1992.

Smart, James D. *The Teaching Ministry of the Church: An Examination of the Basic Principles of Christian Education.* Philadelphia: Westminster, 1954.

Steinmetz, David C. *Calvin in Context.* New York: Oxford University Press, 1995.

Stout, Jeffrey. *Democracy and Tradition.* Princeton and Oxford: Princeton University Press, 2004.

————. *Ethics After Babel: The Languages of Morals and Their Discontents.* Princeton: Princeton University Press, 1988.

Tanner, Kathryn. "Theological Reflection and Christian Practices." In *Practicing Theology: Beliefs and Practices in Christian Life.* Edited by Miroslav Volf and Dorothy C. Bass. Grand Rapids: Eerdmans, 2002.

Torrance, Thomas F. *The Trinitarian Faith: The Evangelical Theology of the Ancient Catholic Church.* Edinburgh: T & T Clark, 1988; paperback ed., 1993.

————. *Trinitarian Perspectives: Toward Doctrinal Agreement.* Edinburgh: T & T Clark, 1994.

Toulmin, Stephen. *Cosmopolis: The Hidden Agenda of Modernity.* New York: The Free Press, 1990.

Turcescu, Lucian. *Gregory of Nyssa and the Concept of Divine Persons.* American Academy of Religion Academy series. Edited by Carole Myscofski. Oxford: Oxford University Press, 2005.

Van Dam, Raymond. *Becoming Christian: The Conversation of Roman Cappadocia.* Philadelphia: University of Pennsylvania Press, 2003.

————. *Families and Friends in Late Roman Cappadocia.* Philadelphia: University of Pennsylvania Press, 2003.

————. *Kingdom of Snow: Roman Rule and Greek Culture in Cappadocia.* Philadelphia: University of Pennsylvania Press, 2002.

Bibliography

Van der Ven, Johannes A. *Practical Theology: An Empirical Approach.* Translated by Barbara Schultz. Kampen: J. H. Kok, 1990; reprint, Leuven: Peeters, 1998.

Vanhoozer, Kevin J. *The Trinity in a Pluralistic Age: Theological Essays on Culture and Religion.* Grand Rapids: Eerdmans, 1997.

Volf, Miroslav. *Exclusion and Embrace: A Theological Exploration of Identity, Otherness, and Reconciliation.* Nashville: Abingdon, 1996.

Volf, Miroslav, and Dorothy C. Bass, eds. *Practicing Theology: Beliefs and Practices in Christian Life.* Grand Rapids: Eerdmans, 2002.

Wendel, François. *Calvin: Origins and Development of His Religious Thought.* Translated by Philip Mairet. Grand Rapids: Baker, 1997, reprint.

West, Cornel. *Democracy Matters: Winning the Fight Against Imperialism.* New York: Penguin, 2004.

Westerhoff, John H. *Will Our Children Have Faith?* Minneapolis: Winston-Seabury, 1976.

"The Westminster Shorter Catechism." *The Constitution of the Presbyterian Church (U.S.A.): Part I: Book of Confessions.* New York and Atlanta: Office of the General Assembly, 1983.

Whitaker, E. C. *The Baptismal Liturgy.* 2nd ed. London: SPCK, 1981.

———. *Documents of the Baptismal Liturgy.* 2nd ed. London: SPCK, 1970; paperback ed., 1977.

White, James F. *The Sacraments in Protestant Practice and Faith.* Nashville: Abingdon, 1999.

Wittgenstein, Ludwig. *Philosophical Investigations.* 2nd ed. Translated by G. E. M. Anscombe. Oxford and Malden, Mass.: Blackwell, 1958.

Wuthnow, Robert. *The Restructuring of American Religion: Society and Faith Since World War II.* Princeton: Princeton University Press, 1988.

Yarnold, Edward. *The Awe-Inspiring Rites of Initiation: The Origins of the RCIA.* 2nd ed. Edinburgh: T & T Clark, 1994; Collegeville, Minn.: Liturgical, 1994.

———. *Cyril of Jerusalem.* The Early Church Fathers series. Edited by Carol Harrison. New York: Routledge, 2000.

Zizioulas, John D. *Being as Communion: Studies in Personhood and the Church.* Vol. 4, *Contemporary Greek Theologians.* Crestwood, N.Y.: St. Vladimir's Seminary Press, 1993.

Index of Subjects and Names

Ambrose of Milan, 71, 82, 124

Anabaptism, 138, 140, 146, 148, 149, 156, 159

Anointing, 24, 33, 84, 85, 86, 87, 88, 143, 144, 156, 219

Anthropology, theological, xxi, 8n.14, 105n.118, 125, 174, 190

Apokotastasis, 94

Apollinarianism, 72

Apophasis, 72, 125, 127, 195, 208, 209, 227, 229

Apostles' Creed, 20, 28, 30, 149, 164, 167, 169, 171, 173, 174, 179, 180, 181, 190

Apotaxis (renunciation), 19, 35, 83, 84, 89, 95, 143, 148

Arianism, 80, 98

Aristotle, 122

Athanasian Creed, 124, 169

Athanasius, 80, 89, 123, 124, 173n.168

Augustine or Augustinian, 49, 70, 71, 81n.44, 82, 124, 146, 149, 153, 154, 155, 156, 157n.125, 161, 173n.168, 174, 183, 198n.8, 226

Baptism, x, xiii-xv, xxii-xxv, 1-10, 13-25, 28-38, 55-56, 63-68, 83-97, 142-61, 192-96, 218-21; education and, xxiii, xxv, 13-14, 25-28, 36-38, 63-68, 112-24, 127-28, 174-83, 185-90, 192-96, 212-15, 222-34; infants, 6-7, 13, 23-26, 55n.46, 89, 143-46, 151, 159-61, 166, 169-70, 175, 181, 186, 220, 223-24; religious practices and, xxii-xxiii, 2-8, 227-28; Trinity or trinitarian doctrine and, 8-35, 55-56, 66-68, 97-112, 126, 163-74, 184-85, 192-96, 203-13, 225-26, 229. *See also* Sacraments

Baptismal names controversy, 150-51

Barth, Karl, xvii, 51-55, 58, 70, 137n.27, 155, 184, 205, 211, 212, 223

Basil of Caesarea, x, 71, 72, 73, 74, 75, 76, 77, 78, 80, 81, 82, 83, 99, 100, 112, 122, 123, 124n.170, 172. *See also* Cappadocian Fathers

Bass, Dorothy, xiin.4, xiii, xxii-xxiii, 2n.2, 39, 59, 227

Beauty: divine, 92, 93, 94, 113, 115, 118, 121, 205; general, 11, 212; human, 94

Bible. *See* Scripture

Binitarianism, xvi, 174

Body (embodiment), xi, 1, 32, 33, 55, 67, 68, 84, 87, 88, 90, 95, 118, 188, 194, 216, 227, 235

Body of Christ, 8, 16, 22, 24, 31, 148, 150, 156, 161, 165, 205, 218, 233

Book of Common Worship, 1, 15-27

Bouwsma, William, 133-38
Boys, Mary, 60, 199n.10
Brown, Peter, 6n.24, 78, 79 n. 39 and
    n.40, 80n.43, 123n.169
Browning, Don, xv-xviii, xix
Browning, Robert, 63-64
Bucer, Martin, 137, 145

Caldwell, Elizabeth Francis, 64-65
Calvin, John, xxvi, 8, 27, 69-70, 124, 131-
    90, 191-99, 206, 208-9, 212-13, 215, 218,
    219-20, 223, 225, 226, 229-30, 233, 235
Cappadocia, xxvi, 73-79, 86
Cappadocian Fathers, x, 45, 53, 69-71,
    72-83, 85, 99-100, 103n.113, 117, 123,
    124-28, 173, 213-14. *See also* Basil of
    Caesarea; Gregory Nazianzen; Greg-
    ory of Nyssa
Caroli, Pierre, 137, 169-70, 173
Catechesis, catechetical, x, xiin.3, 41-42,
    71, 86-87, 118-20, 144-45, 169, 180-87,
    220, 224, 232
Catechism, 169-73, 177, 180-82, 185
Catechumenate, 63, 71, 82, 145, 176-77,
    186, 190
Chalcedon, Council of, xxi, 164, 165
Charry, Ellen, 41, 44-45, 172n.165
Christendom, 78, 132, 196
Christian education, 56, 57-68, 117, 185,
    204-6, 212-16, 235-36; as para-liturgi-
    cal practice, 36, 128, 177-78, 186, 222-
    31. *See also* Pedagogy
Christian identity, xiv, xxvi, 19, 34, 62,
    67, 199n.10, 201-16, 227-30, 232, 236
Christian life, x-xi, xxiii, 4, 7-8, 21, 27,
    29-30, 33, 37, 39, 41, 44, 62, 67-68, 83,
    113-14, 116-19, 125-27, 163, 172, 175, 177-
    78, 183-84, 192, 196, 215, 219, 220, 225,
    227-28, 230, 233-34
Christology, xviii, xxi, 19, 29, 150, 163-65,
    193
Chrysostom, John, 24n.37, 71, 82, 83,
    84n.57, 86, 87, 128, 129n.173
Church school, 10, 25, 221-32

Confirmation, 13, 26-27, 86n.62, 143-45,
    182n.188, 219-20
Congregation(s), x, xii-xiv, xx, xxiv-
    xxvi, 1-28, 37-38, 40, 58, 59-60, 64, 173,
    179-81, 191, 194, 217-34, 235
Constantine, 77-78
Constantinianism, 43, 128, 196
Constantinople, Council of, 78, 81, 82
Contemplation, 91n.80, 92, 94, 108, 112,
    123
Cottret, Bernard, 132-42
Covenant, xxi, 15-19, 27, 146-49, 155, 160,
    164, 170, 181-82, 224, 230
Crucifixion, xviii, 53-54, 95-96, 165, 193-
    94, 219-20, 234
Curriculum, xi, 116-17, 128, 150, 181, 185-
    86, 223-28, 230
Cyprian of Carthage, 143n.54, 144, 182
Cyril of Jerusalem, 63n.65, 71, 82, 87

Daniélou, Jean, 72n.8, 77n.32, 82, 114, 125
Darkness, illuminated, 72, 91n.80, 108,
    109
Democracy, xi, xii, xiv, xv, xxvi, 47, 49,
    199, 201, 209, 210, 211, 213, 215, 223,
    227, 228, 230
Dewey, John, ix, xi
Discipleship, xi, xxv, 31, 66-68, 180, 186,
    188, 205, 221-34
Discipline, 109, 139, 181-82, 187-89
Divinization, 126
Doctrine(s), 41-57, 97-100, 161-63, 183,
    190, 192-94, 202
Doxology, 8, 37, 54, 97-100, 104-5, 114-15,
    126-28, 166, 178, 190, 195, 196, 218
Dykstra, Craig R., xii-xiii, xxii-xxiii,
    2n.2, 39, 59, 176n.176, 227

Easter, 11, 86-88, 137, 182
Ecclesial traditions: Eastern, 20, 24n.37,
    72, 83-86, 99-100, 124-25, 152, 173, 230;
    Western, 20-21, 23-24, 26, 41, 43-44,
    73, 83-84, 86, 99-100, 124, 125, 142-45,
    164, 173, 185, 190

Eck, Diana, xivn.6, 203-4, 211n.34

Election, 17, 157-60, 166, 186-87

Enlightenment, xvi, 3, 44-46, 53, 197-99, 210. *See also* Modernity

Epiclesis, 23, 32

Eucharist (Communion or Lord's Supper), 5-7, 21, 25-27, 32, 63-65, 87-88, 96, 110, 113, 139, 143-44, 169, 181-82, 187-88, 218-19, 220-21, 225-26, 235

Eunomius, 80, 81, 97, 115, 126

Excommunication, 134, 139

Faith, x, xi, xii, xiv, xxi, 7, 26, 37, 89-91, 98, 104, 105, 108-10, 119-21, 154, 155, 157-61, 164, 166, 170-71, 175, 176, 179-80, 181-82, 186-87, 196, 202, 206

Farel, Guillaume, 136-37

Feuerbach, Ludwig, 49-50

Fichte, J. G., 45, 48-49, 52, 54

Forgiveness, xxiii, 37, 39, 156, 158, 164, 170, 175, 218, 227

Formation (of faith), xiin.3, xiv, xxii-xxiii, xxv, 7, 15, 32, 34, 36-37, 55-56, 68, 117-19, 178-79, 182, 191, 203-16, 221-34, 235-36. *See also* Christian education or Pedagogy

Foster, Charles R., 58-59

Fowler, James W., xii, xv-xvi, xx-xxi, 2n.1, 56n.47, 59, 202

Freedom, xix, 46, 48-49, 54, 94, 119, 159, 175, 176, 199, 203-4, 214-15

Gardner, Howard, 129n.174

Geneva, xxvi, 136-42, 147, 151-52, 180, 182-83

God, doctrine of: Persons, xx, xxii, 29-30, 33, 53, 61-62, 78, 81, 98, 101-6, 111, 126, 128, 166-68, 172-74, 193-94, 205, 212-16; Father, xxii, 23-24, 29, 31-32, 61-62, 98, 102-4, 106, 121, 131, 148, 152-53, 163-66, 169, 171, 184, 193-94, 207; Son (Jesus Christ), ix-xi, xvi, 8, 16, 20, 29, 31, 51-52, 53, 61-62, 67, 80, 87, 89-90, 95-96, 98, 103-5, 115, 118, 120, 121, 148, 150, 154-55, 159, 163-66, 169, 171, 178, 184, 193-94, 211-12, 220; Holy Spirit, xi, xiv, xvii, xix, 1, 16, 22, 24, 31-32, 61-62, 81, 85-86, 101-5, 118, 119-20, 148-49, 157-61, 164-66, 172, 173, 175, 178, 184, 186-87, 194; as Mother, 105, 111. *See also* Trinity; Trinitarian Theology

Gospel, 147, 154, 157, 179, 219

Grace, xxiii, 35, 36, 39, 65, 90-91, 98, 102-3, 104, 108, 110, 111, 119, 131, 146, 148, 154-55, 157-59, 163-66, 168, 175, 176n.176, 183, 184, 186, 187-89, 218, 220, 223, 225-26, 234

Great Commission (Matt. 28:16-20), 15, 29, 99

Gregory Nazianzen, x, 70n.2, 72, 76, 77, 78, 80, 81, 83, 99, 124n.170, 172, 173n.168, 212. *See also* Cappadocian Fathers

Gregory of Nyssa, x, xxvi, 69-130, 220, 223; similarities to and differences from John Calvin, 131-33, 184, 191-97, 206-9, 235

Groome, Thomas, 59, 60, 63, 199n.10

Grosse Pointe Memorial Church, x

Gunton, Colin, 69-70

Harris, Maria, 59, 63n.64

Hegel, G. W. F., xxi, 49, 51-52, 54

Holy Spirit. *See* God, doctrine of: Holy Spirit

Homoousios, 78, 80, 167

Humanism (Christian), 122, 134-36, 140, 195, 200

Identity, xiv, xxvi, 17, 34, 62, 67, 199n.10, 201, 203-16, 220, 227, 229-30, 232, 236. *See also* Openness

Idolatry, 51-52, 127, 139, 151, 157, 160, 167, 195, 213, 223

Illumination (spiritual enlightenment), 91, 112, 120

Index of Subjects and Names

Jaeger, Werner, 71n.4, 112-13, 117-20
Jerome, 81, 124
Jesus Christ. *See* God, doctrine of: Son (Jesus Chist)
Johnson, Maxwell, 86-87, 142-45, 156, 217, 219-21

Kant, Immanuel, 45-48, 51-52, 54, 197
Kantianism, vii, xviii, 48-50
Kelly, J. N. D., 20n.29, 41
Kierkegaard, Søren, xxi, 229
Knowledge: of God, 46, 126-27, 157, 162, 174n.171, 185; scientific *(scientia)*, 43-44. *See also Apophasis;* Reason

LaCugna, Catherine Mowry, x-xi, 42-44
Laird, Martin, 90, 91n.80, 108-9, 119n.151, 121, 122
Language, xx, 28-33, 47, 92, 99, 100, 106, 109, 111, 120, 127, 153, 195, 208-9, 219, 225
Lent, 86-87
Life cycle, 35, 37-38, 59, 230-31
Liturgy, 6, 8, 60, 63-65, 128, 145, 180, 186, 218, 226, 228, 232; Gregory of Nyssa's baptismal liturgy, 83-89; John Calvin's baptismal liturgy, 142-53; PCUSA baptismal liturgy, 14-25
Loder, James E., xx-xxi, 59
Lord's Prayer, 149, 180
Love: divine, xi, xxii, 37n.50, 49, 53-55, 62, 91, 95, 111, 121, 161, 194, 215-16, 226; human, xviii, xx, 30, 37n.50, 196, 214-16
Luther, Martin, 145-46, 190

MacIntyre, Alasdair, 2-4, 197n.6
Macrina, 75-76, 123
Marx, Karl, 3n.7, 49-50
McDougall, Joy, 53
McKee, Elsie, 139n.36, 146n.70 and 71, 147, 149n.91, 180-81
Melanchthon, Philip, 173n.168
Milbank, John, xiv, 199

Mission of God *(Missio Dei),* 35
Modalistic moralism, 47
Modernity, 2-3, 45-52, 60, 131-32, 197-200. *See also* Enlightenment
Moltmann, Jürgen, x, xxi-xxii, 35n.49, 52-57, 59, 69, 128, 193-94, 213-14
Moore, Mary Elizabeth Mullino, 65
Moral monotheism, xvi-xvii, xx, 206
Mortification and vivification, 148, 166, 170-71, 178, 184
Multiple Intelligence Theory, 129
Murphy, Debra Dean, 60-62, 197, 199n.10
Mystagogical catechesis, x, 186, 217, 219-20, 232
Mystery, x, xxi-xxii, 30, 34, 37, 43, 46, 53, 98, 101-10, 113-14, 117, 119-20, 122, 125-28, 165, 166, 172, 190, 194-96, 206-13, 218-20, 226, 229, 234, 236

Name(s): baptismal controversy over: 150-52; divine: xxii, xxvi, 23, 29-30, 32-33, 42, 69, 84, 87n.66, 97-101, 105-6, 121, 126, 131, 149, 152-53, 156, 167-68, 171, 179, 196, 207, 209, 212-13, 215-16, 220, 225, 233-34, 236
Naphy, William, 140n.37 and 41, 141n.44, 150-53
Nelson, C. Ellis, 58
Neo-Aristotelian, xiii
Neo-Arianism, 72, 76, 80-81, 126
Neo-Kantianism, xviii, xxi
Nexus (baptism-Trinity-pedagogy), xiii, 37-38, 40, 125-29, 183-90, 191-206, 217, 222, 227-32, 235
Nicea, Council of, 42, 44, 81, 123, 164
Nicene orthodoxy, 72, 100, 125, 131, 170, 171
Niebuhr, H. Richard, xvi, xvii, xx-xxi
Niebuhr, Reinhold, xvii

Old, Hughes Oliphant, 142-46, 149n.89, 186

Openness, xxvi, 62, 201-16, 227-36. *See also* Identity
Origen, 74, 89, 117, 120, 123, 143n.54
Osmer, Richard R., xvin.9, xx-xxii, xxiv, 59-60, 62

Pacini, David, 4n.2, 198n.8, 200n.11, 207n.28
Paideia, 75-76, 79, 112-13, 117, 128
Pannenberg, Wolfhart, 41, 43-44
Participation *(metousia)*, 86, 88, 90, 92-94, 96, 105, 115, 119, 126-30, 184, 193
Paul the Apostle, 37, 51, 90, 105n.118, 110, 114, 121, 158, 168, 170, 233
Pazmiño, Robert, 61-62, 201
Pedagogy: divine, 61-62, 111-12, 119-22, 121-22, 178-79, 208; domestic, 26, 149-50, 177, 179-81, 185-86, 189, 229-32; ecclesial, xiin.3, xiii, xv, xxiii, xxv, 4, 6-8, 25-28, 33, 36-38, 56, 59-68, 71-72, 112-29, 132, 174-90, 192-96, 204, 211-16, 220-34
Pelikan, Jaroslav, 99-100
Perichoresis, xxi, 53, 62, 128
Plato, 112, 122
Platonism, xiii, 91, 114
Plotinus, 122
Pluralism, 3, 198-99, 203-13
Pneumatology, xviii, 159, 166, 173
Pneumatomachianism/ Pneumatomachoi, 72, 81
Postmodernism, 45, 62, 125, 130, 197
Practical reason, 46-48, 224
Practical theology: paradigms, xv-xv; Trinitarian, xxv, 47, 49, 53-57, 60, 66-68, 125-26, 132, 191-216, 233, 235-36
Practices: core constituting, xxiii, 4-8, 67, 225-27; liturgical, 4, 41-42, 60, 97, 100, 156; MacIntyre and, 3; para-liturgical, 36, 128, 177, 186, 222, 224-25, 228; religious, xii-xiii, xxii-xxiii, 2, 4, 6, 21, 39, 41-42, 55, 58-59, 66, 97, 126
Pre-modern, 44-45, 196-98
Presbyterian Church (USA) [PCUSA],

x, xxv, 1, 5-7, 13-14, 17, 18, 24-25, 27, 28, 30, 36, 38, 58, 142, 217, 219, 220
Progress, perpetual, doctrine of, 112, 115, 118, 127
Promises: divine, 16, 29, 148-49, 154-55, 156, 164, 170, 178, 181, 184; human, 24, 26, 155, 189, 231
Prosper of Aquitaine, 41-42
Providence, xxi, 111, 135
Pseudo-Dionysius, 72, 125

Rahner, Karl, 43, 52-53
Reason, 2-3, 45-48, 91n.80, 92, 106-11, 122, 126-27, 198-200
Reed, Roy, 63-64
Reformation, 38, 44, 45, 63, 136, 144, 145
Reformed tradition, x, xv, 5-8, 13, 17, 19, 21, 26, 51, 52, 53, 69-70, 131, 142, 145, 149n.89, 173n.168, 175, 218, 220
Regeneration, 90-91, 94-95, 98, 103, 116, 120, 131, 148, 166, 168, 170
Religious education, xiin.3, 60, 64, 65
Resurrection: of Jesus Christ, 8, 16, 22, 31, 53, 88, 95, 96, 98, 113, 131, 148, 150, 154, 155, 157, 164, 165, 168, 171, 178n.178, 180, 181, 184, 224; of other humans, 27, 31, 51, 94, 95, 105n.118, 114, 156
Revelation, 6, 46, 51-52, 61, 99, 110, 112, 113, 168, 185, 205, 207, 208, 229
Richard of St. Victor, 226
Riggs, John, 145, 160n.132

Sachs, Jonathan, 191, 203-4, 208-11
Sacrament(s): general, 4-7, 63-65, 97, 153-57, 178n.182, 180-81, 188, 222, 225-27, 235-36; Baptism, x, xiii, xxii-xxvi, 1-38, 39-40, 41-42, 55-57. 63-68, 83-100, 101-6, 111-12, 113-23, 125-29, 142-61, 163-90, 192-96, 200-201, 205-6, 211-13, 216, 217-21, 223-24, 227-34, 235-36; Eucharist, 5-7, 14, 21, 25, 26, 32, 64-65, 87-88, 96, 110, 113, 139, 182, 187-88, 218-19, 220-21, 225-26, 235
Sanctification, 65, 102, 149, 171

Schleiermacher, F. D. E., 50-52, 54
Schmemann, Alexander, 7-8, 34n.46
Scripture, x, xxi, 5, 6, 14, 29, 52, 102, 109, 110-12, 117-21, 127, 134, 137, 140, 145, 150, 151, 153, 156, 169, 171, 172, 177, 184, 189, 190, 195, 198, 208, 223, 224, 225
Servetus, 140-41, 170
Sin, 16, 19, 22, 29, 31, 35, 37, 51, 84, 89, 90, 91, 111, 144, 148, 149, 156, 158, 163-66, 169, 170, 171, 174, 175, 178, 184, 218, 223, 229
Smart, James D., 57-62, 67
St. Peter's Presbyterian Church, xiv, 8-28, 39, 217-34, 235
Stoicism, 122, 134, 135
Stout, Jeffrey, xiv-xv, 2n.3, 3, 201, 210-12
Strasbourg, 137-38, 147, 172, 173
Syntaxis (adherence), 19, 83, 84, 87, 90

Teaching, methods of, xi, 123, 222, 228-33
Ten Commandments (Decalogue), 150, 179-81
Tertullian, 143n.54
Theodore of Mopsuestia, 71, 83, 86, 87
Theodosius, 78, 82, 132
Theory-practice relationship (praxis), xvii, xxi, 7-8, 43-44, 52-53, 97-100, 161-62
Torrance, T. F., 69, 124, 155n.118, 173
Transformation, xx, xxi, 16, 27, 31, 35-36, 53-56, 59, 66, 88, 93, 102, 105, 109-16, 118-19, 148, 157, 172, 175-76, 177, 214, 236
Toulmin, Stephen, 200
Trinitarian theology: baptism and, xiii, xxiii, xxv, 15, 28-35, 83, 96-98, 118-19, 126-27, 163-74, 183, 189, 192-93, 195-96, 205, 229; doctrine of, x-xiii, xvii, xxi-xxii, 67, 69-71, 72, 93, 100-112, 137, 163-74, 185, 189, 192, 205, 207; economic,
43, 168, 181; ecclesial pedagogy and, 57-63, 65, 113-18, 121-22, 183, 190, 195, 212-13, 223, 225; immanent 43; practical character of, x-xii, xvii, xix-xx, xxii, xxvi, 1, 8, 23, 37, 41-57, 66-68, 162, 193-95, 204, 214, 225, 229; social doctrine of, xxii, 213-15. *See also* God, doctrine of; Nexus (baptism-Trinity-pedagogy)

Unity and differentiation: divine, xx, xxii, xxvii, 29-30, 46, 49, 101-5, 107, 166-73, 212-15; in liturgy and sacraments, 7-8, 188; social ideal, xiii-xiv, 30, 107, 213-15, 234-35

Van Dam, Raymond, 73-82
van der Ven, Johannes, xvi, xviii-xix
Vanhoozer, Kevin, 201n.15, 206
Virtue, 2, 44, 93, 108, 111, 118, 119, 122, 175, 196
Vocation, 17, 19, 35, 67, 127, 149, 185-89, 230, 232
Volf, Miroslav, 193n.1, 203-4, 206n.25, 233-34

West, Cornel, 199
West Syrian liturgy, 19, 84n.57, 85-86, 89, 131
Westerhoff, John, 58, 221
Whitaker, E. C., 19n.26, 24n.37, 83-86
Wisdom *(sapientia)*, 43-44, 162, 207
Word, 5-7, 105, 106, 110, 120-23, 147, 156, 170, 172, 177, 180, 183, 207, 211, 218, 222, 225-26, 235
Worship, 11-14, 42, 64, 66, 99-100, 139, 153, 180, 183-85, 199n.10, 217-21, 225-26, 228

Zwingli, Huldreich, 145-46, 155, 184

Index of Scripture References

OLD TESTAMENT

Genesis
17:12   161
17:14   160

Ezra
9:2   160

Psalms
124:8   147

Proverbs
10:20   110

Song of Songs
2:5   121

Isaiah
6:13   160
49:2   121

NEW TESTAMENT

Matthew
3:13   168
19   150
19:13-15   149

22:30   182
28:16-20   126
28:18-20   15, 29, 36
28:19   xxii, 87, 99, 168
28:19-20   99
28:20   153

Luke
20:27-40   105n.118
20:35-36   94n.93

John
1:3-4   49
3   86
13:25   120
14:23   121

Acts
2:9   74
2:39   15n.20, 161
8:16   168
13:48   158
17:28   37
19:5   168

Romans
6   86, 96, 178n.178
6:3-4   15
8:15   158

1 Corinthians
7:14   160
11:17-34   182
13:12   110

2 Corinthians
3:18   105, 115
12:4   110

Galatians
3   105n.118
3:26-27   168
3:27-28   15n.20
4:6   158

Colossians
1   95

Hebrews
1:3   110

1 Peter
1:23   158
1:29   15n.20

1 John
1:1   110
4:8   121
4:20-21   215-16